THE LAKELAND ONE HUNDRED

Contents

For the volunteers of the
Mountain Rescue Services

Many thanks to:

The publishers for their patience as this book
went way over schedule.

Paul Buttle of Amadorn Publications for his
offer of help when it was needed.

My sister for providing a home from home.

Barbara Woodward (of the lightning fingers).

Page 1: On Great End overlooking Sprinkling Tarn.
Page 2 and 3: On Striding Edge, part of Walk 11.

First published in 1996 by
CollinsWillow
an imprint of HarperCollins*Publishers*
London

© John Drews 1996

The author asserts the moral right
to be identified as the author of this work

A CIP catalogue record for this book
is available from the British Library

ISBN 0 00 218751 5

Photographs by John Drews
Additional photographs by Paul Buttle:
page 57: Bow Fell and page 87: Stony Cove Pike

Colour reproduction by Saxon Photolitho, Norwich, UK
Printed and bound in Italy by LEGO SpA, Vicenza

AUTHOR'S DISCLAIMER

Although the author encountered no difficulty of access
on the routes described, and while considerable effort has
been made to avoid so doing, the inclusion of a walk in this
book does not imply that a right of way exists in every case.
Readers are also advised that changes can occur to
the landcape which may affect the contents of this book.
The author welcomes notification of any such changes.

THE
LAKELAND
ONE HUNDRED

Circular Walks to the 100 Highest Peaks in the Lake District

JOHN DREWS

CollinsWillow
An Imprint of HarperCollinsPublishers

Introduction

I admit it was becoming somewhat embarrassing – a Lakeland author who had never been on Scafell Pike.

No matter how I pleaded that my visits to the Lake District were purely for pleasure and not for 'peak bagging', the gaps in my education caused a titter. Usually, I revelled in the argument that I was not unfamiliar with the mountain summits, having enjoyed a great number of them countless times. Furthermore, if one of the major peaks does not lie on the route to any of my favoured locations (notably the high tarns), then I have no interest in it. Why waste good swimming, fishing and camping time to indulge someone else's passion? My unvisited peaks could be set aside for another day, year, or lifetime.

However, the message finally got through that I might just be missing out on something good, and a whole new Lake District opened up for me.

I wondered how I should go about the challenge. With a few glaring omissions, I had already scaled many of the popular peaks. Short of visiting every other one, there were no accepted criteria by which I could target the best of them. Therefore, to rank the mountains simply by height seemed to be the most logical approach.

It began modestly, then grew almost into an obsession. I thought of 'doing' the top 30 peaks, but perusal of the maps suggested too many walks – some too short, others over long – to justify that particular number. Fifty or sixty seemed reasonable, but closer

Left: Wast Water from Lingmell.

research proved the idea to be impractical when weighed against the 'ground rules'.

These are shared by many fell walkers, and although not written in stone, it maximises enjoyment to observe them whenever possible. For example, the tedium of back tracking should be avoided, for convenience all routes should return to their starting points, and separate routes should not overlap. Most importantly, routes should make maximum use of existing footpaths and rights of way. This is both to stay within the law and to avoid the risks of twisted ankles and rapid tiredness that 'virgin' ground generates.

Eventually, perhaps inevitably, I toyed with the figure 100. Things began to fall into place, often with astonishing convenience. The result is a book with a total of twenty-one walks that demonstrate the most economical routes to the 'Lakeland 100'.

While compiling my own table of the highest peaks, I was surprised to discover numerous discrepancies in published lists; a hard and fast ruling of what actually constitutes a separate peak was required, but not immediately forthcoming. Eventually, consultation with the National Parks Authority, The Royal Geographical Society and The British Mountaineering Council ascertained that there is only one accepted ruling.

In 1989 and 1990, using the new Ordnance Survey metric maps and their own survey equipment, John and Ann Nuttal published *The Mountains of Wales*, followed by *The Mountains of England*. In 1995 Michael Dewey published his *Mountain Tables*. In

these books there are two classifications: separate mountains and subsidiary mountain tops. Both agree that to qualify at least as a subsidiary mountain top, a peak must be 610 metres (2000 ft) or more above mean sea level, and have an ascent of at least 15 metres (50 ft) from surrounding ground on all sides.

That is the ruling by which I have compiled the Lakeland 100. Michael Dewey also states that to qualify as a separate mountain, the 15 metre height difference above surrounding ground must increase on a sliding scale if two peaks are within 3 kilometres of each other. The scale increases to 120 metres if the peaks are only 0.5 kilometres apart. This, however, is not relevant to the Lakeland 100, as there are only 78 separate mountains in the Lake District, some of which are below the height of subsidiary tops.

This will lead to some surprises for knowledgeable Lakeland walkers, with old favourites such as Mardale Ill Bell and Sergeant Man failing to qualify because they never really existed! However, a good number of virtually unheard of peaks are brought into play now, offering ample scope for new adventures.

The longest walk is approximately 12 miles, which will not sound very difficult to a seasoned hiker. Remember though, that these walks link separate peaks and include repeatedly steep ascents with some taxing descents. With that in mind, I feel that 12 miles is a sensible limit, with 4½ miles a rewarding minimum.

All the routes satisfy the ground rules: each returns to its starting point; only 5 miles from a total distance of around 178 miles involve backtracking; and the only overlapping of routes comes in the Derwent Fells, where two routes share a half-mile section. Maximum peaks, minimum effort. And all this with the knowledge that you are going to see the most spectacular landscape in England from the highest possible vantage points.

Each walk represents a separate chapter of the book. Because of the distances involved, and the obvious need to keep these to a minimum, it has not always been possible to offer start/finish points at popular locations. Roughly half the routes begin at relatively remote sites, but this of course will not present any problem to motorists.

Each chapter contains information regarding accommodation (of all types), plus directions to nearby pubs – I am told this will be warmly appreciated. Also, mention is made of the nearest shops for those of you who, like myself, always forget some vital item.

A brief summary of the route is included at the beginning of each chapter. This describes the start point, the distance of the walk, the degree of difficulty and an estimation of how long it is likely to take. The longest routes are best tackled during the summer months when daylight hours are long.

I have included colour route maps in each chapter, but an Ordnance Survey map and compass should always be carried, as their use is the only way to regain your bearings should you become confused. The relevant OS map for each route is mentioned in the summaries. At least one photograph has been taken either of each peak, from each peak, or somewhere along its slopes. I hope this

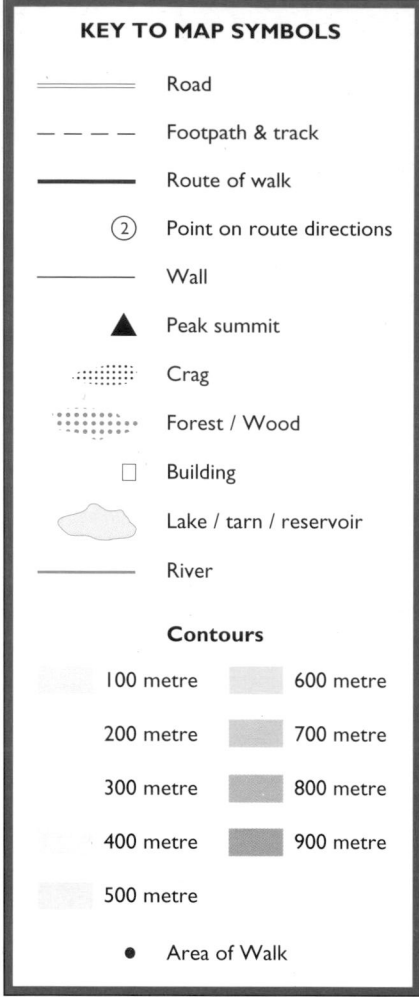

KEY TO MAP SYMBOLS

════════	Road
– – – –	Footpath & track
━━━━━	Route of walk
②	Point on route directions
────────	Wall
▲	Peak summit
⁙⁙⁙⁙	Crag
⁘⁘⁘⁘⁘	Forest / Wood
☐	Building
◌	Lake / tarn / reservoir
────────	River

Contours

	100 metre		600 metre
	200 metre		700 metre
	300 metre		800 metre
	400 metre		900 metre
	500 metre		
●	Area of Walk		

will give you an accurate preview of what can be expected from the walks.

Those unfamiliar with the Lake District will probably have heard tales of how quickly the weather can change here and wondered if the stories are somewhat exaggerated. Please be informed that they are not. Bright sunshine can become driving rain and dense cloud in minutes, usually when one is least prepared for it. Fortunately, the reverse also is true. There is no

need to break the bank in order to remedy this. Most outdoor shops stock breathable waterproofs at reasonable prices, and you should always find a place in your day-sack for them. Also, regardless of what the good folk in the pub might say about the weather, always check the updated Lakeland forecasts on 01768 775757.

There is no doubt that the fells are seen at their best when the summits have a sprinkling of snow. Cold, clean air and practically unlimited visibility, together with ice and snow flakes sparkling in the low angled sunlight, can create unforgettable impressions. Of course, extra consideration must be taken as to where to place one's feet and exposed places such as Sharp Edge should be avoided, but on the whole do not be deterred by a little of the white stuff. It is only when the weather line speaks of 'cornices' and 'drifts' that the peaks should be left to experienced winter walkers. However, no matter how sparse and patchy the snow covering might appear, *any* snow means that an ice axe, and some tuition in its proper use, is an absolute must.

Whatever the weather, carry plenty of food and liquids. Chocolate bars and especially jelly cubes will provide instant energy. Also, drinking from open streams (white, fast-flowing water only) will always put a spring in your step and conserve your canteen for when it is really needed.

It is my intention to set a challenge for readers of this book. I hereby declare that I will buy a full barrel of beer from any chosen Lakeland pub, for the first person who completes the described routes of the Lakeland 100 – blindfolded!

The Mosedale Round

A demanding route that features a footpath renowned as one of the most breathtaking in England.

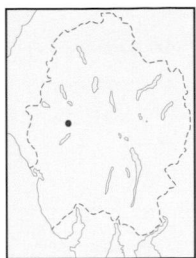

There can be no more inspirational a place than Wasdale from which to commence an odyssey of Lakeland's mountains. On entering the valley, first-time visitors will stare in awe across England's deepest lake to Illgill Head's dramatic screes. Delight and open-mouthed admiration will continue as the valley's only road passes England's highest mountains to arrive at Wasdale Head. Here, further progress by road is barred by encircling peaks, all of which are held in great esteem by walkers and climbers alike.

Despite Wasdale's remote location, accommodation should not be a problem. A youth hostel can be found at the south-western entrance to the valley, on Wast Water's shore. At the opposite (north-eastern) end of the lake, the National Trust operate an excellent campsite. Bed and breakfast is available around Wasdale Head itself, where those of you with deeper wallets can enjoy the comforts of the

The view on looking backwards during the ascent of Red Pike.

hotel or its self-catering apartments. A small camping field lies next to the hotel car park, very handily placed for the public bar but lacking amenities of its own.

Supplies and equipment for the walk are available from the shop opposite the bar, although campers must bring basic fare (bread, eggs, etc) from elsewhere.

The Mosedale Round's route summary names seven peaks. Three are merely subsidiary tops, and two of these require very little effort to ascend. The other subsidiary is Pillar Rock, the only peak of the Lakeland 100 that is beyond the capabilities of ordinary fell walkers or even scramblers. Although classed as an 'easy' climb, only experienced rock climbers should attempt its ascent, and then only in dry, calm conditions.

Walkers can console themselves with the knowledge that the route practically touches upon Pillar Rock's eastern side, and the descent from Pillar overlooks the Rock's summit.

The remainder of the route is demanding, but extremely rewarding. In particular, the famous High Level Route from Pillar to Looking Stead is one of Lakeland's most exciting footpaths. A word of warning though: if there are any (and I do mean *any*) snow or ice patches on this footpath, it should only be used by walkers equipped with an ice axe and crampons. In such conditions, those not suitably equipped must use the alternative route above the ridge down to Looking Stead. This warning is not exaggerated – take it from one who found out the hard way, and is lucky to have survived.

If all this sounds rather gloomy, then be assured that this route is perfectly safe during the summer months, and will prove immensely enjoyable.

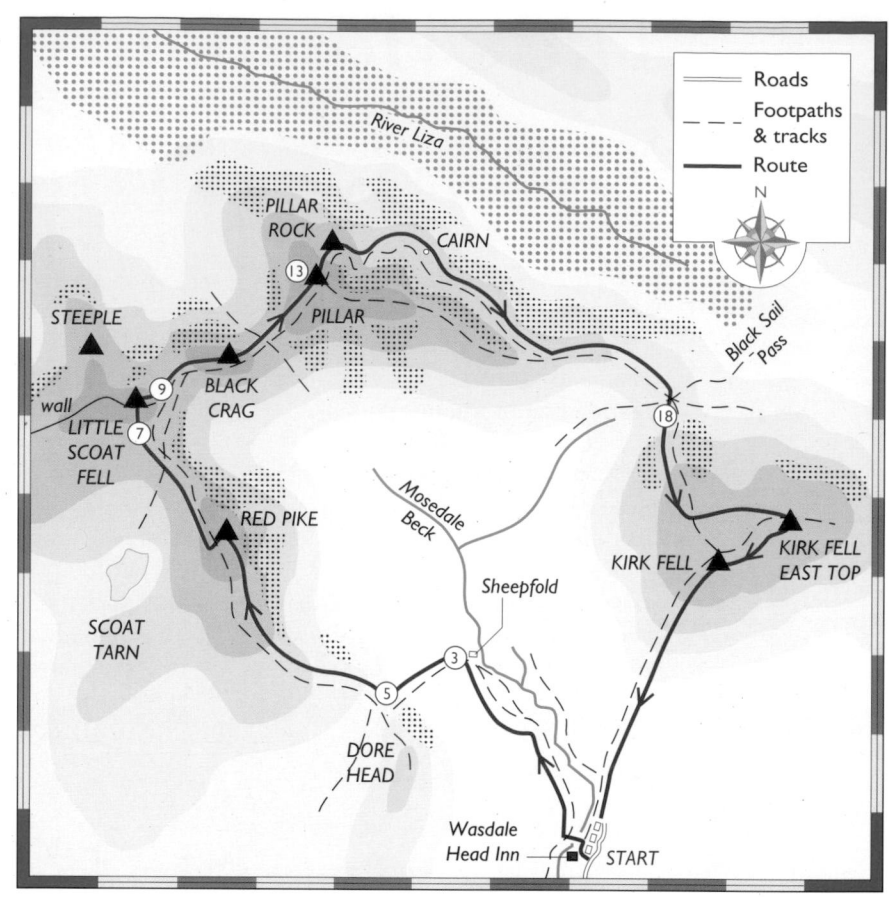

Peaks of top 100 on this route:
12 *PILLAR*
   892 metres (2926 ft)
30 *LITTLE SCOAT FELL*
   841 metres (2759 ft)
34 *BLACK CRAG*
   828 metres (2716 ft)
36 *RED PIKE – MOSEDALE*
   826 metres (2709 ft)
43 *KIRK FELL*
   802 metres (2631 ft)
53 *KIRK FELL – EAST TOP*
   787 metres (2582 ft)
59 *PILLAR ROCK*
   780 metres (2559 ft)

Start/finish point: Wasdale Head Inn (GR 186088)

Map: Ordnance Survey Outdoor Leisure Maps 4 and 6 (1: 25 000)

Distance: Approx 8 miles

Total ascent: Approx 1345 metres (4413 ft). These figures exclude Pillar Rock.

Difficulty: A testing route, with some extremely steep climbs and descents. Sometimes uncomfortable underfoot. Exposed positions on the High Level Route from Pillar. The final descent (from Kirk Fell) is the steepest.

Time: Allow 7 hours (plus 1½ hours if climbing Pillar Rock).

Route directions

1 At Wasdale Head's inn, pass between Ritson's Bar and the apartments, then turn right alongside the beck.

2 Cross the stone bridge, then follow the path that leads to the right (north) between the walls, temporarily leaving the beck.

3 On entering Mosedale, the path returns to the beck. Follow it until reaching an old sheepfold. Here a steep, grassy track leads up the fellside on the left (west), toward a distinctive scree run.

4 Climb the grass track to the scree, then cross over to the northern side at a suitable point to pick up a path that climbs steeply alongside the scree. This leads to the col on Dore Head.

5 Turn right (north-west) on Dore Head, following the path towards Red Pike.

6 On the final approach to Red Pike, the path skirts to the right (east) of a cairn on a rocky knoll. Carry on along your present heading where the path becomes very faint. Soon, it reappears, passing slightly to the left (west) of the highest ground. Detour across to this, to find the summit cairn directly above the crags.

7 From Red Pike return to the path and follow it north-west. This leads down to a saddle, after which the path forks. Both branches skirt to the right (west) of the facing slope of Little Scoat Fell. For the most direct approach, leave the path now and go straight up the slope, but don't stray too far left.

8 On the top a wall runs from east to west, across the true summit. Cross the wall near to its eastern end for the best views.

9 From Little Scoat Fell follow the wall to its eastern termination (merely a few paces) then descend on the same heading towards the ridge. Here, the route returns to the path from Red Pike.

10 Follow the path north-east onto Black Crag's ridge. The obvious summit lies on the left (northern) side of the ridge.

11 From the summit continue north-east, dropping steeply to pick up the main ridge path. This descends to Wind Gap's col.

12 Go straight across the crosspath in the col. Pillar's south-western ridge lies directly ahead, and a number of tracks can be seen clearly on it. Take whichever you like as they nearly all converge on the higher ground, where a series of cairns mark the way to the summit.

13 From Pillar head due north to a small stone shelter. A few paces to its right (east) a small cairn marks the beginning of the High Level Route.

14 This narrow path descends very steeply over crags and scree toward Pillar Rock's unmistakable pinnacle. Before reaching a shelf (Shamrock Traverse) across sheer walls, a path can be seen leading towards Pillar Rock. Heed the warnings in the route description; this is NOT a walkers' route.

15 On no account should you stray from the path anywhere on the High Level Route. On entering the Shamrock Traverse, a one-step section of smooth rock leaves no room for error, after which the traverse itself is much more comfortable. On leaving it, the path becomes faint but can be seen descending an extremely steep scree run to where the path regains clarity and leads to Robinson's cairn. From the cairn continue across the crags to where the path approaches the ridge top.

16 Bear right onto the ridge, then turn left (east) along the main pathway.

17 This skirts slightly below the highest point of Looking Stead, then descends to the Black Sail Pass.

18 Go straight across the major crosspath here, bearing due south up the ridge of Kirkfell Crags.

19 A line of fence posts marks the way towards the summit. Leave the path before reaching the highest point and bear to the left (east), towards Kirk Fell – East Top.

20 Return westward from here, past the tarns and up to Kirk Fell's major summit.

21 From Kirk Fell descend south south-west to pick up the path that leads back down to Mosedale Beck.

22 Follow the beck down stream to return to the inn.

Beginning from the hotel, the route crosses an old packhorse bridge then rises gently to Mosedale's narrow entrance between Yewbarrow and Kirk Fell. Mosedale Beck crashes down alongside the path as the valley basin appears ahead. Within the valley the beck assumes a leisurely flow and our path continues alongside it, surrounded by steep fellsides. Sca Fell and Scafell Pike appear to the rear above Lingmell, while ahead and to either side, all the fells of the route are on display.

One of the steepest ascents in this book follows a narrow scree run up to Dore Head's grassy col. Lungs and legs will demand brief respite here, where Kirk Fell's pyramidal form appears simply enormous on the opposite flank of Mosedale. Far below, the narrow valley empties into Wasdale Head's colourful network of fields, before Lingmell and the Scafells present a spectacular background.

There is still a lengthy ascent to be made before reaching Red Pike's summit, but the gradient is more kindly and the ever expanding panorama is a great incentive over the final approach.

Eventually the route arrives on Red Pike (peak number 36) at an altitude of 826 metres (2709 ft).

The summit cairn is perched precariously above Mosedale's precipitous western crags, so close to the rim that not one more step can be taken. A tentative look over the edge reveals the valley head, before the ground soars up to Mosedale's encircling heights of Black Crag, Pillar and Kirk Fell. Beyond these, the arc from north-east to east presents Dale Head, Brandreth and Green Gable, with Great Gable looming directly above Kirk Fell. Further still in the same arc are the long sweep of Helvellyn's range and High Street.

From east to south, the outlook becomes even more attractive where

The picturesque packhorse bridge at the rear of the Wasdale Head Inn.

Steeple and Ennerdale Forest viewed from Little Scoat Fell.

the Scafells descend into a distant picture embellished by Burnmoor Tarn and the Old Man of Coniston.

Yewbarrow and Illgill Head begin the quadrant from south to west, introducing Wast Water's southern reaches. Seatallan and lesser hills roll down to the coastal plains and a vast seascape. The Isle of Man is seen to great advantage from here, but unfortunately so is Sellafield's industrial sprawl.

As a foreground to this bright western semi-circle, Red Pike's more rounded contours are a marked contrast to the Mosedale side, and descend into Scoat Tarn's unseen combe. From north-west to north, both Little Scoat Fell and Pillar obscure distant views.

The route continues along the ridge, descending into a saddle between Red Pike and Little Scoat Fell. Leaving the path now on the most direct approach, a short ascent leads to Little Scoat Fell's summit at 841 metres (2759 ft). This is ranked as peak number 30.

The true summit appears to be where a wall cuts across the way, running from east to west along the fell top. This of course would be a most uncomfortable viewing platform, and the finest outlook is gained by crossing the wall to a small cairn that can be seen a few yards ahead, very close to the rim of Little Scoat Fell's northern crags.

Despite the title, this is definitely the highest ground of both Little and Great Scoat Fells. The northern view that had been obscured on Red Pike is wide open now, on another breathtaking vantage point above rugged cliffs. Immediately beneath one's feet, the ground plummets into Mirk Cove, then descends further to Ennerdale Forest. This long, green belt will stay in view practically all the way until the route descends back toward Wasdale.

The triangulation point on Pillar's summit.

Jagged buttresses form the arc of Mirk Cove, curving round to Steeple's distinctive pinnaçle. On the opposite (east) side, Black Crag's northern spur completes the arc, beneath the impressive outline of Pillar.

All this rocky grandeur is only the foreground to the picture. From the depths of Ennerdale Forest, the land soars to the great ridge of High Crag, High Stile and Red Pike (Buttermere), then continues westward over Starling Dodd and Great Borne. A small portion of Ennerdale Water can be seen beyond Steeple, leading to the coast and a sighting of southern

Ennerdale Water and the coastal plain as seen from Black Crag.

Scotland. Above the Buttermere Trio's ridge, the Derwent Fells lead round to the Skiddaw group and Blencathra.

Elsewhere, Little Scoat Fell's own ridge removes any depth to the panorama, but nothing of note has been added since the summit of Red Pike. In any case, it is doubtful that anyone would remove their attention from the captivating scene presented by Mirk Cove.

A narrow ridge links Little Scoat Fell with Pillar, forming part of the great wall around Mosedale Head. The subsidiary top known as Black Crag is simply the highest point of this ridge, and is very quickly gained after a short, steep descent over Little Scoat Fell's rocky eastern arm.

At 828 metres (2716 ft) Black Crag's rocky top is ranked as peak number 34. Its location between Little Scoat Fell's and Pillar's major mountain ridges offers excellent views to both south and north.

Mosedale lies on the southern side of Black Crag's ridge, presenting an outlook over Wasdale Head to the Scafells similar to that enjoyed from Red Pike. To the north, Mirk Cove and Windgap Cove fall down to Ennerdale Forest and a superb view down almost the full length of Ennerdale Water.

Looking back along the ridge, Steeple and Little Scoat Fell lead to Red Pike, topped by Seatallan and the coast. Red Pike descends toward Dore Head and Yewbarrow's long top.

Looking down on the distinctive Pillar Rock from Pillar.

With mighty Pillar standing so close, one will be keen to press on and complete the ascent to the route's highest point. A very steep path leads up Pillar's south-western ridge onto the broad top at 892 metres (2926 ft).

Although ranked among the top 100 as peak number 12, Pillar has greater esteem among walkers than that figure suggests. The all-round panorama is magnificent, but the extensive nature of the upper dome requires an amount of wandering if all the views are to be seen at their best. The whole western semi-circle is bright with seascape and coastlines. In this section, Loweswater has entered the picture beyond Ennerdale Water in an attractive cluster of minor peaks above the Great Borne/Starling Dodd ridge. The Isle of Man floats above Little Scoat Fell and Steeple in a scene completed by a bird's-eye view of coastal towns. Yewbarrow introduces the misty distances of the southern outlook, before the Scafells fill the horizon.

An intricate array lies to the east, where Great Gable is dominant among closer peaks that include Kirk Fell and Glaramara. Above and beyond these are Ill Bell, Red Screes, High Street and of course, the Helvellyn range.

The east-to-north quadrant continues over the Dodds to Blencathra and the Skiddaw group, beyond a fine display of the Derwent Fells.

By far the most impressive outlook lies immediately to the north, which is exactly where the route takes us. On approaching Pillar's northernmost stone shelter, the ground underfoot disappears to reveal a very special scene. Pillar's northern crags fall over

Pillar Rock's eastern face viewed from the High Level Route.

2000 ft into Ennerdale Forest's narrow upper reaches, where the Buttermere Trio's ridge forms the opposite flank. This would be a stunning picture even if there was nothing else to enjoy. However, Pillar Rock rears straight up out of the mountainside beneath one's toes, clearly displaying its fascinating table top.

The High Level Route across Pillar's northern face begins now, descending steeply over jagged crags towards Pillar Rock. Soon, the path reaches a rock shelf traversing the sheer mountain walls. This is known as the Shamrock Traverse. Near here, climbers can take the path that leads towards a deep cleft (Jordan Gap) within Pillar Rock. This leads to the 'slab and notch' ascent, but as previously stated, it is only for experienced rock climbers.

For the record, Pillar Rock's summit stands proudly at 780 metres (2,559 ft). This means that for most people peak number 59 will remain tantalisingly out of reach. I should point out that apart from the uniquely aerial vantage point, the ascent of Pillar Rock is not really worth the effort. If you should find the challenge irresistible, tackle it with someone who has already climbed the 'slab and notch' route.

The High Level Route continues from the Shamrock Traverse, constantly twisting and turning, rising and falling through a series of coves. The rock scenery is of the highest calibre throughout this crossing, until the path emerges near Looking Stead. A short descent to the Black Sail Pass is followed by the last strenuous effort of the day as the path climbs towards Kirk Fell's double summit.

On Kirk Fell looking across to Great Gable.

Near the top, a subsidiary peak can be seen to the left (east) of the highest ground, beyond a declivity holding two small tarns. This is Kirk Fell – East Top. The summit cairn is on a knoll above Boat How Crags at 787 metres (2582 ft). It is ranked as peak number 53.

The view across the crags into Ennerdale is good, but cannot compare with the excitement of the High Level Route. The true summit of Kirk Fell is close by, and the overall panorama is better described from there.

The summit cairn and shelter stand at 802 metres (2631 ft), qualifying Kirk Fell as peak number 43. Great Gable is very close in the east, and is by far the most dominant feature. The Langdale Pikes lie further afield in the south-east, before the line of sight comes round to a wonderful view of the Scafells.

Wasdale Head's network of drystone walls viewed from Kirk Fell.

As Kirk Fell stands directly above Wasdale Head, a few paces southwards from the summit cairn will reveal a view across the fields and down the lake. This particular outlook generates a very strong sense of height owing to the mountain's extremely steep southern slope (it is down this slope that our path will return to Wasdale).

Elsewhere, practically all the peaks visible from previous viewpoints are still apparent, despite Great Gable's attempt to hog the picture.

Wasdale Head and Ritson's Bar beckon far below on the final, knee-straining descent. Eventually, the path returns to the welcoming bank of Mosedale Beck, with the inn just two minutes away.

This walk, and particularly the view from the High Level Route, will remain forever an embarrassing memory for me. Nevertheless, I will describe the reason for my discomfort

Above Boat How Crags on Kirk Fell – East Top.

in the hope that the tale will prevent readers from committing similarly stupid acts.

On a wonderfully clear March day, I set off 'safe' in the knowledge that the isolated snow patches visible on the summits did not represent any danger. Would I need an ice axe today? Not me, mate. And footwear; rigid winter boots, or lighter 3-season type? Surely the latter would suffice, especially for a sure-footed 'expert' like myself.

On Pillar's north face, snow and ice-filled gullies were scattered across the mountainside. However, between the snow were long stretches of dry ground – just enough to be seductive.

Within a split-second of my inevitable slip, the rocks were flashing by at an unbelievable speed, and somewhere below were Pillar's sheer cliffs.

On The Way

Pillar Rock is the only peak of the Lakeland 100 that can only be tackled by experienced, suitably equipped rock climbers.

Eventually, a soft patch of snow halted the fall about 30 yards from total disaster.

Battered, shocked and unable to move in any direction, I had 2 ½ hours to gaze at the scenery before the Cockermouth Mountain Rescue Team found me, and a further 2 hours before the blessed sound of the helicopter. My saviours were highly amused to find themselves assisting a guide book writer, and kindly returned to the scene the following day to find my camera. (Thanks, Mike!)

The Scafell Massif

A memorable journey of distant panoramas and dazzling heights over some of Lakeland's most rugged terrain.

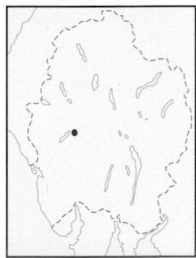

The big one. Eight miles over eight peaks including the highest point in England, plus peak numbers 2, 3, 5, 6 and 9 of the Lakeland 100. Four of the peaks are merely subsidiary tops, requiring little effort to visit once their parent mountains have been gained. However, the major summits are separated either by considerable distances or by deep divides.

Although the route is demanding, it passes through spectacular rock scenery and incorporates an exciting scramble within the appropriately named Lord's Rake. Distant panoramas and dizzying heights occur regularly along Lakeland's most rugged terrain, a journey that will remain forever in the memory. Even the most

Great Gable from Lingmell's lower cairn.

experienced walkers should not underestimate this route – that way, it will prove memorable for the right reasons.

The massif could be described as one great block of rock that nature has attempted to slice into three portions. Great End, with the subsidiaries Broad Crag and Ill Crag form the top (north-eastern) piece, after which the ground dips into a col linking Piers Gill and Little Narrowcove. Across this, Scafell Pike (peak number 1) and Lingmell join in the centre section before Mickledore's awesome divide. Sca Fell stands on the other side, with a subsidiary top and Slight Side, which fails to qualify as another subsidiary by just 1 metre in height separation.

If you feel that this is a pedantic ruling, then both Slight Side and Middleboot Knotts can be included in an extended route that covers all ten peaks of the entire massif.

Middleboot Knotts is represented by the peak symbol on the summary map alongside Piers Gill. At 703 metres (2306ft) it is ranked as peak number 110. With that extra metre of separation, Slight Side's altitude of 762 metres (2500ft) would qualify as joint peak number 71. It is located at the southern end of the massif and is easily accessible from Sca Fell's summit, followed by a reasonably comfortable descent via Long Gill and Maiden Castle.

All eastern and northern faces of the group are extremely rough and precipitous, but both Lingmell's and Sca Fell's western slopes (although steep) are generally smooth. These fall into Wasdale, so, as with Chapter 1, this celebrated valley provides the base for the route.

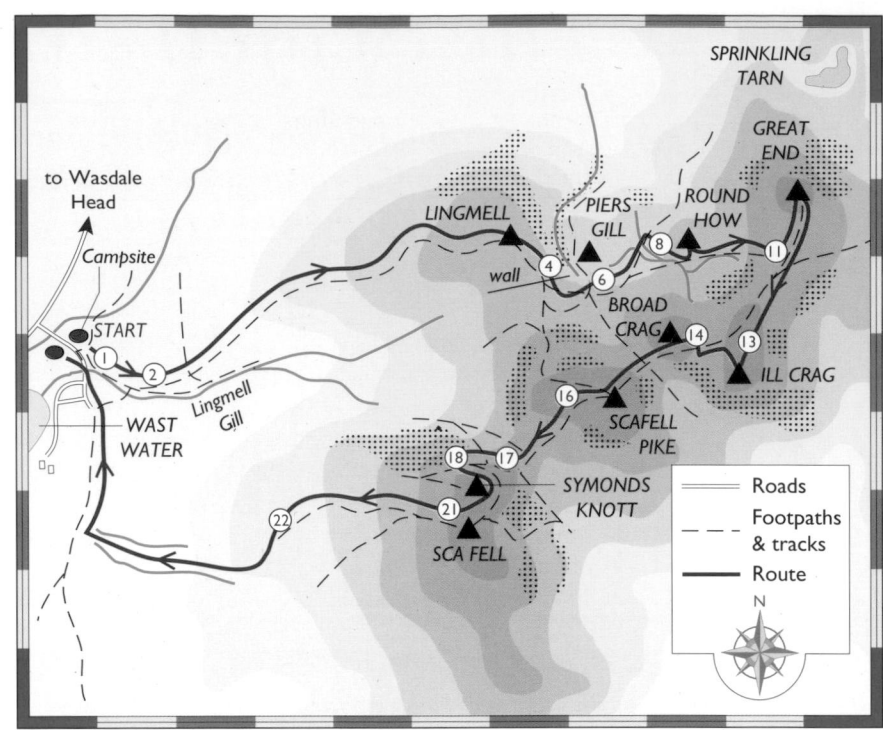

Peaks of top 100 on this route

1 *SCAFELL PIKE*
   978 metres (3208 ft)
2 *SCA FELL*
   964 metres (3162 ft)
3 *SYMONDS KNOTT* (Deep Gill Buttress) 959 metres (3146 ft)
5 *ILL CRAG*
   935 metres (3067 ft)
6 *BROAD CRAG*
   934 metres (3064 ft)
9 *GREAT END*
   910 metres (2985 ft)
46 *LINGMELL*
   800 metres (2624 ft)
81 *ROUND HOW*
   741 metres (2431 ft)

Start/finish point: Wasdale National Trust Campsite and Car Park (GR 183074)

Map: Ordnance Survey Outdoor Leisure Map 6 (1: 25 000)

Distance: Approx 8 miles

Total ascent: Approx 1490 metres (4888 ft)

Difficulty: A series of steep climbs and descents, with uncomfortable, boulder-strewn sections approaching Ill and Broad Crags. The final ascent is the most difficult, incorporating scrambles up Lord's Rake and the West Wall Traverse. Despite the popularity of these two sections they should not be underestimated. Lord's Rake can be particularly hazardous on busy weekends, when careless feet above dislodge scree stones.

Time: Allow 7 ½ hours

Route directions

1. Whether starting from the National Trust campsite or its car park, follow the path that leads south-east on the northern bank of Lingmell Gill.

2. At the footbridge continue on the present side of the beck, then take the left branch where the path forks. This leads up Lingmell's south-western ridge.

3. After the steepest part of the ascent, the path skirts to the left (west) of Goat Crags, but carry straight on if you prefer a more direct approach. (Lingmell's summit lies directly ahead.)

4. From Lingmell, take the path that leads south-east above the crags into a col. Cross the broken wall, then immediately turn left on the path alongside it.

5. Follow the path as it branches away from the wall in order to join the Corridor Route. Turn left here.

6. Then bear right (east) on the corridor route, away from Piers Gill.

7. When the path assumes a northerly heading, a very faint track branches off to the right then becomes clearer as it climbs alongside Greta Gill below Round How's southern flank.

8. After the steepest part of the gill, leave the path to complete the ascent of Round How.

9. From Round How, return to the path and follow it to the east, heading toward the col on the ridge.

10. A steep scramble emerges on the col above Calf Cove. Turn left (north) on the final ascent to Great End

11. From Great End, return to the col and join the path coming up from Esk Hause, heading south-west. The way becomes very rocky, but is clearly marked by cairns. Remember that the route stays on the ridge top.

12. The ridge widens onto a plateau. A minor peak can be seen ahead at the south-eastern end of the plateau. This is Ill Crag. Bear left off the path to visit the summit.

13. Return to the main path, then descend westward to a shallow col. Here, the path traverses Broad Crag and a detour to the right (north) is necessary to reach the summit.

14. Return to the path, then follow it south-west into the deep col of Little Narrowcove. Go straight across the crosspath in the col to begin the ascent of Scafell Pike.

15. On the summit the ground is covered in rocks, effectively disguising the initial descent into Mickledore. Head west past the trig point, then bear to your left (south-west). Very quickly the path becomes obvious and is marked by cairns. Ensure that your heading is south-west or you might return to the Lingmell col.

16. The path descends to Mickledore, then runs into the face of Sca Fell. Go across Mickledore's col, then turn right (west) on the uppermost path.

17. This descends to the unmistakable entrance of Lord's Rake. Enter the scree gully and scramble up toward what appears to be the top exit. Perhaps 10 yds from this exit (or skyline), climb left out of the gully on a clear path that enters another gully (West Wall Traverse).

18. Another steep scramble emerges between two crag tops. Bear to the right (west) onto the top of Deep Gill Buttress (Symonds Knott).

19. Sca Fell's summit cairn lies about 250 metres to the south on the other obvious high point.

20. From the summit cairn go back perhaps 20 paces to where a clear path heads down to the west.

21. The track is sometimes clear, sometimes invisible. If in doubt, simply ensure that you do not stray to the right (northward). The heading is west and south-west, keeping on relatively comfortable slopes until reaching a considerably steeper gradient.

22. Bear to the left (south) above the steeper slopes until reaching the gentler inclines around Groove Gill. From here, descend westward wherever you feel comfortable, to the major track from Burnmoor Tarn.

23. Turn right (north) on this, back to the campsite.

Both Lingmell and Sca Fell tower directly above the campsite on Wast Water's shore. The route begins here, alongside Lingmell Gill. The beck effectively divides the two mountainsides, rising to a skyline formed by both Scafell Pike's and Sca Fell's dramatic crags.

Height is gained very quickly on Lingmell's clearly defined south-western ridge, where the rear view down the lake becomes ever more far reaching. The steepest part of the ascent leads to a false summit, with the consolation of a considerably gentler gradient. Goat Crags' knolls lie immediately ahead, but they must be crossed before the true summit is revealed a little further ahead.

A short climb leads to the rocky top of Lingmell, peak number 46, at an altitude of 800 metres (2624 ft). On the final approach, one's attention is captured by the tall, surprisingly elegant cairn. On reaching it, a few more paces to the rim of crags will provide a just reward for the strenuous effort of the ascent.

Fanciful superlatives often are written about Lakeland views, but the splendour of the scene that unfolds here cannot be exaggerated. It is simply stunning.

On The Way

At 1490 metres (4888ft), the total ascent of the Scafell Massif is the highest of all routes of the Lakeland 100.

Immediately beneath one's toes, Lingmell Crags plunge over 1000 ft into the savage ravine of Piers Gill. From its depths, another 700 ft of rough mountainside falls to the foot of Great Gable, which appears impossibly steep as it soars above even our present viewpoint.

The line of sight is across Piers Gill to Styhead Tarn, then on to Borrowdale. This section of the panorama forms a perfect quadrant from north to east, with distant landmarks completing one of

Lakeland's finest pictures. Notable among these are Skiddaw and Blencathra, with Clough Head leading to the Helvellyn range.

Another impressive vista lies to the other (western) side of Great Gable. Here, the Derwent Fells lie in a narrow arc before Kirk Fell's closer mass introduces the peaks of the Mosedale Round. Looking further round to the west, Haycock leads to Seatallan beyond Yewbarrow.

Middle Fell and Illgill Head's screes rise on either side of Wast Water in the south-west, with a soft background of coastal plains and the sea. From south to east, the great bulk of Sca Fell, Scafell Pike and Broad Crag are almost in touching distance, completely obscuring further views.

The route descends slightly to a col between Lingmell and Scafell Pike, then swings eastward on a path that leads directly above Piers Gill. Joining the famous Corridor Route, the path continues above and below harsh crags to a point where Greta Gill flows down from Great End.

Leaving the path here, the route heads into a secluded hollow within the heart of the massif. Round How stands guard at the entrance, where a short ascent alongside the stream comes round to the peak's southern and south-western base. Very little height or distance lies between this base and the summit of a peak that is probably the most surprising inclusion in the top 100. How many fell walkers, I wonder, have even heard of it?

Standing a touch closer to Broad Crag than it does to Great End, Round How could be described as a subsidiary of a subsidiary. Nevertheless, at 741 metres (2431 ft) it is classed as peak number 81.

Encircled by major peaks, it adds nothing to the distant views seen on

Looking back over Round How and Great Gable on the ascent of Scafell Pike.

A pleasant aspect from the lower slopes of Great End.

Lingmell, but the surrounding crags are truly memorable, particularly where Lingmell presents its most impressive face above Piers Gill. Moreover, the outlook across the deep, rugged void to Great Gable retains all its drama.

The most pleasing characteristic though, is the location beside the 'secret' little valley. One can stand on Round How looking down on the Corridor Route, and then look up to the Great End/ Broad Crag ridge, knowing that it too will be busy. Meanwhile, the sheltered hollow lies in blessed repose between the two thoroughfares.

The route leads to the far end of the hollow where a very steep scramble emerges on a col (Calf Cove) above Esk Hause. At this point we have arrived on the main ridge, very close to Great End.

A short ascent arrives between two cairns on the rocky top. The first (south-eastern) cairn marks the summit at an altitude of 910 metres (2959 ft). This is ranked as peak number 9. Once again, it is necessary to walk a few paces towards the rim of the mountain in order to enjoy the finest viewpoint. Great End is the north-eastern termination of the main Scafell block, and it does not go out with a whimper. A series of deep gullies are etched into the northern wall, climbing over 700 ft to their rugged exits on the mountain top. Peering through these 'windows', visitors are treated to a Lakeland scene of exceptional beauty enhanced by a giddy sense of height.

Sprinkling Tarn lies far below on the broad ridge of Seathwaite Fell. The tarn's arrowhead north-eastern tip points directly to a series of interlocking ridges as they descend another 1600 ft into Borrowdale. Derwent Water, Keswick and Skiddaw lie beyond the valley, with a hazy coastline way off in the distance. This picture alone is worth the effort of the entire journey.

I am convinced that there is a power in rock, and I have felt its influence most strongly when below here, at Sprinkling Tarn. Camping by the shore one September weekend with a friend, we knew that our evening's regulatory bottle of Scotch would have absolutely no effect; we were too keenly aware of an energising force emanating from the great massif above us. This

On Ill Crag, looking up towards the brooding Scafell Pike.

rejuvenation cannot be explained merely by reference to fresh air and exercise. Be as sceptical as you like, but I believe that the power is one of the reasons why so many people are attracted to mountains, an attraction they find so difficult to explain.

If you are still reading, there are more excellent views from Great End's summit, interrupted only in the south-west. Here, the great massif's ridge leads to nearby Ill and Broad Crags with Scafell Pike appearing above them.

In the north-west, Great Gable is still the pick of the mountains that lie before distant coastlines and the Isle of Man. Blencathra, the Helvellyn range, and the High Street range are all in the north-eastern quadrant, leading round

to the Kentmere peaks in the east. The Langdale Pikes begin the final sector, with Windermere, Esk Pike, the Bow Fell/Crinkle Crags ridge and the Coniston group.

After returning to the col above Calf Cove, the route continues south-west along the ridge. Stones and boulders lie underfoot on a somewhat irksome crossing before reaching a much more comfortable plateau. Ill Crag lies at the south-eastern end of the plateau, and requires hardly any time to scale, although the ground again is a little tricky. The summit stands at 935 metres (3067 ft), qualifying this subsidiary as peak number 5.

Nothing of significance is added to

the panoramas, but there is a strong sense of height here. Immediately below, Little Narrowcove's deep chasm falls into the head of Eskdale, presenting a superb southern picture over Harter Fell and the Duddon Valley. Esk Pike and Crinkle Crags are very eye-catching now, before vast lowlands lead down to the sea.

Broad Crag is close by on the south-western end of the plateau. Again, little climbing is necessary, but the top is formed by a great pile of volcanic boulders which must be trodden with care. The summit stands at 934 metres (3064 ft), so this seemingly anonymous pile is in fact peak number 6.

The finest outlooks are north-west to Round How and Great Gable, and west to Lingmell. Although it is tempting to step in their direction in order to add fuller depth to the scene, it should be remembered that there is nothing new to see, and wandering above these crags is very dangerous. Conserve your energy, and prepare for the strong mountaineering flavour of the central and southern sections of the massif.

On The Way

The crossing from Scafell Pike to Sca Fell requires a descent of almost 150 metres into Mickledore, then a scramble up Lord's Rake and the West Wall Traverse.

The summit of Scafell Pike is less than 200 ft above the point where our route returns to the path. However, a descent into Little Narrowcove's col must first be made, before a steep climb onto the rocky, desolate dome of England's highest mountain.

A large stone platform marks the summit at 978 metres (3208 ft), from where all other mountains but Sca Fell take on the appearance of foothills.

Despite the breadth of Scafell Pike's upper dome, there is appreciable depth to the whole panorama. From north to east, the scene is particularly intricate beyond Broad and Ill Crags.

At our present, supreme elevation, even Great Gable fails to penetrate the skyline, topped by Grasmoor and other Derwent Fells. Sty Head, the Jaws of Borrowdale and Derwent Water lie beneath the Skiddaw Group and Blencathra, before the eye passes to the north-east where Great End rises

On the rocky barrens of Broad Crag.

A beautiful October morning on Scafell Pike.

loosening thousands of tons of rocks.

The col links to a ledge beneath a rock wall, where walkers have a choice of three routes. The most direct of these is through a cleft in the rock, then over a slab known as Broad Stand. This way requires agility and a steely nerve. It is a route better suited to mountain goats than walkers and it should be avoided. A slip here would

above Broad Crag. Above Great End, Clough Head and Great Dodd begin the long march of the Helvellyn range.

High Raise and Esk Pike are above Ill Crag, topped by Red Screes and the High Street range. The Kentmere peaks appear above the Langdale Pikes, then Bow Fell introduces Windermere, lowlands and the distant Pennines.

In the south-east, Crinkle Crags begin a less complicated outlook that passes over the Duddon Valley and the Coniston Group to Black Combe. Sca Fell dominates immediately to the south-west, falling toward Wast Water and a bright coastline. Sellafield's stacks are unavoidable in this quadrant, lying directly beneath a floating image of the Isle of Man.

Middle Fell, Yewbarrow and Mosedale run from west to north-west beneath Seatallan, Haycock and all the peaks of the Mosedale Round. The Buttermere trio stand above Kirk Fell, where the Solway Firth and southern Scotland lead back to Grasmoor.

This is not the most dramatic panorama in the Lake District, but it is

of course the most extensive and finely detailed. For me, the most striking aspect of Scafell Pike is its sheer dominance over surrounding mountains. In particular, I remember the first time I saw Blencathra from here and was reduced to laughter by its tiny, insignificant appearance.

A cairned path descends south-west over the rocky ground, arriving on the narrow col of Mickledore amid breathtaking scenery. To the left (south-east), steep slopes fall towards the head of Eskdale with similarly precipitous screes plunging to the right, bound for Brown Tongue and ultimately for Wasdale.

Directly ahead, the col runs into the north-eastern wall of Sca Fell, with the mountain's awesome crags and buttresses towering above to a jagged skyline. Screes and rock-falls are all around, many of them having been formed as recently as 1958 when terrible storms ravaged the Scafells,

The panoramic view on looking south from Sca Fell.

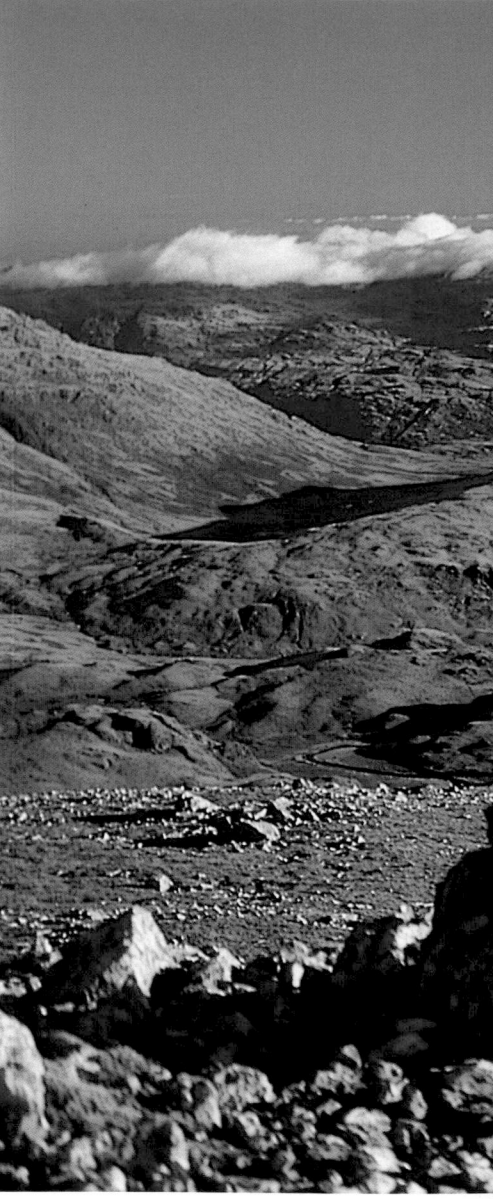

be calamitous. Another way is to descend to the south-east then climb Sca Fell's eastern face, passing close to Foxes Tarn. The most interesting way is on a path that hugs the base of the rock walls, on a narrow ledge above the screes and Mickledore's gaping western chasm. This leads down to the entrance of Lord's Rake, a steep scree-filled gully between buttresses. It is unique among Lakeland pathways and concentration must be maintained on its ascent.

Only the first section of the Rake is climbed, then the route follows the West Wall Traverse into Deep Gill. The drama continues here, and the climb remains very steep. Looking back down through the gully walls gives a sense of adventure that is surely the height of any ordinary walker's ambitions.

Eventually, Deep Gill emerges between two pinnacles, where the route curves round the rim of crags onto Symonds Knott (better known as Deep Gill Buttress). Ranked as peak number 3, this subsidiary top stands at 959 metres (3146 ft).

Symonds Knott has a much finer location and deserves greater acclaim

Symonds Knott viewed from the exit of the West Wall Traverse.

than its parent body. It stands directly above Sca Fell's and Scafell Pike's daunting cliffs – the most impressive crags in Lakeland. Here, the naked savagery of the scenery forcibly reminds all visitors that they are above England's grandest rock mansions.

However, for a more comprehensive panorama one must leave the crags and continue southwards for about 250 metres to the cairn that stands at 964 metres (3162 ft). This is the true summit of Sca Fell, and is ranked as peak number 2.

All eyes will be drawn southwards now, where the outlook could not be in greater contrast to the northern crags. This is a view of boundless distances and soft textures. Sca Fell's ridge runs down to Slight Side which introduces Eskdale,

the Duddon Estuary, foothills and wide coastlines beyond undulating lower ground and a cluster of bright tarns.

Of the major mountain groups, only Coniston's lies within the southern semi-circle, leading eastwards to Crinkle Crags and Bow Fell. Beyond these, the Pennines return one's attention to far off places. The misty, dreamlike images are enhanced in the south-west and west where Wast Water leads to the plains, and the Isle of Man.

Wasdale's western fells, the Mosedale Group and the Buttermere Trio come round to the north-west and the Solway Firth. The Derwent Fells, Great Gable and the Skiddaw Group are northwards, leading to Blencathra and of course, Scafell Pike.

Remarkably, Helvellyn is missing from the view, but Nethermost and Dollywaggon Pikes display the course of its ridge. Finally, the High Street range and the Kentmere peaks occupy the eastern vista.

All that remains of the journey is a descent of Sca Fell's deceptively long western slope into Wasdale. Middle Fell and Yewbarrow lie on the far shore of the lake as the path leads down towards them, but considerable time passes before they draw tangibly nearer. Eventually, the route drops steeply alongside Groove Gill to a major track linking Wasdale with Eskdale. A captivating view of Wasdale Head and its encircling peaks is a fitting finale to the day's splendours before the track returns to the campsite.

The Seathwaite Round

Lakeland's brooding mountain giant, the Old Man of Coniston, looms over a walk which is steeped in the traditions of the area's industrial heritage.

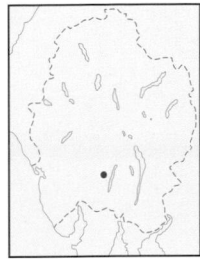

The hard volcanic rock of the Coniston Fells rises straight out of Torver's moorlands. This is the most southerly of Lakeland's major mountain groups, with its southern ramparts formed by the renowned Old Man of Coniston and Dow Crag.

Standing above Coniston Town and the moors, they command an uninterrupted view over the lowlands to the sea. Their high, rugged profiles dominate the scene for miles from the south and east, proving an irresistible magnet for walkers. The number of visitors is boosted by an industrial heritage that has left the eastern side of the group riddled with old mines and quarries. Therefore, the great majority of 'explorers' approach the peaks from the town and lake, heading

Dow Crag's forbidding eastern walls tower above Goat's Water.

directly for the crags, combes and jagged spurs of the eastern faces.

The opposite side of the group falls over smoother contours into the high valley occupied by Seathwaite Tarn, and then down to the long, peaceful flow of the Duddon Valley. This enchanting, fertile vale separates the Coniston group from the western hills all the way up to Cockley Beck. From there, the Wrynose Pass effectively cuts off the group from the central mountains.

The road from Cockley Beck is the only entrance into the valley from the north. As the road continues alongside the River Duddon, forested fellsides climb steeply to a succession of overhanging pinnacles. The great bulk immediately to the east is formed by Grey Friar; the final peak of a walk over four of the top 100. For this reason, the Duddon Valley offers a more logical start point for the route than the more popular Coniston side.

About two-thirds of a mile before the road reaches Seathwaite's tiny settlement, a minor track branches eastward, heading for Coniston via the Walna Scar road. This quickly becomes impassable for vehicles but it terminates in a small parking area where a track comes down from Seathwaite Tarn. This is an ideal base for the nine mile walk for day visitors.

Those wishing to stay longer can find a camp site at Turner Hall Farm near Seathwaite. A little further down the valley is the Newfield Inn which offers accommodation. Campers should ensure they bring everything needed for their stay, otherwise they might find themselves on an expedition to Broughton-in-Furness – all the way down at the Duddon estuary.

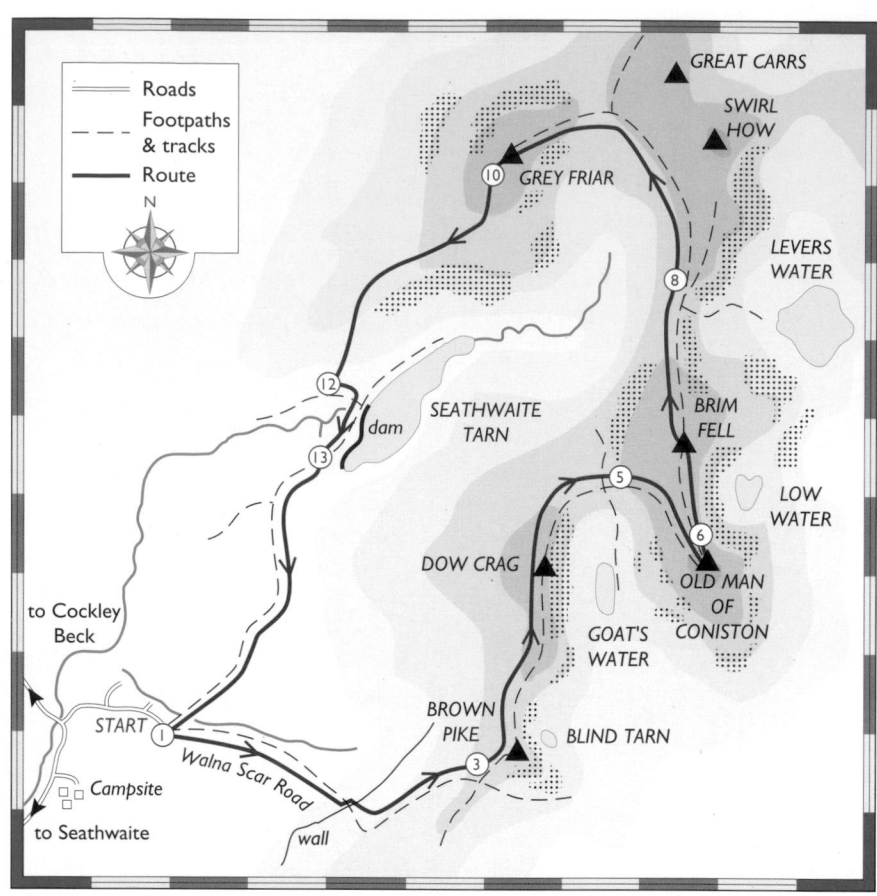

Peaks of top 100 on this route
41 OLD MAN OF CONISTON
     803 metres (2634 ft)
48 BRIM FELL
     796 metres (2611 ft)
60 DOW CRAG
     778 metres (2552 ft)
67 GREY FRIAR
     770 metres (2526 ft)

Start/finish point: Termination of tarmac lane where the Walna Scar Road begins on its Duddon Valley side (GR 239968)

Map: Ordnance Survey Outdoor Leisure Map 6 (1: 25 000)

Distance: Approx 9 miles

Total ascent: Approx 905 metres (2969 ft)

Difficulty: A lengthy, somewhat tiring first ascent (to Dow Crag). Uncomfortable underfoot on Dow Crag and on its descent. There is no visible footpath on the descent from Grey Friar. Care must be taken here not to stray southwards too early. Head south-west on the grassy slopes until reaching a point where the gullies offer a comfortable approach to Seathwaite Tarn

Time: Allow at least 6 hours

Route directions

1 From the parking area, leave the main track and follow the path to the right (east) signed 'Walna Scar'.

2 The path is clear all the way to the ridge top, turning north-east on the upper section of the ascent near Walna Scar quarries, then curving eastward again.

3 On the crest of the ridge, turn sharp left (north-east) at the crosspath, heading up to Brown Pike.

4 The ridge top path continues northwards over Buck Pike and Dow Crag, then descends to Goat's Hawse.

5 Go straight across the col, and take the major path that heads south-east up to the Old Man of Coniston.

6 From the summit, turn back northwards and stay on the ridge top path, going past the path that leads back to Goat's Hawse.

7 The way is clear over Brim Fell, then down to Levers Hawse.

8 Continue northwards along the ridge, climbing away from the deepest part of the hawse. Watch for a minor path that branches left now, and follow its course slightly below the ridge top, curving westward.

9 Continue to bear left (west) when the path is joined by another that comes down from Great Carrs. This leads onto Grey Friar.

10 From the summit there is no clear path on the ground. Head south-west down the ridge, taking care not to stray too far south until the crags below offer safe passage.

11 On the final part of this descent, head south and down to the footpath that approaches Seathwaite Tarn.

12 Follow the path that runs alongside the tarn, crossing over the footbridge and the dam.

13 Leave the tarn at its southern tip, heading south-west on the major track. This leads down to the parking area.

Looking down on Levers Water from Levers Hawse.

On starting out, Walna Scar's ancient thoroughfare provides a clear path towards the declivity between Brown Pike and White Maiden.

Initially, the way is rocky and appears to be impassable for any wheeled transport despite its old title as a road. Mountain bikers are often seen here, but they are forced to carry their bikes over much of the ascent. The modern classification of Walna Scar is that of a bridleway – a fact that must have escaped the attention of the convoy of motorbike scramblers who roared past me here one September morning. They were in sight for no more than three minutes, but within earshot for at least fifteen. Immediately ahead, the mountain ridge completely obscures further views and the path can be seen leading all the way to the skyline. Because of this, the long and sometimes steep ascent can be tiresome, with the walker keen to gain a ridge crest that does not approach as quickly as is hoped. However, there is compensation to the rear, where the Duddon Valley unfolds and Harter Fell's forested eastern slopes provide contrasting shapes, colours and textures. Also, over the left shoulder, the great bulk of the central fells lead to an ever more impressive Scafell group.

The route approaches Lakeland's oldest slate quarries, their abandoned workings still evident in a few waste heaps below White Maiden. A sharp turn northwards leads across White Maiden's north-western contours, eventually emerging on the ridge where the outlook suddenly changes. Coniston Water and Grizedale Forest lie ahead, beyond the broad sweep of Torver Common. To the south are

Climbers brave Dow Crag's eastern face.

miles of moorland and plains leading to estuaries and the sea's silver-blue haze.

A clear path follows the ridge over Brown Pike, where Blind Tarn is revealed below. Tucked neatly into a pocket high on the eastern slope above the moors, this fascinating little water is the first of five tarns on the route.

On the Way

Sharing the same grid reference northing (978), both Dow Crag and The Old Man of Coniston are the southernmost peaks of the Lakeland 100.

A few more paces lead on to Buck Pike, where a glance backwards over Blind Tarn shows Brown Pike's steep, forbidding crags in stark silhouette against the soft background of the seascape. Immediately below the right hand, the ground falls ever more steeply to the entrance of Goat's Water's combe. The Old Man of Coniston's south-western slopes are the dominant feature there, practically filling the entire quadrant from east to north.

One more short ascent over increasingly rocky ground leads to Dow Crag's summit at an altitude of 778 metres (2552 ft). Although ranked at a lowly 60, this peak has one of the most spectacular precipices in Lakeland. It falls almost vertically to screes and a mass of boulders around Goat's Water, over 900 ft below. Five narrow gullies are etched into the face of the cliff, one of which forms an exhilarating scramble. All this makes Dow Crag very popular among rock climbers, and there are invariably whole teams of them to be seen roped together from base to summit.

Great care must be taken when

peering from this pinnacle into the combe – the jumble of summit rocks and boulders can be very treacherous. It is better to keep one's curiosity in check and wait for the excellent view of these crags and the combe that comes in the next section of the route.

The opposite side of Dow Crag could not be in greater contrast to its eastern bowl, with rounded grassy slopes leading down to the Duddon Valley. Beyond the valley, Eskdale lies between a chain of lower fells and the long line of Cumbria's western coast.

The estuaries and Morecambe Bay continue the bright horizon in the south, while the Old Man's massive bulk denies anything else immediately to the east. Although Helvellyn's range is north-east leading to Blencathra and Skiddaw, and the Scafells are on full display, Dow Crag will remain in the memory not for its mountain views, but for its striking sense of height.

The col of Goat's Hawse forms a natural link between here and the ridge of Coniston Old Man, Brim Fell, Swirl How and Great Carrs. It is highly unusual to find a col at the head of a

combe, as these are usually formed by steep crags. Separate glaciers flowed from the Old Man, one into Goat's Water's combe and the other down to Seathwaite's valley. Intervening ground became narrower under the grinding ice to form the col over which the route passes.

Here, the full majesty of Dow Crag's famous eastern wall can be appreciated as it towers above the tarn's boulder-strewn hollow.

The Old Man's smooth western slope is in marked contrast to Dow Crag's jagged cliffs, and a comfortable ascent leads to the summit of this Lakeland favourite at 803 metres (2634 ft). An extra couple of metres can be climbed to the large stone platform that serves as a base for the summit cairn. Once again, it is the bright and bracing southerly aspect that most takes the eye.

In the semi-circle from east to west, the vast green southern lowlands are packed with detail. Before a background of the Pennines, Windermere lies to the east with Claife Heights, Esthwaite Water and

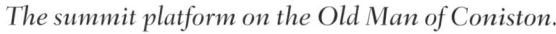

The summit platform on the Old Man of Coniston.

Grizedale Forest. Coniston Water stretches out below, while both Torver and Beacon tarns glint in the wide Torver Commons. Blind Tarn can still be seen in the south-west, perched defiantly above steep grassy slopes that fall all the way to the lake. Beyond all these, the Kent and Leven estuaries flow into Morecambe Bay, and the Duddon estuary heads in a more westerly direction out to sea and the Isle of Man.

A triangulation column and a memorial to the author Arthur Ransome stand a few yards north of the platform, above the rugged combe of Low Water. Looking north-east now, the whole tarn can be seen with the southern tip of Levers Water peeping over the foot of Raven Tor. Immediately east of Levers Water, a series of high, knobbly ridges fall down from Wetherlam and Black Sails toward Coniston Water and the town.

Further afield, the Kentmere peaks and High Street range lead northward to Helvellyn then Blencathra.

Swirl How and Great Carrs are close by at the northern end of the Old Man's ridge which removes any depth to the scene in that direction. Far to the north north-west are Skiddaw and company, with a superb display of the entire Scafell massif above Grey Friar in the north-west. Completing the circle, distant Wasdale's western peaks and Illgill Head continue round to Dow Crag.

For centuries the Old Man of Coniston has been central to countless legends and myths. Long before mine shafts and quarries infiltrated the mountain, there were stories of nether-world inhabitants within 'the high rock'. Bogart's, the 'little people' and earth spirits are but a few of the subjects regularly associated with this brooding giant.

Does world peace and harmony sound appealing? I hope so, because according to the Aetherius Society, this could be achieved if sufficient numbers of us were to pray from the summits of certain mountains throughout the world. The Old Man of Coniston, of course, is one of these, charged with power channelled through the society's founder and president Sir George King.

On The Way

Coniston Water was the lake on which Sir Donald Campbell broke the world water speed record. He died whilst attempting to better it and his body was never recovered.

While in a Yogic trance, this worthy soul received transmissions emanating from spiritual beings on Venus and Mars, who guided him throughout the three year period of 'Operation Starlight'. From 1958 to 1961 he visited designated peaks across the globe, chosen for their locations at intercepting 'lines of force' and their potential as store houses for cosmic forces.

For the record, the recommended method of praying is to stand with outstretched arms, palms facing outwards and ahead. Concentrating on a white light that radiates from the heart and palms, one appeals to the higher powers for their assistance in ridding the world, nay the solar system, of any nastiness. Light-hearted (never disrespectful) tone apart, I think I shall give it a try. What harm could it do? Intriguingly, this mountain was the location of a celebrated flying saucer sighting.

Levitating along the ridge, 'the way'

On Brim Fell looking towards Swirl How and Great Carrs.

Low Water as seen from the Old Man of Coniston's summit.

lies northwards for the short distance to Brim Fell. At 796 metres (2611 ft), the summit is merely the highest point of the ridge before the ascent to Swirl How. A few rocks are scattered around the broad, generally grassy hump which is ranked as peak number 48. Steep crags fall eastward toward Low and Levers Waters' dramatic combes, which are separated by the long rough buttress of Raven Tor.

Similarly, there are crags on the western side that fall a greater distance into Seathwaite Tarn's high valley. Beyond the head of the valley, Grey Friar is growing ever larger while both Great Carrs and Swirl How lie directly ahead. With the Old Man and Dow Crag to the rear now, all the earlier mountain ranges are still visible as the path descends gently on the narrowing ridge towards Levers Hawse.

Of all the Lakeland publications I have read, by far the most enjoyable is *The Shining Levels* by John Wyatt. It is not a guidebook, but an account of the author's early years in the Lake District having settled here as a lowly estate worker. He went on to become the head warden of the national park and the author of many more fine works. In his 'Reflections on the Lakes', one passage describes the sudden sensation of somehow having been magically transported to another mountain range – an illusion caused by mist on the fells. My most striking experience of this occurred here, en route to Swirl How.

I already knew the area very well and was striding confidently toward Levers Hawse through a dense cloud. Momentarily, a window opened through the veil to reveal the mountain ridge fall away ahead of me, with a lake

The summit of Grey Friar, with Goat's Hawse in the middleground.

of perhaps the size of Buttermere thousands of feet below and about 2 miles away. Such a sight is impossible on this ridge.

The mist closed and I froze, totally bemused. Imagine stepping out of your front door one morning only to see the Taj Mahal at the end of your street and you will begin to appreciate the shock. The thoughts one has at such a moment are extremely bizarre, ranging from time-warps to the possibility of having awoken from some dream-like state. In the absence of any further sensory input I decided that I had no option other than to carry on. Within 30 yards I discovered the ridge 'precipice' was no more than a jumble of stones and that 'Buttermere' was a tiny pool of rainwater, with both size and distance wickedly distorted by the translucent light and mist.

The route branches away from the main ridge, curving westward around the head of Seathwaite Tarn's valley. This large water unfolds below, its southern tip pointing down to the Duddon Valley. Above the northern tip is the faint track that used to serve an old copper mine.

This is a very quiet area and Grey Friar is the least frequented peak of the Coniston Group. The path joins another from Great Carrs in the Fairfield Col, where the Wrynose Pass lies immediately to the north. Turning south-west to complete its curve, the path begins its final ascent on to Grey Friar's rounded summit dome.

Surprisingly, very little can be seen of the Duddon Valley from the summit, and Seathwaite Tarn is hidden beneath Grey Friar's southern crags. A number of small cairns are scattered around the top, with two

Atop Grey Friar, looking towards Harter Fell and Dunnerdale.

major piles constructed on rock outcrops. The southerly one is the true summit at a height of 770 metres (2526 ft). This is peak number 67, standing somewhat alone despite the proximity of Great Carrs and Swirl How.

The great divides of the Duddon Valley and the Wrynose Pass isolate Grey Friar from other peaks to the west and north, with Seathwaite's deep valley head lying between here and the Old Man. The Goat's Hawse col is seen face-on now, leading to Dow Crag's pointed pinnacle.

The Scafell massif is by far the most impressive aspect of a mountainous panorama, displaying its full range in the north-west. Crinkle Crags and

Bow Fell climb away from Wrynose, leading to the far northern cluster of Skiddaw's group and Blencathra.

The Langdale Pikes are closer as the gaze turns towards the east, where the Helvellyn range comes across to Fairfield and companions. Extensive sea views are still on offer, with Devoke Water in the western foothills the only tarn or lake visible.

Descending by way of the south-west ridge around knolls and through grassy gullies, the route arrives at a footpath near Seathwaite Tarn. Deep, clean water lies immediately below the left hand as a clear track crosses a footbridge above the outflow, then continues on a long walkway above the dam. A look back from here over the

water will present a wonderfully atmospheric image of the entrance to the valley head. Grey Friar's crags form the ramparts on the nearside, with Raven Nest How standing guard opposite. Between and above them, Swirl How's great ridge marches across the skyline.

Leaving the tarn at the southern tip, a wide, clear track heads toward the Duddon Valley. There is still a considerable distance to walk, but the descent is gentle and very comfortable across moorland. On a clear day, the setting sun will be ahead, above the network of walls and fields around Tarn Beck. Eventually, the track leads back to the parking area.

The Greenburn Round

A five-hour adventure designed to serve as a practical introductory route for inexperienced walkers.

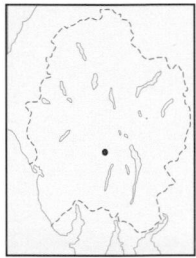

The Wrynose Pass falls eastward into Little Langdale's pastoral charms. Before reaching Little Langdale Tarn, the road is met by another that comes down from the high basin of Blea Tarn, providing a link with Great Langdale.

Castle Howe's rocky pinnacle stands guard at the confluence of these avenues, displaying a prominence and command far greater than its modest height suggests. Here, very close to Fell Foot Farm and the ancient meeting place of Ting Mound, a crook in the road offers a few parking spaces. Despite its remote, rustic location, this is the most convenient starting point for a 6 ½ mile walk over four of

Looking back to Great Carrs from the summit of Swirl How.

Lakeland's top 100 peaks that include that old favourite, Wetherlam. However, make sure that you have everything needed for a day on the fells; there is nowhere in the immediate vicinity to buy provisions, and nothing in the way of accommodation save for a hotel east of Little Langdale Tarn. The nearest campsites are in Great Langdale, ideally placed for those who are choosing their routes in book order.

As stated in this chapter's sub-title, the Greenburn Round has been separated from the main Coniston Group in this book in order to present a rewarding excursion for walkers who are not yet ready to tackle the major routes.

For seasoned campaigners who might prefer to conquer the Lakeland 100 by the least possible routes, the peaks of the Greenburn Round can be linked to those of the previous chapter.

Begin from Coniston town and take the path alongside Church Beck, crossing Miners Bridge. After the bridge take the track that branches to the right, heading for Hole Rake. Where this begins to skirt to the east of the Lad Stones/Wetherlam Ridge, branch left (due north) and climb the ridge to Wetherlam's summit. From there, follow the Greenburn Round route in reverse to Great Carrs. Descend from Great Carrs to the Fairfield Col and pick up the path to Grey Friar. From the summit, follow the Seathwaite Round route in reverse all the way to the Walna Scar Road. Turn left (east) on this and follow it back to Coniston.

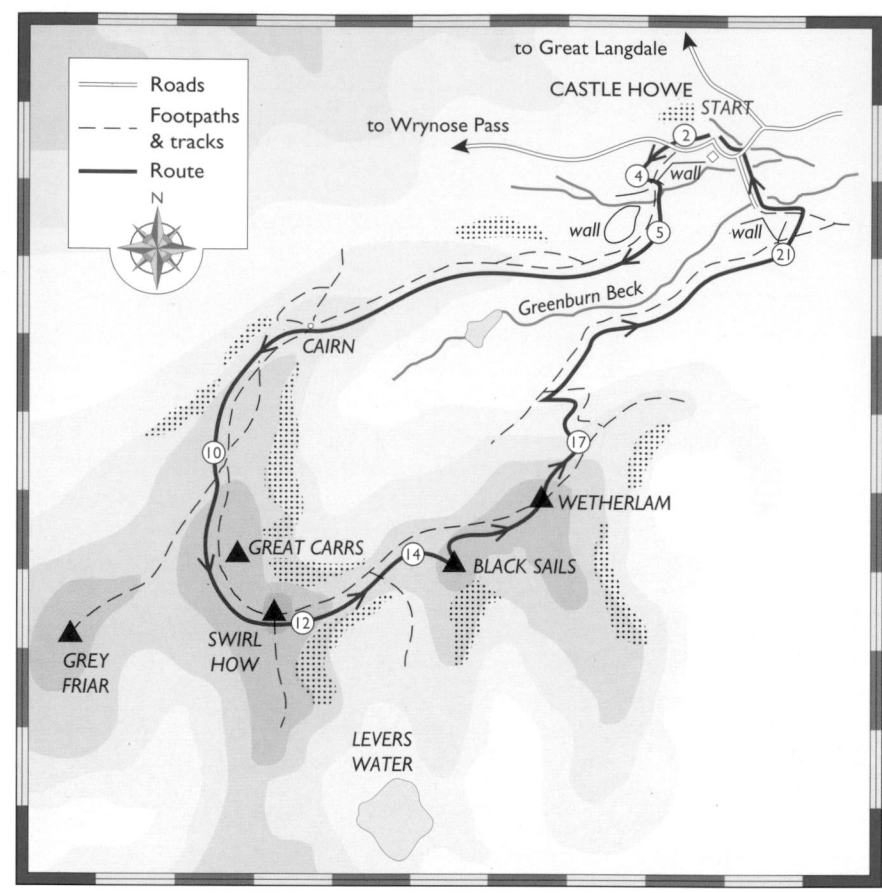

Peaks of top 100 on this route
44 *SWIRL HOW*
    802 metres (2631 ft)
55 *GREAT CARRS*
    785 metres (2575 ft)
72 *WETHERLAM*
    762 metres (2500 ft)
79 *BLACK SAILS*
    745 metres (2444 ft)

Start/finish point: Small parking spaces in crook of road immediately north of Fell Foot Farm, Little Langdale (GR 298033)

Map: Ordnance Survey Outdoor Leisure Map 6 (1: 25 000)

Distance: Approx 6½ miles

Total ascent: Approx 895 metres (2936 ft)

Difficulty: Once having located the Rough Crags/Wet Side Edge Ridge, the route is quite straight forward although particular attention must be paid to note 10 in the route directions. From Wetherlam there is an extremely steep descent to Birk Fell Hawse, and the path from there to Greenburn can be difficult to locate. This path also is very steep over its initial descent (very good practise for more demanding routes).

Time: Allow 5 hours.

Route directions

1   From the small parking spaces at the sharp bend immediately north of Fell Foot Farm, head west on the road toward Wrynose Pass.

2   Turn left (south) through the first gate off the road (this is about 200 yds distant).

3   Through the gate a path runs alongside a wall. Follow this to the stile which comes immediately after a gate.

4   Bear to the right after crossing the stile, and head straight up the mound ahead. A cairn appears on the mound, marking a faint track that descends through ferns to a stream (River Brathay).

5   Cross the stones then head up the fellside to the left (east) of the walled enclosure.

6   There is no clear path on the ground, but carry on upward slightly to the left of the main mass of ferns.

7   Start to angle away from the wall as you climb higher, aiming for a generally south-west heading. If you see a small cairn atop a rock, head towards it. After this, another small cairn can be seen on a rock outcrop on the skyline. It does not matter if you cannot locate these cairns, for the general idea is simply to ascend until you can clearly see the long ridge of Rough Crags and Wet Side Edge immediately to the west. Once this is located, head for the clear path that rises up along the ridge through ferns.

8   On the ascent of the ridge (heading west now), the path comes to two cairns. Go past the path that branches to the right here, and carry on up the ridge.

9   The way is clear now up to Wet Side Edge. Carry on past the cairn, where another path falls towards Wrynose.

10 The ridge swings towards the south approaching Little Carrs. Just before the obvious final ascent, a path branches sharp left off the main track, marked by a tumble-down cairn. Follow the left branch here, heading steeply upwards.

11 Now, stay on the ridge top over Great Carrs, then on to Swirl How.

12 Leave the ridge path on Swirl How, and head east on the path across Prison Band. This descends steeply to Swirl Hawse.

13 In the hawse, ignore the path that branches to the right (south-east), and begin the ascent of Black Sails. The heading now is north-east, and the path remains clear.

14 After the steepest part of the ascent, the main bulk of Wetherlam is obvious ahead. Immediately to the right (south), a lesser peak marks the summit of Black Sails. Take a short detour to visit this, then return to the path for the easiest ascent of Wetherlam.

15 On the final approach to Wetherlam, follow the cairns where the path becomes indistinct.

16 From Wetherlam's summit cairn, head north-east to pick up an obvious track down to Birk Fell Hawse.

17 A very steep descent leads to the shallow saddle of the hawse. It is possible to save some distance by continuing north-east along the ridge, but this way is difficult to locate. It is simpler to turn sharp left (west) here, at the small cairn. This leads to a series of small cairns that mark the route down the grassy fellside.

18 The path becomes obvious, and leads partly back up the valley as it continues to descend.

19 Turn sharp right where the path forks, then follow it down towards Greenburn Beck.

20 The path fades approaching the beck, but continue to head down towards the stream and the way becomes obvious.

21 A wide and clear track leads alongside the beck for about ¾ of a mile. You will see where the track comes down to join another, then turns sharp left (in effect doubling back) down to Bridge End. To save a distance of about 400 yds, follow the wall that cuts left, down to the gate above Bridge End House.

22 Go through the gate here, then continue along the farm track to Fell Foot Bridge and the road.

23 Turn left on the road back to the parking spaces.

On starting out, a few paces up the road leads to a footpath that crosses a knoll before dropping gently to a crystal stream. This is the infant stretch of one of Lakeland's most beautiful rivers, the Brathay. A short, steep climb leads up around Hollin Crag where the peaks of the route are on full display ahead, curving around Greenburn's narrow valley. Wetherlam's great bulk dominates this picture, while to the rear the Langdale Pikes soar beyond Blea Tarn's basin.

A relatively level section approaches the eastern end of Rough Crags' and Wet Side Edge's long, narrow ridge. The climbing begins in earnest now, gaining height rapidly and moving parallel with the Wrynose road that lies immediately below the right hand. Beyond the deep recess of the pass, a vast array of peaks begins to unfold, with the Langdales and Bow Fell ranges growing ever more detailed.

Behind, the green lowlands of Brathay lead on to Lakeland's north-eastern fells. This scene will constantly expand over most of the route and will provide the day's most appealing outlook.

Immediately below the left hand, thickly grassed slopes fall down to Greenburn Beck then rise sharply to Wetherlam. Deep in the valley, the remnants of Greenburn Reservoir are a sorry sight nowadays, the only disappointment in an otherwise splendid and contrasting panorama. The reservoir was constructed in the 19th century to provide water power for the few copper mines of Wetherlam's northern face. Elsewhere, the mountain is literally honeycombed with them.

The steepest part of the ascent

Greenburn Valley from Great Carrs.

The airmen's memorial between Great Carrs and Swirl How.

emerges above Rough Crags, but the ridge continues to climb. On reaching Wet Side Edge the view across Wrynose's divide provides a fascinating spectacle of Red Tarn nestled in the high saddle between Cold Pike and Pike O'Blisco.

The ridge begins to curve southwards on the approach to Little and Great Carrs. As more height is gained, a breathtaking view unfolds over the Wrynose and Hardknott passes to Eskdale and the coast. Harter Fell above Dunnerdale takes the eye along with Grey Friar, then the path reaches Great Carr's summit above the precipitous crags and buttresses enclosing Greenburn's hollow.

The Coniston group of Dow Crag, Old Man and Brim Fell can be seen now, close at hand on the southern end of the Great Carrs/Swirl How ridge.

Although an attractive view of the sea and coastal plains has opened beyond these peaks and Grey Friar, this outlook will improve on the next stage of the route. Swirl How itself impedes the view to the south-east.

At 785 metres (2575 ft) Great Carrs is ranked peak number 55 and offers its finest outlook in a northerly semi-circle from west to east. Beyond the Wrynose Pass, the Scafell massif is on full display from Slight Side to Great End, leading on to Crinkle Crags, Esk Pike and Bow Fell. Further afield lies a narrow arc of the Derwent Fells then the distant Skiddaw group and · Blencathra. Beneath these are Cold Pike, Pike O'Blisco and the distinctive sculpture of the Langdales.

Coming round to the east, Clough Head begins the long chain of Helvellyn's range with Seat Sandal, Fairfield, Hart Crag and Dove Crag.

Completing the arc above Greenburn and the colourful Brathay valleys are the High Street and Kentmere ranges.

The ridge top continues to curve from south to east on the short ascent to Swirl How. By the left hand (east and north) are steep crags falling towards Greenburn, while a gentle grassy slope lies to the right. This forms the valley head above unseen Seathwaite Tarn. On the way to Swirl How, the path passes close by a wooden cross within a cairn. It marks the spot where a Halifax bomber crashed in October 1944 whilst on a night flying exercise, killing all eight crew members. A few pieces of wreckage are incorporated into the monument.

An easy climb arrives on the summit of Swirl How at 802 metres (2,631 ft). Ranked peaked number 44, this is the apex of the route. Now, the

Approaching Black Sails, looking south.

southerly outlook has improved throughout a semi-circle from east to west. Wetherlam, Black Sails and their southern spurs fall to a superb view of Coniston Water and Grizedale Forest. Claife Heights separates Esthwaite Water from Windermere, with all of these a foreground for the far distant Pennines. From south to west, Morecambe Bay and the Irish Sea form a silvery haze, where a very good day might reveal a dark outline 'floating' above Grey Friar. This, of course, is the Isle of Man.

Elsewhere, the only notable addition to the mountainous aspects is close at hand, where Great Carrs' broken crags plunge towards Greenburn.

At this point, the mountain ridge continues south towards Brim Fell and Coniston Old Man. Our route leaves the ridge, heading east across the narrow, jagged col known as Prison Band. This leads to Swirl Hawse, forming a link between Swirl How and Wetherlam.

On the steep descent over Prison Band, Levers Water is unveiled to the south, presenting a delightful foreground to the picture of lakes and forests. After Swirl Hawse, the day's final ascents begin on a well-beaten track towards Wetherlam. Before reaching there, a short detour is required to 'bag' the subsidiary peak of Black Sails. This stands slightly south-west of its parent mountain at a height of 745 metres (2444 ft).

Ranked peak number 79, there is little to say about it that cannot be left to Wetherlam's description. It is, in fact, merely the top of an extremely rugged spur that leads up from Coppermines Valley towards Wetherlam. It is wise not to wander too much around this spur, although a

On the descent from Wetherlam.

few paces to the east will unveil a spectacular view of the crags around Red Dell Beck.

One last push is rewarded by the finest views of the route on Wetherlam where the rocky summit is capped by a large cairn at an altitude of 762 metres (2500 ft). Although ranked at a lowly 72, Wetherlam figures prominently in the itineraries of most fell walkers owing to its fortunate location.

Strictly speaking the mountain belongs to the Coniston group, but in effect it is separate from them. Standing to the north of the main group, it is the last mass of high ground before Little Langdale introduces a magical view of lowlands immediately to the west and south of Ambleside.

Wetherlam is also slightly east of the Coniston group, which allows a virtually uninterrupted view to the south over Coniston Water, then in an arc to the west. This entire quadrant is a vision of fields, forest, lakes, tarns and undulating foothills. Where a line of mountains begins in the west, this arable countryside narrows northwards into the Brathay area, providing Wetherlam with a green patchwork panorama practically all the way from north to south.

All this, of course, is complemented by the vast array of mountains already described. In the north, the Langdales appear deceptively tall, clearly displaying Stickle Tarn high in its magnificent mountain combe. Along the same line of sight, Blea Tarn is in evidence above Little Langdale. These are just two of the fifteen separate waters visible from here, or sixteen if the sea is counted.

Immediately to the south, the land falls over ridges and lower fells that contain the majority of the old mine workings for which the Coniston region is renowned.

On The Way

Some remnants of the halifax bomber that are too large for souvenir hunters to carry away are still visible on Great Carrs' lower slopes.

The initial descent from Wetherlam is very steep, falling approximately 750 ft over a lateral distance of perhaps 600 yds. Some scrambling is necessary here, as the path heads straight down the ridge toward Little Langdale's beckoning pastures.

The ground levels on Birk Fell Hawse, where two return routes are possible. The most obvious way leaves the ridge, heading on a zigzag course over the grassy fellside down to Greenburn. Again, the gradient is very steep for a short while, then eases on a clear track bound for the disused workings below Greenburn Reservoir.

The path fades approaching the mine's remnants, then the old mine track is picked up running alongside Greenburn Beck. This is a typical Lakeland stream, resplendent with numerous short cascades and deep rock pools. At the end of a hot day, it is a more than welcome sight.

The Greenburn round was one of the first routes I walked when compiling this book. With my usual foresight, I had failed to bring a canteen, hoping to come across mountain springs along the way. After all, there are always one or two to be found, are there not? Having crossed the River Brathay, there hadn't been a single drop anywhere on the route.

I should have expected this, as there had been a dry spell of some weeks previously. OS maps mark a stream issuing from Swirl Hawse, but even this had disappeared. The blazing sun was unrelenting throughout the journey, and I have never been more grateful or relieved to discover that Greenburn was untouched by the drought. It must have been a good half-hour before I emerged from those cold crystal pools.

The track continues towards Little Langdale, with Fell Foot Farm drawing ever nearer. The route joins a farm track crossing Greenburn Beck at Bridge End. Back down in the valley basin now, a short stroll through the fields comes to Fell Foot Bridge over the Brathay. From here, two minutes along the road leads back to the parking spaces.

The Bow Fell Ridge

A favourite route through an area of outstanding natural beauty overlooked by the majestic outline of Bow Fell.

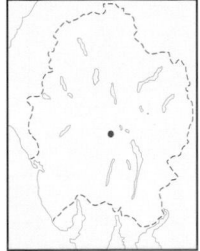

The thought of eight peaks in a 12 mile walk conjures up images of lungs and muscles straining to cope with constantly alternating demands of climbs and descents.

Although this particular walk is indeed tiring, it is by no means exhausting because five of the peaks belong to Crinkle Crags, and the following two are both on Bow Fell. Having gained the first peak (Little Stand), it is surprisingly easy to conquer the sharp undulations of the ridge all the way to Bow Fell. From there, although Esk Pike is separated from the main ridge, it is not far removed.

The entire range marches from south to north, forming the great wall of mountains that effectively blocks Great Langdale's westerly flow. The Band forms Bow Fell's long eastern spur, falling into Great Langdale which then branches to either side of The Band in the forks of Oxendale and

Bow Fell and Shelter Crag – North Top from Shelter Crags.

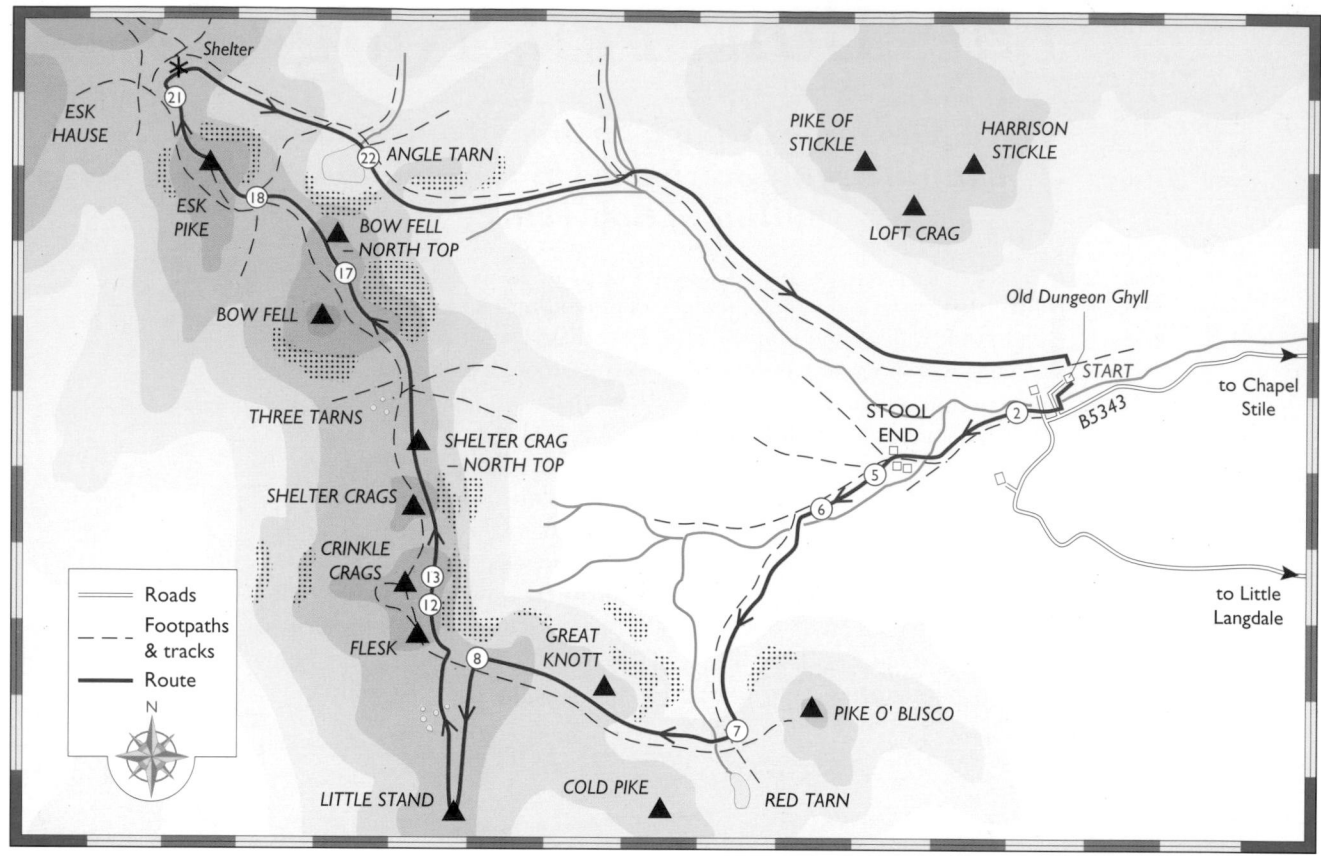

Mickleden. Both of these quiet valleys are incorporated in the route; Oxendale on the outward leg and Mickleden on the return.

Bow Fell's majestic outline stands at the hub of three major valleys, forming an instantly recognisable landmark. It's views, like those from Crinkle Crags are literally breathtaking.

All this natural splendour notwithstanding, an area's popularity depends largely on its accessibility and convenience. In this respect, the Bow Fell ridge is particularly fortunate. At the head of Great Langdale, the legendary Old Dungeon Ghyll Hotel and a large National Trust campsite offer accommodation and refreshment, with supplies and equipment available from Chapel Stile at the eastern end of the valley.

Peaks of top 100 on this route

10 *BOW FELL*
902 metres (2959 ft)

15 *ESK PIKE*
885 metres (2903 ft)

19 *BOWFELL – NORTH TOP*
866 metres (2841 ft)

23 *LONG TOP (CRINKLE CRAGS)* 859 metres (2818 ft)

33 *FLESK (CRINKLE CRAGS)*
834 metres (2736 ft)

39 *SHELTER CRAGS (CRINKLE CRAGS)* 815 metres (2673 ft)

64 *SHELTER CRAG – NORTH TOP* 775 metres (2542 ft)

82 *LITTLE STAND*
740 metres (2427 ft)

Start/finish point: Old Dungeon Ghyll Hotel, Great Langdale (GR 286061)

Map: Ordnance Survey Outdoor Leisure Map 6 (1: 25 000)

Distance: Approx 12 miles

Total ascent: Approx 1235 metres (4052 ft)

Difficulty: Apart from a scramble around 'Bad Step' on Crinkle Crags and some awkward boulders underfoot in various places, the only real difficulty with this route is its length. Ensure to follow the path in the gully of Rossett Gill, *not* the scree run.

Time: Allow 8 hours.

Route directions

1 Return to the road from the Old Dungeon Ghyll car park, and turn right at the T-junction after the bridge.

2 At the following T-junction, go through the gate next to the post box in the facing wall signposted 'Public footpath Oxendale, The Band'.

3 Follow the lane across the fields into Stool End farmyard, then go through the gate at the rear of the farm buildings (this is signposted quite simply, 'path').

4 The path forks immediately after the gate. Bear left following the sign 'Path to Band'.

5 Bear left alongside the wall where a stony track branches right and uphill towards The Band.

6 Take the path that branches left (south) off the main track to a footbridge across Oxendale Beck.

7 The way is clear now, heading southwards and climbing towards the high saddle of Red Tarn. Slightly before reaching the tarn, take the path that branches sharply to the right (west) across the stream, climbing between Great Knott and Cold Pike.

8 Before reaching the top of the ridge, turn left (south) along the ridge.

9 The summit cairn of Little Stand lies approximately ½ a mile along the ridge, atop a conspicuous knoll.

10 From Little Stand, return along the ridge top, heading north past a cluster of tiny tarns.

11 The first major Crinkles lie directly ahead. On approaching them, ensure that you bear to their right (east) to regain the main path. As soon as the path is located, it rises steeply on a north-westerly bearing along the rim of the eastern crags.

12 Follow the path over the first top, Flesk (Crinkle Crags), then continue down to a grassy saddle. When confronted by the boulder obstacle (Bad Step) in a steep scree gully, there is a choice of ways around it. Either locate the grassy path which bears to the left (west) then swings around to regain the ridge top path, or take the more direct route by scrambling up the rock faces to the right (east) of Bad Step.

13 The steep ascent after Bad Step leads to the summit of Long Top. Ensure that you take the northerly path along the main ridge from here, not the one that follows Long Top's lateral ridge to the west.

14 Continue past three more distinct Crinkles (non-tops) then up to Shelter Crags. As the path begins to descend towards the Three Tarns col, a rocky pinnacle can be seen slightly to the right (east) of the main path, this is Shelter Crag – North Top, the final subsidiary top of Crinkle Crags.

15 Regain the path then go straight across the Three Tarns col up to Bow Fell. The summit cairn is atop a large rock outcrop on the western side of the upper shelf.

16 From the summit, return to the path that is visible now only in a line of cairns, and continue to the north.

17 Bear to the right (east) of the path in order to stay on the ridge top and reach Bowfell – North Top. After the summit cairn, head back down to the west and regain the path.

18 This leads down to a crosspath in Ore Gap. Go straight across this, staying on the more obvious path.

19 On Esk Pike bear right on the track that leads directly to the summit.

20 Regain the main path by heading west from the summit, and follow its northerly heading down to Esk Hause.

21 Turn sharp right (east) at the route centre on Esk Hause, descending to the stone shelter. Turn right again at the shelter, ensuring that your heading now is south-east.

22 At Angle Tarn, cross the outflow beck and continue north-east on the major track that climbs up to the col between Hanging Knotts and Rossett Pike.

23 From here, stay on the main path down to Mickleden. Another path joins from the left (north-west) in the valley, then the route bears south-east on an unmistakable track.

24 Stay on this all the way to the gate at the rear of the Old Dungeon Ghyll.

On starting out from the Old Dungeon Ghyll car park, the long line of Crinkle Crags' pinnacles lies directly ahead across Great Langdale Head's green pastures. From this location, various peaks are seen to surround the main valley and its two upper forks. With Side Pike over the left shoulder, the skyline continues clockwise over Pike O'Blisco to the Crinkles/Bow Fell ridge, then around to the right shoulder where Raven Crags fall from the Langdale Pikes. Perhaps it was the encircling effect of all these mountains (or possibly the tighter curve around Oxendale), that the early Norse settlers referred to when naming Crinkle Crags – otherwise it is difficult to imagine how they could equate the ridge with anything circular. ('Kringla' – a circle)

On The Way

On the footbridge over Oxendale Beck there is a dedication to a man who climbed Scafell Pike – on crutches!

A long, flat track leads across the fields to Stool End Farm at the foot of The Band, then into Oxendale where encroaching crags seem to grow higher. On crossing the footbridge over Oxendale Beck, there is evidence of wild winter storms in the wide, boulder-strewn stream bed.

The path begins to climb, heading very steeply towards the pass between Pike O'Blisco and Great Knott. Very soon into the ascent, Oxendale Beck's most interesting tributary can be seen to the north-west where Whorneyside Force crashes below Hell Gill's dramatic ravine. As more height is gained, The Band no longer obscures Bow Fell's summit, while the Langdale Pikes are on display to the rear above Great Langdale's graceful curve. After a relatively level section above Browney Gill, the path traverses crags bearing the ominous title of Black Wars. Here, Hell Gill looks particularly impressive to the rear, while nearby, the towering crags of Great Knott

A cold November day on Little Stand.

Oxendale on the approach to Flesk.

enjoy a powerful but temporary pre-eminence.

Approaching a high saddle cradling Red Tarn, the path follows Browney Gill through a rugged gorge of distinctly red tinted stone and shale, then turns westward to skirt Cold Pike. Another steep ascent emerges on the col between Great Knott and Cold Pike where Crinkle Crags forms a jagged skyline. At this increased height, a much wider panorama has opened up, displaying both Skiddaw and Blencathra above the High Raise ridge. Helvellyn's range has appeared beyond the Langdales, while Windermere glistens in the south-east. Coniston's group dominates the southern sector beyond the wide void of Wrynose Pass, and it is in that direction that the route heads now, having finally gained the great Crinkle Crags/Bow Fell ridge.

A short stroll along the stony plateau leads to a cairn atop a rock outcrop on Little Stand. At 740 metres (2427 ft) this is peak number 82. Somewhat disappointingly, the summit is too far back from the ridge's southernmost crags to offer a bird's-eye view into the Wrynose Pass – it would be necessary to descend over the lower knolls of Red How and Ravens Nest to enjoy that particular scene. However, the complex arrangements of rocks and stones on the summit provide a fascinating foreground for surrounding fells and more distant views.

Wetherlam, Great Carrs, Swirl How and Grey Friar are nearby, commanding one's attention to the south and south-east. Harter Fell is prominent among vast swathes of the Dunnerdale and far south-western fells, with lowlands and the sea beyond all these.

Of course, there is much more to the panorama than this, but a more detailed description is better left till the major summits. However, bearing in mind that Little Stand is merely a starter before the main course of the ridge, if you seek solitude and a particularly rugged Lakeland atmosphere, then this unfrequented, restful spot will prove memorable.

The first 'Crinkle' beckons to the north. After passing over the intervening rocks of Stonesty Pike and a cluster of tiny tarns, the route returns to the main path coming up from Red Tarn and begins the ascent of Crinkle Crags proper.

There is a distance of approximately 1 mile from this position across the ridge to the Three Tarns col. Be prepared for an exhilarating crossing of no fewer than seven 'Crinkles', four of which are ranked within the Lakeland 100. By 'prepared' I am not implying any imminent physical difficulties, but suggesting that an acute awareness of

one's surroundings will be particularly rewarding now. The sheer desolation of the buttresses, crags and gullies that form this ridge creates an overwhelmingly rugged yet beautiful impression. The scene constantly changes from one dramatic picture to another, with dizzying views of Oxendale and Great Langdale immediately below the right hand and the wild grandeur of fells and crags around Mosedale below the left.

On The Way

There are in fact five seperate pools of water at Three Tarns. The forgotten two are the first to be passed on the route.

The first Crinkle that can be classed as a subsidiary top is indeed the first pinnacle along the ridge, and this is gained very quickly. Various cairns mark the summit at an altitude

of 834 metres (2736 ft). Ranked peak number 33, it does not appear to have an official title, although Michael Dewey names it 'Flesk (Crinkle Crags)'. The most impressive outlook from here is to the east, down the gullies falling through Great Cove into Oxendale.

The second Crinkle lies approximately 300 yards to the north beyond a grassy saddle, and is clearly the highest pinnacle. Before gaining the summit, the route arrives at an obstacle known as 'Bad Step'. It consists of a large boulder blocking the most direct path within a scree filled gully. Having successfully negotiated this minor inconvenience, the way is clear once again to Long Top – the true summit of Crinkle Crags. The immediate surroundings are a shade gentler than the main body of the ridge, with a shelf extending westwards. Of the two obvious summit cairns, the northerly one is the highest at 859 metres (2818 ft), qualifying Long Top as peak number 23.

As one would expect from such a precipitous ridge, the views have both depth and distance, although a few paces to either side are necessary to fully appreciate them (not too many paces, mind!). Beyond Mosedale and Hard Knott, an exquisite picture is presented by Eskdale and the Duddon Valley as they flow south-westerly to the sea, separated by Harter Fell and Lakeland's south-westernmost chain of lower fells. With the Dunnerdale Fells the only other landmarks of any stature, this quadrant is a marked contrast to the remaining panorama.

Illgill Head lies due west above Eskdale Fell, introducing the rugged sculpture of the Scafell massif, Bow Fell and Esk Pike. These are all close at hand and present daunting faces that plunge into the remote passes

Relaxing on Long Top (Crinkle Crags).

Looking down from Shelter Crag – North Top on a moody spring afternoon.

above Eskdale and Mosedale Heads. The declivity of Mickledore is particularly pronounced beneath Scafell Crag, with a clear distinction between the subsidiary tops of Broad and Ill Crags.

This great mass effectively obscures more distant views in the west to north quadrant, although Crag Hill manages to stake a claim for the Derwent Fells and Ullock Pike is visible in the north above Glaramara's ridge.

From north to east, however, the outlook is packed with peaks both near and far beyond Crinkle Crags'

awesome eastern cliffs. Oxendale and Great Langdale lie below, leading to the near cluster of Langdale's Pikes and the High Raise/Ullscarf Ridge. Far to the north are Skiddaw's group and Blencathra coming round to the Dodds and Helvellyn's long range which gives way to Fairfield and Great Rigg. Further removed and more easterly are the High Street range and a full display of the Kentmere peaks.

From east to west, the Coniston group are totally dominant before gentler, forested contours bejewelled by Windermere, Esthwaite Water and

Wise Een Tarn.

Continuing northwards, the path passes above a wide scree gully followed by three more Crinkles in quick succession. Despite their prominence and popularity, none of these three possess the necessary height separation to qualify as subsidiary tops. Further along the ridge, the more imposing bulk of Shelter Crags lies before Bow Fell's pointed silhouette. At 815 metres (2673 ft) Shelter Crags is peak number 39, but has nothing of note to add to Long Top's description. The ridge

Top: A summer sunset viewed from Bow Fell.

Above: A springtime afternoon on Bowfell – North Top.

marks the apex of our route. The entire upper shelf consists of naked, broken rock, with the summit proper formed by an enormous pile of boulders on the western rim of the shelf. At 902 metres (2959 ft) this is peak number 10 and a favourite of many fell walkers.

The summit rocks are piled so steeply, and have such a pointed formation that the views on all sides have some depth to enhance their far reaching panoramas. Looking back along our route over the cliffs of Bowfell Links, Great Knott and Crinkle Crags form a delightfully rugged foreground to a skyline composed of the Coniston Group. Crinkle Crags' western ramparts fall into Mosedale and Ling Cove which lead into the still enchanting picture presented by the Duddon Valley and Eskdale. Undulating lower fells and foothills in this quadrant lie before the Esk Estuary and the sea, generating a marked sense of the height of our viewpoint.

Slight Side begins the Scafell massif, which for me is the most impressive yet somewhat forbidding aspect of the entire vista. Our more northerly position has unveiled the Derwent Fells in the north-west and north, while the Solway Firth is visible to either side of them. Beneath this complex skyline, the continuation of our route can be seen crossing Ore Gap up to Esk Pike.

From north to east, Bow Fell's visible boundary of rocks hides the mountain's awesome eastern precipices. Beyond their rim, the great valley of Langstrath falls away between a foreground of Glaramara, the Ullscarth/High Raise ridge and the Langdale Pikes. A multi-pinnacled skyline lies beyond all these, beginning with Skiddaw's group and a section of the seldom seen Caldbeck Fells.

begins to descend from here toward Three Tarns. Along the way, the path skirts to the left (west) of a distinctive rocky tower named in mountain tables as 'Shelter Crag-North Top'. Although this has a much lower altitude than the three non-qualifying Crinkles, its height separation is sufficient to merit a place in the top 100. At 775 metres (2542 ft), this is peak number 64.

A short, steep descent leads into the Three Tarns col where our path crosses a major thoroughfare linking Great Langdale with one of Lakeland's most remote areas and thence with Eskdale. Despite the title of 'tarns' the waters here are little more than rock pools, but they offer welcome resting places among rocks and grasses before the push up Bow Fell.

A short but very steep ascent arrives on the boulder-strewn summit which

Blencathra and Souther Fell lead round to Clough Head and the Dodds, then onto Helvellyn's ever present range. A distant, compact cluster formed by High Raise, Rampsgill Head and Kidsty Pike can be seen above the Fairfield/Great Rigg ridge, then High Street introduces the Kentmere peaks.

From east to south-east, Great Langdale lies before lesser fells, lowlands and Windermere with a background of the distant Pennines. Pike O'Blisco commences the march of more serious fell country with Red Tarn below Wetherlam completing the circle back round to the Coniston group.

Before leaving the mountain, a slight detour is taken from the path onto the rocky eastern rim in order to visit Bowfell – North Top. This is the high point on the eastern crags before the ridge top heads down towards Hanging Knotts – Bow Fell's northern rampart. Care must be taken on the rough ground here if one is to enjoy the view from these crags overlooking

Mickleden. If it were not a feature of the top 100, I doubt if anyone would ever visit this practically anonymous spot. Nevertheless, at an altitude of 866 metres (2841 ft) it is classed as peak number 19.

On The Way

From Esk Pike (the final peak), there is a total descent of 825 metres (2706ft) and a distance of 4.5 miles back to the Old Dungeon Ghyll.

Regaining the main path, the route picks its way over rocks and boulders as it moves parallel with the ridge, then swings westward down to Ore Gap. This pass was named after the iron ore trail from Eskdale to Langstrath which crosses our path in the deepest part of the col.

From here, a short ascent leads to the summit of Esk Pike at an altitude of 885 metres (2903 ft). Ranked as

peak number 15, this mountain is the pivot of a great semi-circular range around the head of Eskdale that incorporates both the Bow Fell ridge and the Scafells. This favourable location offers excellent views from the stony top, particularly of the Scafells' eastern crags which lie immediately across upper Eskdale's divide.

Above the ridge from Ill Crag to Great End, Haycock, Red Pike and Scoat Fell have entered the scene with Great and Green Gables much more prominent now. The Derwent Fells occupy an arc from north-west to north, where Derwent Water is another new addition. A short stroll northward from the summit cairn will reveal Angle Tarn and Langstrath, presenting a wonderfully atmospheric foreground for the mountain chains already described.

A busy track, which we will join shortly, is seen skirting the tarn en route to a col below Rossett Pike which lies before the rugged outline of

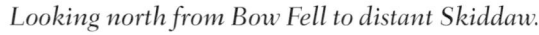

Looking north from Bow Fell to distant Skiddaw.

Looking north from Esk Pike.

Langdale's pikes. With the exception of a short ascent from the tarn to the col, it is downhill all the way home now, heading initially for Lakeland's most famous pass on Esk Hause.

This grassy plateau is at the hub of Lakeland's major mountain ridges, and a likely place for the uninitiated (or the over confident) to become disorientated. Two distinct crosspaths share the plateau: a higher one in the saddle between Great End and Esk Pike and a lower one marked by a star shaped shelter. As both points are linked by a clear track, it is easy to confuse one with the other. Walkers coming up from Angle Tarn are especially liable to error – mistaking the path to Scafell Pike for the continuation of the bridleway to Sprinkling Tarn. This is exactly how I got lost on my first visit to Esk Hause, with the happy consequence of finding a more direct route through a delightful, lonely valley to Lingmell, and then straight to my original destination of Wasdale!

Heading south-east from the hause, our route joins the well beaten track down to Angle Tarn's enchanting combe where Bow Fell's northern crags tower above the clear waters. After a short ascent to Rossett Pass, a very steep but firmly constructed path leads down into Mickleden's wide glaciated valley. Roughly half way into the descent, the path passes a grassy mound marked by a stone cross. Known as the 'Old Woman's Grave' there are two accounts that relate to her identity. Either she was a traveller on her way to collect an annuity, or she was a pack-woman who regularly sold her wares at the farms of Great Langdale. The grave marks the spot where her body was found.

On reaching the valley basin, a long trek along a section of the Cumbria Way follows the course of Mickleden Beck, flanked by the Langdale Pikes and The Band. This final leg of the journey is on a relatively flat, comfortable surface, which one's muscles and knees will be very grateful for.

Eventually, the pace quickens as the scent of fine ales is detected on a soft evening breeze, and the bridleway arrives immediately at the rear of the Old Dungeon Ghyll.

The Langdale Pikes

A short but visually spectacular walk from a popular valley, leading over one of Lakeland's most renowned skylines.

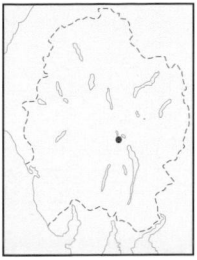

Among walkers and climbers, Great Langdale is one of Lakeland's most favoured valleys. Many trails lead into the fells from here, visiting the cluster of high peaks between the valley's westernmost reaches and Wast Water. But the main reason for Langdale's popularity is the group of peaks known collectively as the Langdale Pikes that lie to the east of the main bulk.

Individually named Harrison Stickle, Pike of Stickle and Pavey Ark, they dominate the skyline on the only two possible approaches into Langdale for motorists. These are from Skelwith Bridge via Chapel Stile (the main avenue), or through Little Langdale passing by Blea Tarn. This secondary route enters Great Langdale at the Old Dungeon Ghyll Hotel, right at the foot of the Pikes. From here, the

Stickle Tarn from the summit of Pavey Ark.

impression of their height is almost overpowering and it comes as a surprise to note that the highest peak, Harrison Stickle, is only ranked at number 85 in the Lakeland 100 and that neither Pike of Stickle nor Pavey Ark make the list at all.

Thunacar Knott is very close to the Pikes, and fortunately any circular route linking it with Harrison Stickle would logically pass over Pavey Ark. Also, since it is inconceivable that anyone would ever ascend Harrison Stickle yet fail to visit Pike of Stickle, I have extended the route to accommodate that very worthy pinnacle. This indulgence will not cause any inconvenience but it will demonstrate that the attraction of the Pikes is not in their height, but in the grandeur and diversity of the views they offer.

The most logical approach to Langdale is on the A593 from Ambleside or Coniston, turning onto the B5343 at Skelwith Bridge. After passing Elterwater, the road arrives at the village of Chapel Stile; the gateway to Great Langdale. There is a large store here, stocked with outdoor equipment and clothing, groceries, film etc – everything that you might need. A little further on, as the road begins to leave the village, you will see a farm gate on your left, crudely signposted 'camp site'. This is the Baysbrown Farm site. Although the facilities here only amount to toilets and a drinking water supply, the camp field itself is enormous, ensuring a degree of privacy regardless of the number of visitors. As a bonus, Great Langdale Beck runs along the northern perimeter of the site, and this particular stretch of water has a clarity that must be seen to be believed.

The route itself begins a further 2 miles along the road at the New

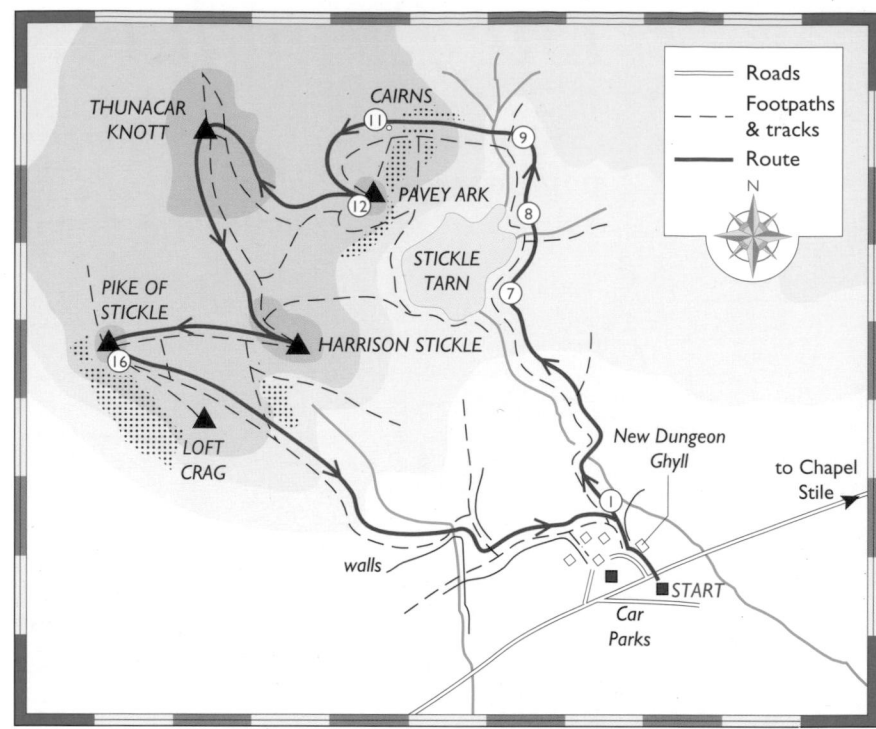

Dungeon Ghyll Inn and Hotel, and the Sticklebarn Tavern, where bunkhouse accommodation is available. Half a mile further is another campsite owned by the National Trust which offers all the facilities one would expect (and all the crowds).

At the inn and hotel, there is a large National Trust car park, another on the opposite side of the road, and parking spaces at the inns. Footpaths lead to the rear of Sticklebarn Tavern where the walk begins.

Peaks of top 100 on this route
85 *HARRISON STICKLE*
736 metres (2414 ft)
95 *THUNACAR KNOTT*
723 metres (2372 ft)

Start/finish point: Car parks at Sticklebarn Tavern, Great Langdale (GR 295064)

Map: Ordnance Survey Outdoor Leisure Map 6 (1:25 000)

Distance: Approx 4½ miles

Total ascent: Approx 720 metres (2362 ft)

Difficulty: Two steep ascents before reaching Pavey Ark, and a short scramble up Pike O'Stickle. One very steep but short section of descent after Loft Crag.

Time: Allow at least 4 hours.

Route directions

1 The paths from the National Trust car park and Stickle Cottage merge at the rear of Sticklebarn Tavern, where the path immediately forks. Take the right branch here, in effect straight on, and upwards alongside the fence and Stickle Ghyll.

2 Cross the footbridge and continue upwards with the stream to your left.

3 Cross the stile and carry straight on (another path joins from your right at this point).

4 Where two stone flags cross a minor stream, a path branches to the right, away from the stream. This heads for the tarn via a higher level, but ignore it – it is not very interesting.

5 From this point there are various places where the Ghyll can be crossed, and the ascent can be continued on either bank. Personally I prefer the present (eastern) side as there are more enjoyable rock-steps here.

6 Arriving at Stickle Tarn, there are three choices of routes. If you wish to climb Pavey Ark by either Jack's Rake or Easy Gully, take the path along the southern and western shores of the tarn. This leads to a point above fallen rocks, at the base of a buttress above the north-western tip of the tarn. From here a grassy slope leads to the left (south-west) into Jack's Rake. The more obvious gully to the right (north) is Easy Gully.

This leads up to join the main route of North Rake, but not before an awkward obstacle of jumbled rocks at the head of the gully. If you choose Jack's Rake, remember that after you emerge from the section that follows a small part of Great Gully, you should bear to the right where there appears to be a choice of paths. This will lead you through the shallow saddle between a distinctive rock outcrop and the mountain top, to emerge about 100 yards to the left (south) of the summit cairn.

7 To follow the main (and easiest route) at Stickle Tarn, follow the path along the eastern shore opposite Pavey Ark.

8 Cross the inflowing stream at the tarn's north eastern corner, and continue along the path that runs parallel to Bright Beck.

9 Where the path bears left follow it across Bright Beck.

10 The path up North Rake is clearly seen now, heading steeply up ahead and sheltered on either side by crags.

11 Where it emerges at the top cairns, turn left (south) for about 200 yards, crossing the remains of the wall wherever you feel comfortable.

12 From Pavey Ark, Thunacar Knott lies to the west. Follow the cairns that lead down past the small tarns, then bear to the right. Many paths interlace hereabouts, but Thunacar's dome is unmistakable once you

have skirted the knoll that lies between it and Pavey Ark.

13 From Thunacar Knott, a grass path can be seen leading south towards Harrison Stickle. Follow this to the northern flank of the mountain, where the path becomes much clearer over the final, short ascent.

14 From Harrison Stickle head due west down the steep shale path. Where this forks bear right (in effect straight on), into the hollow.

15 The track up to Pike of Stickle is clearly seen ahead. From the sign above the 'factory' screes, various paths lead up the final stage of the mountain – take whichever you fancy.

16 On leaving, come back to the screes, then the hollow, and bear right along the path that skirts the eastern base of Loft Crag.

17 After the steepest part of the initial descent, where the path becomes grassy, ignore the minor track that branches left.

18 Where the path arrives at some cairns, bear to the right, continuing your descent.

19 After crossing Dungeon Ghyll, turn immediately to the right, over the stile.

20 Follow the path down and turn left through the gate.

21 This leads back to the point where the original paths merge at the rear of Sticklebarn Tavern.

The first peak on our itinerary is Pavey Ark which represents the second of two distinct steps on the outward leg of the route. The first step is the hanging valley beneath Pavey Ark that contains Stickle Tarn, which outflows into Stickle Ghyll.

Immediately on starting out, both hearing and vision are subjected to Lakeland's magical treatment. Harrison Stickle towers above, as the path follows Stickle Ghyll's gorge upstream. Numerous falls provide the sound, with the water resting every few yards in tempting rock pools.

Initially, the gorge is tree lined, mainly with Rowans, and the going is comfortable although quite steep over the firmly constructed path of stones and boulders. After a footbridge, the trees begin to thin out, and Harrison Stickle is no longer in view, hidden temporarily by Thorn Crag. To the rear, Great Langdale begins to unfold with the heather decked top of Lingmoor Fell and Side Pike prominent. Windermere comes into view over the walker's right shoulder, with Wrynose Fell over the left.

As more height is gained, Harrison Stickle is unveiled once more ahead, together with the upper heights of Pavey Ark. The going becomes very steep and a little scrambling is necessary in places, but this serves only to make the ascent even more enjoyable. The tallest waterfalls are soon reached, and the panorama continues to expand to the rear, where Wetherlam, Great Carrs and Swirl How appear beyond the long ridge of Wrynose Fell and Pike O'Blisco. Then, a distant Old Man of Coniston can be seen between Wetherlam and Swirl How.

The massive bulk of Pavey Ark's eastern wall looms ever larger ahead, as the path climbs over some rock formations to reach the top of our first step and reveal the jewel in Langdale's crown; Stickle Tarn.

It will probably have taken between 45 minutes and an hour to reach this point, and no doubt you will rest here a while, looking across the tarn to Pavey Ark which soars another 750 feet above the water's surface. Two narrow paths can be seen traversing the awesome wall of the mountain. One branches northwards, the other southwards. The latter is known as Jack's Rake, Lakeland's most renowned scramble. A brief description of both routes is included in the route section for those who fancy the challenge.

On The Way

Despite the towering appearance of its crags, at an altitude of 700 metres Pavey Ark's summit fails by 15 metres to qualify for the Lakeland top 100.

Sergeant Man lies due north from the tarn, and its distinctive pinnacle can be seen clearly ahead as the main route leads up alongside Stickle Tarn's main inflow, Bright Beck. After crossing the beck, a steep ascent takes us up scree and broken stones in the gully known as North Rake. A slight detour to the left, when Easy Gully joins our path, is recommended for the view through the cleft.

Emerging at the top of the rake, a short stroll over rocks and boulders leads to a truly breathtaking spectacle on the summit of Pavey Ark. At a height of 2296 feet this does not qualify for the highest 100, but you will appreciate now why the Langdale Pikes are so esteemed. Directly beneath your feet lie the shimmering waters of Stickle Tarn, 750 feet below. Some 1200 feet under the tarn, Great Langdale snakes out towards the vast south-eastern panorama. Over to the right (south) Harrison Stickle stands guard over the gateway to the tarn's

Deft footwork on Thunacar Knott.

deep mountain combe.

Immediately to the north lies the broad, grassy hump of High Raise with Sergeant Man. Moving eastwards, the Dodds lead on to the Helvellyn range up to Fairfield. Then come the eastern fells and a horizon formed by the distant Pennines. The peaks around Kentmere give way to closer fells around Great Langdale, with Rydal Water, Windermere, Elter Water and Esthwaite Water clearly visible. Then the ground rises again in the Coniston group up to Bow Fell and the Scafells. After that, the close bulk of Thunacar Knott rather dampens the effect of the view from west to north.

You won't be in a hurry to leave this wonderful spot, but later the path makes a short descent over rocks, then leads past a cluster of tiny tarns, and up the grassy flanks of Thunacar Knott. Moving to the north west now, the summit is soon gained amid an area of small striated rocks, at an altitude of 723 metres (2372 feet). This is ranked peak number 95.

The view to the north-north-west is no longer obstructed by High Raise, allowing Skiddaw and a small section of Bassenthwaite Lake to enter the picture. The Derwent Fells are more prominent now, and to the west there is no mistaking the fact that the Scafells are the roof of England. The uppermost cone of Pike O'Stickle makes its introduction close at hand in the south west, but overall our present position is the least distinguished part of the route. This is due to the wide expanse of Thunacar Knott's high ground, and the only reason for our visit is to 'bag' it.

With no reason to linger here, Harrison Stickle beckons to the south. An easy crossing leads down gently to the beginning of the short climb up its northern flank. Blea Tarn comes into

Looking into Great Langdale from Harrison Stickle.

view beyond Side Pike, then the path arrives on the extensive, rocky summit of the mountain at an altitude of 736 metres (2414 feet) – ranked 85th.

Due west, and close at hand, Pike O'Stickle's domed summit looks remarkably unappealing, almost comical from the present viewpoint – but that impression will be totally reversed when the path finally arrives there.

It is to the south and east that Harrison Stickle offers its finest outlook. From the south-eastern summit cairn (there is another one to the north-west), the eye is taken by the broad sweep of Oxendale, and then onto the greater part of Langdale, which can be seen now in much more detail. Stickle Tarn is still apparent, presided over by the daunting face of Pavey Ark. Far away, the distinctive shape of Wise Een Tarn on Claife Heights has revealed itself. The full array of the Coniston group is open to view, in the form of Wetherlam, Coniston Old Man, Swirl How, Great

Carrs and the tip of Dow Crag.

Now the route drops steeply over rocks and shale into the peaty hollow between the two major pikes. Along this section some very large boulders have been incorporated into the path by builders who must have possessed the strength of Hercules. After crossing a narrow stream in the deepest part of the hollow, the path emerges above steep screes which mark the site of one of Langdale's neolithic axe head 'factories'. A small sign here discourages passers-by from souvenir hunting on the screes, as this practice has led to erosion of the site. The gradient should act as a deterrent in itself and I know that at least one person has paid the price of over eagerness with his life.

A short scramble up the eastern side of Pike of Stickle's dome leads onto the summit at 709 metres (2326 feet). Practically all the landmarks previously listed can still be seen from here, but now the sense of height is dramatically enhanced by the deep,

Climbers on Loft Crag, viewed from Pike of Stickle

wide chasm of Mickleden that lies directly below. Across the valley, the land rises sharply to Bow Fell's majestic pinnacle, which forms the highest point of the long mountain chain immediately to the west, incorporating the Crinkle Crags ridge. Slightly further afield, the Scafells lead onto that most distinctive of all Lakeland peaks; Great Gable.

Loft Crag lies very close to the south-east with our vantage point ideally placed to view its cliffs falling into Mickleden. Look closely and invariably you will see the tiny shapes and movements of rock climbers inching up the walls.

This position marks the end of the route's ascents. From here it is downhill all the way back to Sticklebarn Tavern, a return that takes about an hour. The path skirts Loft Crag, then drops steeply over iron tinted shale and stone. Along the way a spectacular view of wide, green pasturelands appears to the right, where Mickleden, Oxendale and Great Langdale conjoin. As more height is lost, the crashing sounds of Dungeon Ghyll Force will tempt you to take the short detour to your left, where a minor track branches through the ferns.

All that remains is the crossing of Dungeon Ghyll's stream before the path returns to the rear of the inns. As with walks 3 and 4, ambitious hikers might wish to combine the Langdale Pikes with the peaks of Walk 7 – the Central Ridge. The most feasible way of doing this is to commence from Stonethwaite in Borrowdale and go via Dock Tarn to Coldbarrow Fell. From there, the peaks of both routes lie southwards, with a return through Langstrath.

The Central Ridge

An isolated and generally unfrequented walk that begins as a long climb and finishes as a steep descent from Codale Head.

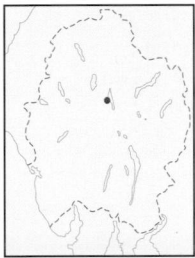

The true central range of Lakeland's mountains is formed by the relatively unsung undulating ridge that rises at Bleaberry Fell near Keswick before rolling southwards all the way to Great Langdale. After passing over High Seat and High Tove, this lonely ridge falls down toward Blea Tarn then climbs to Ullscarf and High Raise in the very heart of the mountains. Here, more popular trails lead both across the ridge (linking Grasmere with Borrowdale), and further along it to Langdale's busy pikes.

Understandably, most walkers who pass over High Raise also take the time to visit Sergeant Man's distinctive little

Thirlmere, and the route's start point, viewed from Steel Fell.

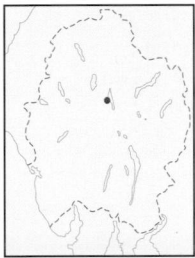

pinnacle. The superb view is the main reason, but many are drawn here by Sergeant Man's reputation as the southernmost peak of the great High Raise dome. In this they are mistaken, for Sergeant Man lacks the necessary height separation to qualify as an individual summit.

There *is* a subsidiary peak on High Raise, but it is formed by the rocky outcrop that lies immediately to the north-east of Sergeant Man, and is named on OS maps as Codale Head. It is doubtful that the few people who pass over this jumble of boulders and rocks are aware of its significance, or its place within the Lakeland top 100.

Codale Head can be grouped with High Raise and Ullscarf to form a very stimulating 9 mile walk over generally unfrequented ground. Although the starting point of the route is close to the A591, it lies in the quiet woods around Thirlmere and is far removed from any major accommodation centres. There are a number of campsites between Thirlmere's northern tip and Keswick, but otherwise the realistic bases for this route are Grasmere and Ambleside. All provisions for the day must be brought from the towns.

Approaching the end of the route, walkers who still feel reasonably energetic can enjoy a view of Thirlmere and Helvellyn (as depicted on page 65) by staying on the ridge top after Brownrigg Moss.

Continue on the main path alongside the fenceposts, then bear left on the summit of Steel Fell where the path forks. A path descends Steel Fell's northern ridge, eventually returning to the road and Thirlmere. Follow the minor road back to Dob Gill.

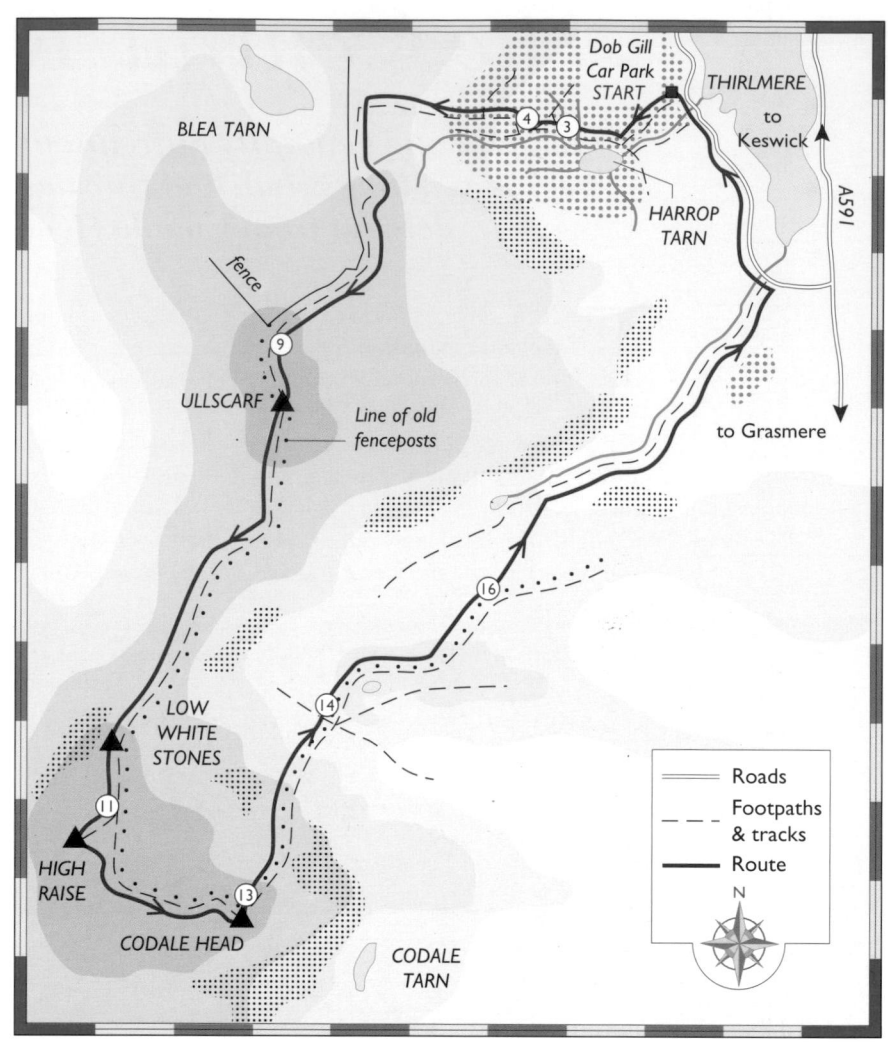

Peaks of top 100 on this route:
71 *HIGH RAISE – CENTRAL*
    762 metres (2500 ft)
90 *CODALE HEAD*
    730 metres (2395 ft)
94 *ULLSCARF*
    762 metres (2382 ft)

Start/finish point: Dob Gill car park, Thirlmere (GR 316140)

Map: Ordnance Survey Outdoor Leisure Map 4 (1: 25 000)

Distance: Approx 9 miles

Total ascent: Approx 740 metres (2428 ft)

Difficulty: The climb to Ullscarf is long and somewhat tiring, but displays wonderful scenery. After descending to Greenup Edge, another steep climb is required to High Raise. The section to Codale Head is very easy, followed by a steep, sometimes tricky descent. Later, the descent above Wyth Burn also is steep.

Time: Allow 5½ hours.

Route directions

1   Follow the Armboth Road off the A591, passing alongside Thirlmere's western shore. Take the path from the rear southern corner of Dob Gill car park. This leads steeply through woods until reaching a major track that skirts Harrop Tarn.

2   Turn right here (west), following the sign marked 'White route'. This is not the most direct route to Ullscarf, but it is by far the easiest to follow.

3   After leaving the tarn, the track climbs gently then forks. Take the left branch signposted 'Public bridleway Watendlath'.

4   Follow this for about 100 yds up to where direction markers stand on each side of the track. ('Blea Tarn' has been scratched onto one of the markers). Follow the minor path that branches to the right here, up the wooded slope.

5   Before long, another path branches to the right. Go past this and follow the 'Bridleway' sign.

6   The path reaches a double gate at the boundary of forest and open fell. Carry on upwards after the gates on the most obvious path, ignoring any minor branches to the right.

7   At the top of the rise, the path crosses a narrow plateau (the ground can be quite boggy here) and approaches a fence. Turn left (south) and continue alongside the fence; a faint path marks the way.

8   A path can be seen bearing slightly to the left and climbing steeply toward Standing Crag. Follow this to the highest ground and locate the ridge top fence. Now simply stay alongside the fence as it leads in a generally southerly direction.

9   Before reaching Ullscarf's summit, the modern fence turns sharply right (north-west). Continue to the south here (straight on), following a broken line of old iron fence posts. Eventually, these lead to the summit cairn.

10 The fence posts mark the way for the majority of the route from now. Follow them southwards from Ullscarf down to Greenup Edge, where more uncomfortable boggy sections have to be negotiated. Continue up past Low White Stones to the north-eastern cairn on High Raise.

11 At the cairn leave the line of fence posts and follow the path that branches right (south-west). This leads across to the true summit.

12 Head south-east across the summit plateau, returning to the path that follows the line of old fence posts. These lead directly over the outcrop of Codale Head. From Codale Head, the fence posts are intermittent but can still be followed. A faint path runs alongside them, heading north-east.

13 After a long and steep descent the route arrives at a crosspath. Go straight across this, then go past the path that branches to the right.

14 Pass to the left (west) of Brownrigg Moss Tarn, then follow the fence posts, heading slightly uphill once more towards a small crag.

15 A faint track follows the fence posts on a long, straight descent after leaving the tarn and crag, heading north-east. Close to the bottom of the descent (where the line of posts bears slightly to the right heading toward another ridge tarn), leave the line of posts and bear to your left (north north-east).

16 There is no path to show the way, but carry on downhill, heading roughly for the point where the visible end of Ullscarf's ridge meets Helvellyn's skyline. This leads quickly to the path above Wyth Burn.

17 Follow the path to the north-east (downstream).

18 Stay on your present side of the stream all the way down to the fields and the road at Stockhow Bridge.

19 Turn left (north) on the road, and then either continue along the road to Dob Gill or go through Stockhow Bridge car park to the lakeside path. This returns eventually to the road, where you should turn right for the short distance to Dob Gill.

From Dob Gill car park on Thirlmere's western shore, a stone path winds steeply up through woodland, passing by waterfalls before reaching Harrop Tarn's enchanting hollow. Across the water, Tarn Crags tower above the trees, exactly in line between our present position and Ullscarf.

Skirting the tarn, the route continues through woods heading due west towards the great central ridge. After ascending approximately 700 ft over a distance of 1 mile, the path emerges onto the open fells. As more height is gained, a wide vista opens to the rear above the forest, where Helvellyn's long range marches across the eastern skyline.

On approaching the plateau between Bell and Standing Crags, this eastern view is obscured by the plateau's breadth, but a superb picture of the Derwent Fells and Skiddaw's range opens ahead. Having gained the main ridge at this point, the route swings southwards, and begins the ascent of Standing Crag. Blea Tarn is

revealed below and to the rear, its north-western tip pointing toward distant Bassenthwaite Lake.

Although Ullscarf appears close to Standing Crag on maps, the approach feels much longer on the ground and it should be remembered that over 100 metres still have to be climbed to the summit. This final section toward the first major objective of the walk can be rather tedious until reaching Ullscarf's upper dome, where all the hard work is rewarded by a wonderful spectacle formed by the entire western panorama. Bassenthwaite Lake and Derwent Water can both be seen in the north-west, but they disappear behind the northern boundary of Ullscarf's broad dome on the final approach to the summit cairn. At 762 metres (2382 ft) this is peak number 94, and as stated, it is to the western semi-circle that one's attention will be riveted.

Due north, Lonscale Fell introduces the Skiddaw Group which fall towards a narrow arc occupied by the now unseen lakes and valleys. The land rises again to the near ridge of Cat

Bells, Maiden Moor and High Spy, above which are the Derwent Fells where Grasmoor, Crag Hill and Grisedale Pike figure prominently.

On The Way

With an altitude of 792 metres (2500 ft) High Raise summit is the apex of the 9-mile long central ridge.

The Newlands trio lies to the north-west with Dale Head presenting its imposing eastern face. As one's gaze continues toward the west and south-west, Rosthwaite Fell takes over the foreground, its ridge lying before the most closely packed segment of the mountain view. From Fleetwith Pike, the Grey Knotts/Brandreth Ridge comes round to both Green and Great Gables beneath a skyline of Kirk Fell, Red Pike, Scoat Fell, Pillar and the Buttermere Trio.

Rosthwaite Fell rises up to Glaramara's ridge and summit, after which Great End and Scafell Pike lead to Ill Crag, which effectively obscures Sca Fell. Esk Pike, Bow Fell and Crinkle Crags come next, before the close bulk of High Raise obstructs any sighting of the Langdales and their companions. Coming round to the south, the Coniston Group is clearly visible, but their appearance will improve later in the route.

Despite Ullscarf's long and rounded summit area, there is sufficient depth in the south-eastern prospect to allow a view of distant Windermere, the lowlands and the sea. Loughrigg Fell and Wansfell Pike can be seen in the same sector, before Heron Pike and Great Rigg form the long ridge up to Fairfield. Far away in the east, the other High Raise and

The western prospect viewed on the descent from Ullscarf.

Rampsgill Head are glimpsed beyond Fairfield and Dollywaggon Pike. From east to north-east there is a full but uninspiring array of the Helvellyn/ Dodds range leading to Blencathra, which completes the circle.

Around 120 metres in height is sacrificed as the route continues to Greenup Edge, passing close by some tiny tarns on the generally wet ground. There is a 'moorish' feel to the immediate surroundings now, but interest is maintained by a magnificent and unusual view of Glaramara's ridge. From our present angle and height there appears a marked distinction between Glaramara's various pinnacles, with the true summit and Combe Head particularly pronounced. In keeping with the mood, a remarkably pointed Honister Crag on Fleetwith Pike can be seen above Glaramara's ridge.

From Greenup Edge, a steep but comfortable ascent leads to Low White Stones on High Raise's northern face, where two high points can be seen a little further along the way, topped by cairns. The path rises to the first (north-eastern) cairn, then branches across the expansive summit plateau to the trig point and large stone shelter at an altitude of 762 metres (2500 ft).

Although ranked as peak number 71, High Raise does not attract the number of visitors that one would expect for such a centrally located peak. When viewed from a distance, its broad, rounded hump looks unappealing and lacks any promise of dramatic outlooks. However, this mountain has a 360 degree panorama that incorporates as many peaks as any other Lakeland viewpoint, and the summit proper is positioned conveniently on the western side of the dome, not at its centre. This allows greater depth to the western scene,

At the trig point on High Raise.

which, as on Ullscarf, is by far the most arresting.

Looking back along the route, the line of sight passes over Low White Stones to Ullscarf, which is capped by Clough Head. Bannerdale Crags and Blencathra lead round to Knott, in the distant Caldbeck Fells, then the Skiddaw group is seen due north.

Beneath this skyline, the High Seat/Bleaberry Fell ridge and Grange Fell fall towards Derwent Water. Lower still, both Sergeant's and Eagle Crags can be seen on High Raise's north-western arm, which then descends toward Borrowdale. Bassenthwaite

Lake lies at the feet of Skiddaw's group, before a background of the Solway Firth and southern Scotland.

Langstrath's deep, wide valley lies immediately below from north north-west to west south-west, and the southern reaches of its beck can be seen snaking up towards Angle Tarn. Across the valley's great void, Rosthwaite Fell displays Tarn at Leaves before reaching up to Glaramara's long ridge. Above this is Dale Head and the High Spy/Cat Bells ridge, topped by the multitude of western peaks listed in Ullscarf's panorama, and the Irish Sea. Of all

The Coniston Group viewed from Codale Head.

these, Great Gable's unmistakable pinnacle is the star of the show.

Allen Crags are clearly visible now, and Sca Fell has appeared between Scafell Pike and Esk Pike. Bow Fell has become the dominant feature in what remains of the western semi-circle, making the Crinkle Crags ridge seem almost insignificant.

Pike of Stickle's prominent dome lies close at hand, slightly below the skyline formed by Cold Pike and the Coniston group. From the present viewpoint, there is a surprisingly wide separation of Pike of Stickle and Harrison Stickle bridged by Thunacar Knott's instantly forgettable grassy hump.

Wetherlam lies due south, after which the visible boundary of High Raise's plateau narrowly fails to obscure the southern lowlands which introduce Morecambe Bay. Coming round towards the east, the plateau's smooth flow is disturbed by the rocky outline of Codale Head. Above this are Wansfell Pike and the far distant Pennines which lead round to Yoke and Ill Bell. Red Screes, Harter Fell and High Street stand slightly above

Dove Crags and Great Rigg's ridges, then Fairfield, Seat Sandal, Wether Hill and St Sunday Crag form the last complex section of the eastern skyline.

Matters are greatly simplified now, as Dollywaggon Pike begins the long flow of Helvellyn's range over the Dodds until the circle returns to Clough Head.

A short stroll across the plateau leads past a tiny tarn and back to a line of old fence posts that the main path has followed since Ullscarf. Codale Head's outcrop becomes clearer, and Sergeant Man has appeared slightly to the right (south-west) of the line of posts.

Little time or effort is required to reach the extremely rugged top of Codale Head which stands at 730 metres (2395 ft) and is ranked as peak number 90.

The great bulk of High Raise is behind us now, and the western mountain range has lost its appeal. To the south however, the Coniston Group has grown in stature, standing proudly over a wide and captivating arc of lowlands. Blea Rigg's knobbly ridge

falls away beneath one's feet towards the south-east where Loughrigg Tarn and Windermere gleam brightly. Esthwaite Water and Grizedale Forest lie near the Coniston Fells, with Rydal Water closer at hand in the east.

This is by no means a spectacular mountainous scene, but the lowlands and seascape are a very enjoyable contrast to what has gone before. The Helvellyn range is still very much in evidence of course, forming the background to a fascinating picture of lesser ridges and valleys which the route heads into.

It is downhill practically all the way from Codale Head back to Dob Gill, initially descending north-east above Wythburn Valley.

Losing height rapidly amongst a succession of sharp outcrops and knolls, the path requires a degree of concentration and an occasional short scramble. Heather adds a dash of colour to the thick mountain grasses before the steepest part of the descent is over and the route reaches a crosspath linking Far Easedale with Greenup Edge.

After passing the sheltered hollow and tiny tarn of Brownrigg Moss, our route leaves the ridge, leading down the grassy fellside into a gorge to pick up a path above Wyth Burn. The going becomes steep once again as the gorge narrows and the path picks its way through rocks and grasses above numerous cascades.

Eventually, the crashing sounds of the gorge are left behind as the path arrives in the peaceful fields of Steel End. Steel Fell rises over the right shoulder, with Helvellyn's forested slopes directly ahead. From here, one can choose between a short stroll through the woods along Thirlmere's shore or the simpler route along the road to Dob Gill.

North from Ambleside

An escape from a bustling Lakeland town, through wide green pastures to the superb Rydal/Fairfield ridge, culminating in the challenging ascent to Red Screes.

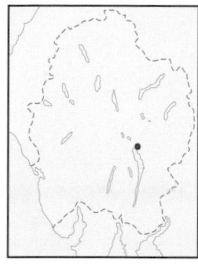

The busy town of Ambleside is a curious location from which to commence a mountain walk. However, it is an ideal base for a trip to five of the Lakeland 100 that lie to the north of the town. At 12 miles this is a long but quite straightforward route, incorporating the full length of the superb Rydal/Fairfield ridge.

After crossing Dove Crag the walk differs from the popular 'horseshoe' route by heading south-east to Red Screes. From there it is downhill all the way back to Ambleside.

There is no shortage of hotel and guest house accommodation here, although surprisingly the nearest camp site is over 3 miles away at Low Wray

Looking over Grasmere's valley to Easedale from Great Rigg.

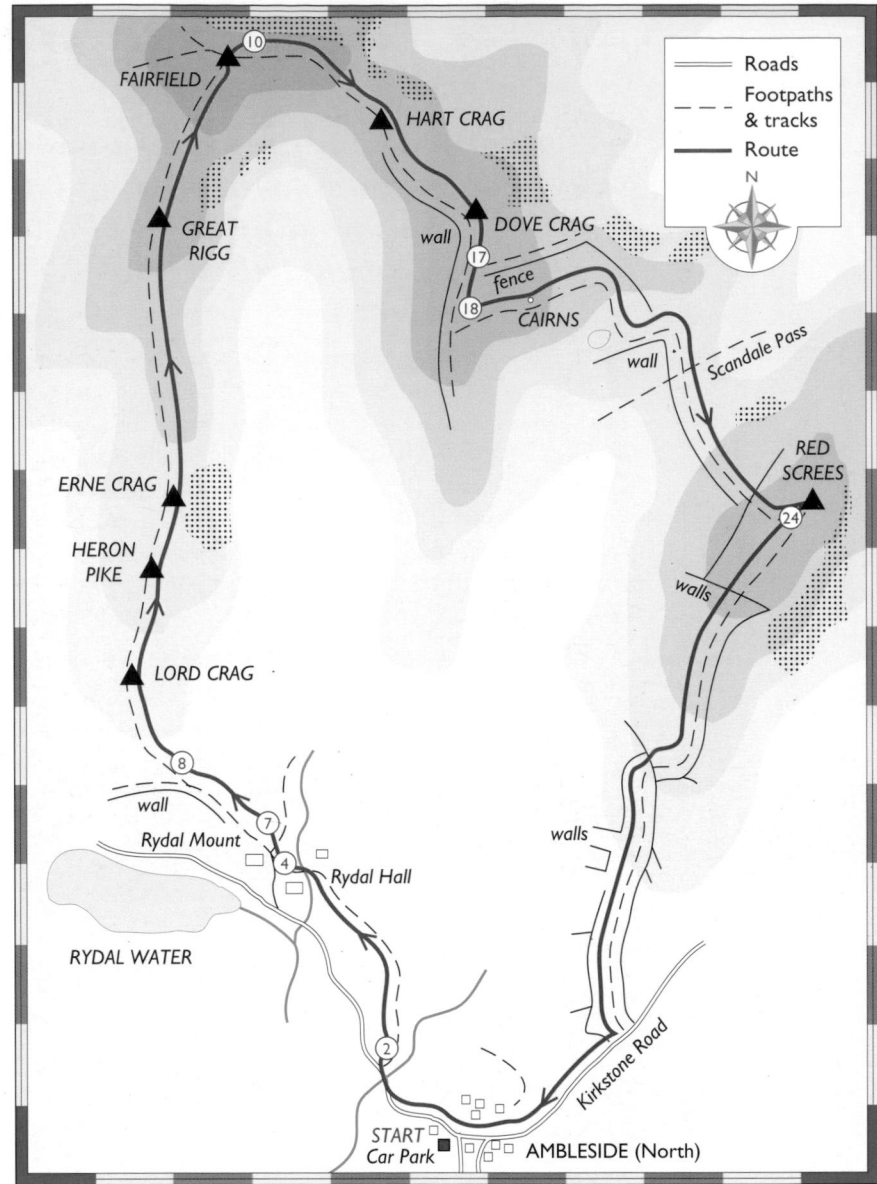

Peaks of top 100 on this route
17 *FAIRFIELD*
    873 metres (2864 ft)
37 *HART CRAG*
    822 metres (2696 ft)
50 *DOVE CRAG*
    792 metres (2598 ft)
62 *RED SCREES*
    766 metres (2545 ft)
69 *GREAT RIGG*
    766 metres (2513 ft)

Start/finish point: Large car park next to Ambleside police station (GR 375046)

Map: Ordnance Survey Outdoor Leisure Maps 7 and 5 (1: 25 000)

Distance: Approx 12 miles

Total ascent: Approx 1190 metres (3904 ft)

Difficulty: The only real difficulty will prove to be the ascent to Red Screes. Be prepared mentally for this.

Time: Allow at least 7½ hours.

(near the castle). Equipment and supplies are available at countless outlets, some of which are so large and well stocked that an enjoyable day can be spent merely browsing around them. As one would expect, pubs, restaurants, cafes and tea rooms abound.

Readers with a taste for the supernatural might be interested to note that the 'little pocket in the fells' described on page 75 was the site of a particularly strange event. The Lake District offers many bizarre legends, most of which are rooted firmly in the past, but this one belongs to modern times.

In his *Reflections on the Lakes* John Wyatt describes the occasion when he was asked to lead a mountain rescue party to the Easedale Fells. The previous evening, two people had reported the sighting of a 'flying saucer', stating that they had definitely seen it go down in the area. The rescue team suspected that the witnesses had actually seen a helicopter, but a search had to be conducted nevertheless.

Having been given reasonably positive directions, the team were confident that the area around Blindtarn Moss would prove to be the location of any evidence.

On arrival, there was nothing to be seen other than a perfectly circular flattened patch of reeds, with no apparent tracks leading to or from it.

Route directions

1 From the car park adjacent to Ambleside police station, turn left on the A591 towards Grasmere.

2 In less than ½ a mile the road crosses Scandale Bridge, after which a large iron gate can be seen on the right (west) side of the road. A wooden sign points through the gateway stating 'Public footpath Rydal Hall'. Follow this sign past the gate house.

3 When the track approaches the hall and out-buildings, look for the footpath signs (turning first to the right, then left).

4 After crossing the stone bridge, the track comes out to a minor road. Turn right here, uphill.

5 Pass Rydal Mount (Wordsworth's home) to your left, ignoring the 'Public bridleway Grasmere' sign. Follow instead the 'Public footpath' sign that points straight on up the road.

6 Go past the sign barring further cars, through the gate.

7 Immediately through the gate, a faint path goes sharp left into a private yard, a central one goes slightly to the left marked 'Public footpath', and a third goes straight on with an 'Agreement only' warning. Take the central path.

8 After passing through a small gate, follow the yellow direction indicator that points to the path leading away from the wall.

9 From this point the path is clear up to the ridge. Stay on the ridge top all the way to Fairfield.

10 From Fairfield head east, following the main path marked by a line of cairns, not the much fainter one slightly to its left on the very edge of the ridge.

11 Follow the path and small cairns down to the col and then up towards Hart Crag.

12 Before the summit, the path bears to the left and slightly downwards. Leave it, bearing slightly to the right and upwards over the rocks, to visit the summit proper.

13 Rejoin the path beyond the summit, heading south.

14 Follow the path down, and then up alongside the wall to Dove Crag. Ignore any faint paths you see leading away from the wall.

15 To visit Dove Crag's summit it is necessary to detour a few yards left (east) from the wall.

16 Continue to follow the path as it descends gently southwards alongside the wall/fence.

17 A fence and path branch left (east) from your track. Go past this.

18 Around 200 yards further on, another path goes to the left, away from the wall/fence. Follow it to the east.

19 This leads to the cairns above Scandale Tarn. Continue past the cairns as the path drops

steeply. This is indistinct in places, but head for the general direction of the tarn.

20 The path skirts the tarn, then comes to a wall and runs down alongside it.

21 At the wall corner follow the path as it turns sharply to the right (south).

22 Now, simply follow the wall down and over Scandale Pass, then up Red Screes. Ignore the crosspath in the pass.

23 Approaching the summit ridge, the wall forms a T. Cross over it, then either continue straight up to join the summit ridge path, or bear to your left towards the easily discernible summit.

24 From the summit, head south along the ridge-top path.

25 The only deviation comes where the path arrives at a facing wall. Follow the 'Footpath' sign to the right, then cross the stile on your left.

26 Ignore any gaps in the walls that follow the path down on each side.

27 Eventually the path arrives at a steel gate, which opens onto the road.

28 Turn right on the road down to the town.

29 Where there is an obvious fork in the road take the right branch.

30 The car park is directly opposite, at the bottom of the hill.

A large car park can be found next to the police station at the north end of the town, on the A591. It is unlikely that you will find a free street parking place at weekends or at any time in high season.

As the walk begins within the town boundaries at the car park, it is necessary to cover the first few hundred yards by road, heading north towards Grasmere. Very soon the long ridge of the outward leg of our route can be seen ahead, with the distinct pinnacles of Lord Crag, Heron Pike, Erne Crag and Great Rigg leading up to Fairfield. To the right (east) of this, the southern end of the Low Pike/ Fairfield ridge is seen climbing away in the distance.

The roadside section is over quickly, after which a comfortable trek alongside a cheerful stream passes through the wide, green pastures and intermittent copses of Rydal Hall Estate. An array of distant peaks are unveiled to the west, with the Langdale Pikes and Bow Fell prominent, then ahead the path up Lord Crag becomes clearly visible.

After winding through the main group of trees and a clutch of rhododendron bushes, Rydal Hall itself appears. This is a private conference and retreat centre operated by the Church of England, complete with its own campsite. The right of way is clearly signposted through the grounds, leading over Rydal Beck and then out of the estate. Within a few paces we pass by Rydal Mount, which proudly displays the legend 'William Wordsworth's home 1813-1850'.

The climbing begins now on a firm stone path that snakes up the fellside. Windermere appears to the rear, and stays in view for practically the entire route. Low Pike's and High Pike's ridge dominate the scene to the west as the path rapidly gains height, heading for the first rock outcrops of Lord Crag. On reaching them, Rydal Water appears beneath us to the west, with the silver ribbon of River Rothay winding from its southern reaches to Windermere. Further along the ridge top, Grasmere is unveiled, with Loughrigg and Silver How forming a foreground for distant mountain ridges, where the Coniston Group is dominant.

Looking over Grasmere to the Coniston Group from Great Rigg.

Temporarily, only distant peaks can be seen as the path undulates through a succession of knolls, then Grasmere reappears. Coniston Water and Esthwaite Water enter the vast southern panorama of lowlands, lakes, tarns and the sea, while to the west the bulk of Red Screes grows in stature.

On the summit of Heron Pike, Great Rigg looms large ahead, with Rigg Crag falling into Tongue Gill's deep valley immediately to the left (west). A slight depression links Heron Pike with Erne Crag ('Erne' – a sea eagle), before the ridge narrows, leading up the steep and stony path onto Great Rigg's magnificent viewpoint, at an altitude of 766 metres (2513 ft). This is ranked as peak number 69. The westward outlook is impressive with a mountain skyline incorporating the Coniston Group, Crinkle Crags, Harrison Stickle, Bow Fell and the Scafells. Due west, Great Gable stands proudly above High Raise, with Pillar, the Buttermere Trio and the Derwent Fells leading to the north-west and Skiddaw. Completing the arc are Dollywaggon Pike, Helvellyn with Striding Edge and Catstye Cam – all seen over the col of Grisedale Hause, above which peeps the tip of Grisedale Tarn.

Easedale Tarn is the pick of five tarns visible from here, tucked neatly in its combe beneath Blea Rigg and Grasmere Common. Immediately to the south of it lies a rounded little pocket in the fells, where there used to be another tarn that dried up. Slightly to the north of the tarn lie the valleys of Easedale and Greenburn, both looking distinctly lonely. The towering southern walls of Fairfield are ahead and slightly to the right (east), leading

Looking southwards to Windermere and the coast from Fairfield.

Top: The north-eastern outlook from the rocky summit of Hart Crag.

Above: Looking westward from the summit of Dove Crag.

fully appreciate the views on offer. Note the marked contrast between the mountain's smooth southern face of Rydal Head and the north-eastern crags. Above these, care must be taken when peering down over the rocky coves and towering buttresses that lead into Deepdale. Beyond this valley the horizon is formed by the High Street range and Kentmere's peaks, with a clear sight of Angle Tarn above Patterdale.

Cofa Pike and St Sunday Crag take the eye to the north, with the full westward mountain skyline previously described still dominant. A short stroll to the west will reveal Grisedale Tarn seated imperiously at the head of the great Grisedale Valley.

To the south, the major lakes and Morecambe Bay can be seen to their best advantage. Other than in cloud of course, this southerly aspect invariably has a bright silvery gleam.

Moving on, the high ridge path follows around Rydal Head, then descends into a narrow col on the extremely rocky approaches to Hart Crag. At 822 metres (2696 ft), the summit area is about 100 yards in length and sports a cairn at each end. This is ranked peak number 37. Now, although the south-westerly and eastern aspects are still impressive, Fairfield and Dove Crag obscure further views from here. The bare, broken rock hereabouts has quickly changed the mood from bright and airy to harsh and somewhat daunting. Suddenly, one is forcibly reminded that this is serious mountain country.

A steep descent over more rock and boulders leads to the col before Dove Crag, where the ground regains a softer texture. After a short rise up the peak's northern flank, we arrive at peak number 50 at an altitude of 792 metres (2598 ft). The only notable additions to

onto the ridge of Hart and Dove Crags. Immediately to the right and behind, the east to south view has suddenly come into its own. Precipitous crags fall to the vast glaciated valley of Rydal, with its beck running the entire length of the vale back to Rydal Hall.

From Great Rigg the push up

Fairfield seems a bit of a slog, but our efforts are rewarded by even more spectacular scenery on the mountain's expansive and stony summit plateau. At 873 metres (2864 ft) this is the apex of the route, ranked peak number 17. It is necessary to move freely around the cairns and shelters here in order to

At the cairns on Scandale Head overlooking Little Hart Crag.

the panorama are the northern end of Ullswater, and a slice of Brothers Water, with the eastward aspect becoming more appealing. To the south-east Red Screes beckons, promising to regain the glories of the route's earlier sections. This is not a false promise.

Beneath Dove Crag's summit, on the north-eastern crags, there is a very popular climbers' retreat known as Priest's Hole Cave. There is some speculation that it is man-made, with a title suggesting the reason.

The route swings east now towards Scandale Pass. Approaching Scandale Head, the ground falls gently to reveal a superb picture, with the tall, elegant cairns on High Bakestones commanding a lofty viewpoint above the pass. Red Screes dominates the scene ahead, clearly displaying the path that climbs its steep north-western slope. To the north-east of the path, Brothers Water lies beneath a background of high peaks, while to the south there remains a clear view of Windermere, far beyond the deep

Looking towards the Kentmere Peaks from the summit of Red Screes.

valley beneath Scandale Head. These two views are separated only by the narrow col of the pass. Directly ahead and below, Scandale Tarn nestles at the feet of an impressive rocky pinnacle known as Little Hart Crag.

This vantage point invariably comes as a welcome bonus for walkers passing this way for the first time – there is nothing on a map to suggest it could be so enjoyable. Considerable height is sacrificed on the way down to the tarn, height which will have to be regained on Red Screes. However, there is no alternative and it should be remembered that the next ascent is the last for the day.

The tarn's surroundings are grassy and very restful. A glance backwards here shows the twin cairns we passed standing sentinel above, silhouetted against the sky. Ahead, Red Screes has grown enormously in stature. Get your head down, try not to think about it, and soon you will be striding past the tarns on the summit ridge, looking at the wide eastern panorama that unfolds beneath your feet. At a height of 776 metres (2545 ft), this peak is ranked number 62.

To study Red Screes' position on a map suggests that Brothers Water and Ullswater will steal the scene, but this is not the case. These two lakes play only bit parts in an otherwise fascinating spectacle. From north-west to north-east, with the nearby eastern heights of Dove Crag providing the most precipitous aspect of the panorama, a profusion of jagged, undulating pinnacles lead over the Helvellyn range to Blencathra. Even more follow on to the mountain range that begins near Penrith. This of course, is the mighty High Street range, and we can see its full array marching in line en route to the south. When this reaches Thornthwaite Crag it is at its most impressive, offering the finest possible viewpoint of Froswick, Ill Bell and Yoke. Beyond these, both Harter Fell and Kentmere Pike cap the horizon.

In the same direction there is a strong sense of height looking down the crags into the Kirkstone Pass, with a bird's-eye view of the inn. To the south, fractions of the major lakes are still apparent along with the sea, while the mountainous skyline to the west continues to display full regalia. The famous sugar loaf aspect of Great Gable is particularly striking now.

The way home is to the south, with long views to the sea and over to the east into Yorkshire. The grassy path falls gently ahead, stretching out clearly all the way to Snarker Pike. Rydal Water comes back into view to the west, presenting a wonderfully tranquil scene as it nestles among a series of overlapping mountain ridges. The going is very comfortable on the approach to the pike, where Ambleside reappears below.

After a long day on the fells, and a 'job' well done, this kind of long, easy descent can be very gratifying. I remember being here one October evening, when the town lights twinkled and Rydal Water gleamed under the fading sky. A few yards to my right, a grinning farm hand was bringing down some sheep, obviously as appreciative of the peaceful scene as myself. Without a word necessary we kept apace down the ridge, stopping occasionally to savour the quite magical atmosphere and, I suspect, more than a touch pleased with ourselves.

On The Way

The return leg of the route from Red Screes is all in descent, losing 726 metres (2381 ft) over a distance of about 3 ½ miles.

Drystone walls conveniently mark the passage down the final stages, until the path deposits us on the Kirkstone Pass road. A short, steep stroll, with Wansfell towering to the left leads back down to town, passing the Golden Rule pub on the way. From here, the car park is one minute away.

Around Kentmere

Dramatically undulating terrain over a distance of 11 miles makes this walk a challenging yet rewarding day out.

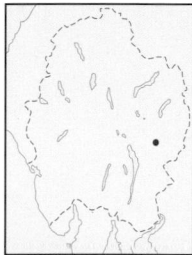

The most easterly route of this book begins at the tiny rustic outpost of Kentmere. With its smattering of farm houses and cottages, the settlement hardly qualifies as a village or even hamlet, although it boasts a fine hall and church.

There is very limited bed and breakfast accommodation in Kentmere itself, and little more in Staveley four miles to the south, where the Eagle and Child offers the nearest hotel rooms. Camping is available to the south of Staveley in the area of Ratherheath Tarn (for details call tourist information on 01539 446499). By road, the only approach to Kentmere is via Staveley (north of Kendal, off the A591), so stock up your provisions from the shops there. Kentmere is a very popular spot with walkers, but parking spaces are minimal. Recently, these have been

A misty autumn morning on Yoke.

Peaks of top 100 on this route
61 *HARTER FELL*
    778 metres (2552 ft)
73 *ILL BELL*
    757 metres (2483 ft)
91 *KENTMERE PIKE*
    730 metres (2395 ft)
97 *FROSWICK*
    720 metres (2362 ft)

Start/finish point: Parking spaces at Kentmere Church (GR 456041)

Map: Ordnance Survey Outdoor Leisure Map 7 (1: 25 000)

Distance: Approx 11 miles.

Total ascent: Approx 1010 metres (3314 ft)

Difficulty: Repeated ascents and descents over a long distance make this a challenging route.

Time: Allow at least 7 hours.

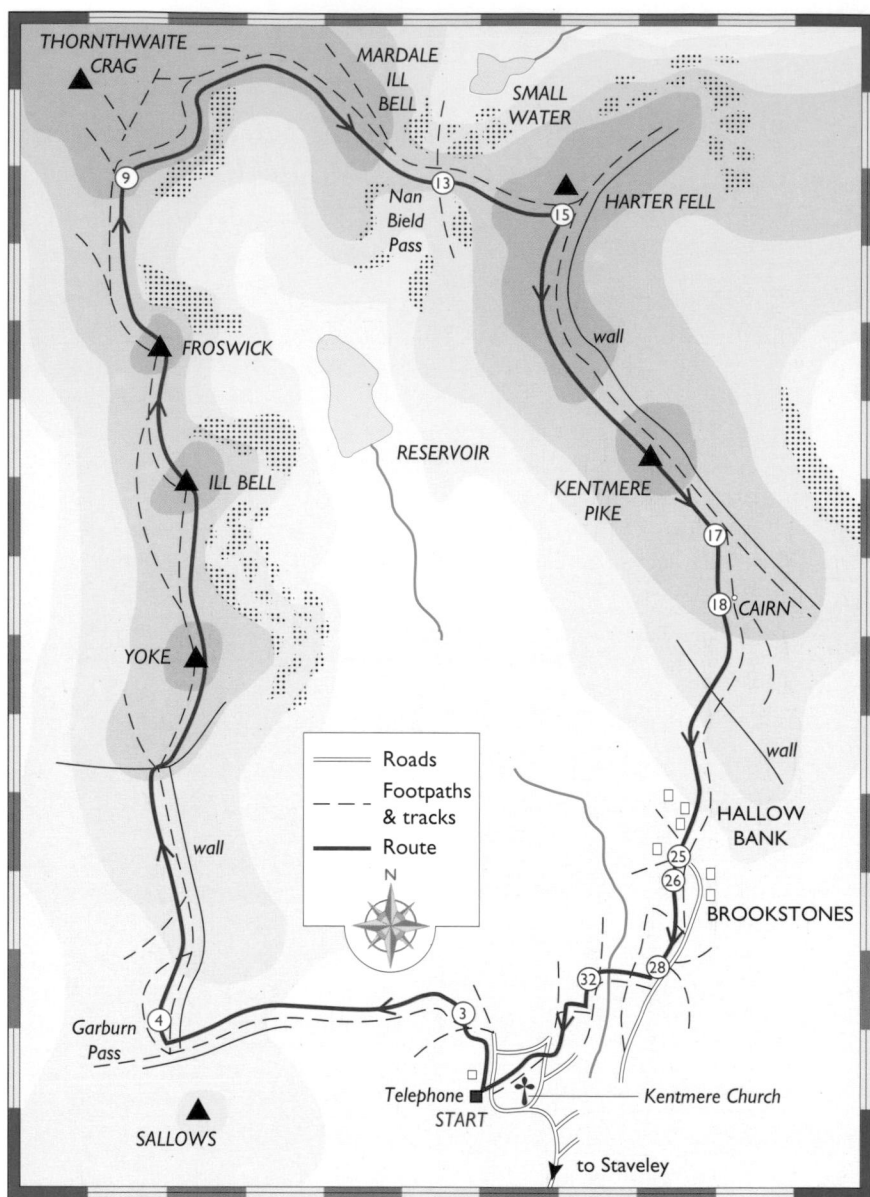

even further restricted, and I recommend that this particular walk should be undertaken on a weekday if possible. It is definitely one to be avoided on Bank Holidays.

The route covers 11 miles, passing over five mountains (or six if Mardale Ill Bell is counted). Of these, Ill Bell, Froswick, Harter Fell and Kentmere Pike belong to the top 100. For added interest, I have included the summit of Yoke on the route, even though it is possible to skirt around the upper heights of this peak. To do so, I feel, would be a waste, as hardly any time would be saved and little effort is required for the additional short ascent.

Readers who are well acquainted with the fells might wonder why both Thornthwaite Crag and High Street have been excluded from this walk,

given that these two peaks are usually associated with the classical 'Kentmere Horseshoe' route. The answer can be found in the next chapter in which they are more conveniently placed for the purposes of this book.

Also, the stated route directions from Kentmere Pike back to the start point might seem complicated, but

they are reasonably easy to follow on the ground. At the cost of some greater distance, a simplified return route can be taken by staying on Kentmere Pike's ridge over Shipman Knotts and Wray Crag until reaching the bridleway linking Kentmere with Longsleddale. Turn westward on this until High Lane, which can then be followed back around to the church.

WALK 9: AROUND KENTMERE

Route directions

1 From Kentmere church, head north on the road past the institute.

2 On reaching two signs, follow 'Public footpath Troutbeck via Garburn 100 yards'.

3 Turn right on the track signposted 'Public bridleway Troutbeck'.

4 At the top of Garburn Pass, Turn right immediately after the gate.

5 Either follow the wall path or take any of the paths that bear away from it should the going become too unpleasant underfoot. These paths return to the wall.

6 A small fenced enclosure marks a particularly boggy section. It is better to go through the gate here, then re-cross the wall a few yards higher.

7 Immediately after crossing a stile, bear to your right (east) and upwards to Yoke's summit.

8 From Yoke, the path is clear all the way across the ridge top, passing over Ill Bell and Froswick.

9 Continue in the same direction (north) from Froswick. On the ascent of the next fell (Thornthwaite Crag), watch for the first path that branches to the right. Take this path keeping to the very crest of the ridge.

10 Stay on this path, curving around the head of the valley.

11 The path curves around to the south-east, passing over Mardale Ill Bell. At this point, another path joins you from your left (north).

12 Carry on south-east to the Nan Bield Pass.

13 A stone shelter marks the crosspath in the pass. Go straight on here (east). This path leads up on to Harter Fell, following a line of cairns on the higher section.

14 At the summit cairn (the first major one), a fence comes up from the north-east, then turns to the south.

15 Follow the path alongside the fence heading south. This leads up to Kentmere Pike.

16 Continue south-east from here, following the wall-side path.

17 Shortly after the wall becomes a fence, the main path veers away from the fence, arriving at a small cairn.

18 At the cairn, the path forks again. Take the right fork here (the most southerly).

19 This leads down to a stile, then on down the fellside heading generally south-west.

20 The path is rather faint in places. Keep on the most well-trodden route where shallow gullies cross over it (at least one of these could be mistaken for a path).

21 Go through a wall gap, after which the path reaches scattered trees.

22 Here, there is a definite fork. Take the most obvious branch to the right, inside the gully.

23 The path comes down to a wall, where at first glance the way appears to be to the left. Turn right here, following the 'Footpath' sign and direction indicator.

24 This leads down to the rear of a white-painted house and ruined barn.

25 Go through the gate, then turn left at the crosstrack.

26 Through the next gate (white), the lane forks. Take the right branch here.

27 This leads to High Lane, the tarmac road. Stay on this, ignoring the track to Mardale that branches right.

28 After passing through a road gate, another 150 yds or so brings you to a 'Footpath' sign. Step over the wall stile here, to your right.

29 The path leads through a walled enclosure of grass and large boulders to another wall stile.

30 Step over the stile, then straight across the lane to another wall stile.

31 Go down to the footbridge, from where the path leads to a wall gap.

32 Through the gap, turn left on the lane.

33 Where the lane forks, take the right branch (towards the gate).

34 Follow the lane past the farm houses, where the lane starts to descend. Watch for a tiny wall gap with a small iron gate on your right.

35 Through the gate, turn left down to the church.

81

Beginning from the church, our first section follows the road heading towards a jagged skyline formed by Castle Crag. This appears to be the head of the Kentmere Valley, but the popular, true upper reaches are hidden from view as yet, tucked between mountains to the north.

Below: A winter afternoon on Ill Bell, looking south.

Bottom: Rest break on Froswick's summit.

Once through the farm houses, the route turns west and starts to climb a stony path, looking down on Kentmere Hall. Rock outcrops and bracken are close at hand, with the valley stretching out over the left shoulder. Over on the western slopes at Green Quarter, a compact network of dry-stone walls catches the eye, as the path

snakes higher towards the Garburn Pass. This is one of Lakeland's ancient thoroughfares, formerly a link between Kendal and Troutbeck. On reaching the skyline between Sallows and Buck Crag, the route leads north over Yoke's grassy southern approaches. The terrain has a distinctly 'moorish' look now, despite rock outcrops and frequent undulations. Many wet peaty sections occur between here and the steeper slopes of Yoke, but these are minor distractions from a mountain view that opens to the west. Suddenly, the Scafell and Helvellyn ranges dominate the scene, quickly followed by the Coniston Group.

Windermere unfolds to the rear as more height is gained, with the bulk of Yoke quite clear ahead. Over to the east, Kentmere Pike is joined by Harter Fell beyond the Kentmere Valley. On the final ascent of Yoke, our line of sight opens ahead to reveal a breathtaking picture of Ill Bell's rugged top and prominent cairns standing proudly before Thornthwaite Crag and Stony Cove Pike.

Once on the summit, Kentmere's deep valley opens immediately to the west, beneath Yoke's precipitous crags. As yet, Froswick is concealed behind Ill Bell but the rest of our route can be seen crossing the head of the valley on High Street's southern flank. From there it leads over Mardale Ill Bell onto Harter Fell and down to Kentmere Pike, all of which are open to view now.

Although all the eminent mountains lie in other directions, the most appealing outlook from Yoke is undoubtedly from south-west to south-east. Here, an undulating array of foothills and lowlands lead round to gleaming Windermere with its cluster of islands.

A slight descent followed by a comfortable climb leads us to the

A summer sunrise on Mardale Ill Bell, overlooking Small Water.

summit of Ill Bell. At an altitude of 757 metres (2483 ft), this is ranked peak number 73.

The rocky top sports three cairns, one of which has been very carefully shaped. This looks over a vast western panorama with major peaks visible in an arc from south-west to north. Morecambe Bay, Windermere and Blelham Tarn begin the picture, after which Wansfell Pike leads on to the Coniston group. The Scafells and ever prominent Great Gable give way to Fairfield and the Helvellyn range. Further north come the Dodds, Blencathra and Bowscale Fell.

Froswick lies to the north, ahead of an impressive view of the deep col between Stony Cove Pike and Thornthwaite Crag. Continuing north-east, Kidsty Pike peeps over the extensive plateau of High Street and Mardale Ill Bell, with Harter Fell and Kentmere Pike lying in wait for us.

Sooner or later, almost everyone who spends much time in mountains or countryside experiences insights of a depth and range proportional to the outward view. The sense of revelation is so strong that it defies dispassionate analysis and any sceptical explanations of 'self delusion'.

It can be in a sunset, with a momentary glimpse and understanding of the complex interaction of the heavens. More often, it comes in the view from some lofty crag that looks down on work-a-day concerns and shows them in their true perspective. I know one man who, simply by observing the curve of a high jet's trail from a mountain top, realised that he was looking at the curvature of the earth and 'saw' the fragility of our ecosystems.

It was during a classic, crisp December afternoon on Ill Bell that I felt my strongest ever rapport with the

Haweswater in drought conditions, viewed from Harter Fell.

natural world. The clear sky's electric blue merged with green, then into yellow above a thin mantle of snow. The laser-like light from our own star was glittering in the frost and ice. Every protruding rock, blade of grass and undulation of the fells was brought into sharp relief along with distant lakes, shining ribbons of streams and isolated pockets of trees. Each individual form was diamond-bright, brittle and complementary to the whole. Somewhere, just beyond the range of human hearing, it seemed as if the universe was resonating like a tuning fork. Each part of creation added to, and was a part of the same vibration, brought to life by the light. Which of course, it is.

I have often visited Ill Bell since that day, and have been on the fells in similar conditions, but the intensity of that moment has never been repeated. Like some particularly humorous event that never seems the same in the telling, I suppose you just had to be there.

The way to Froswick entails a steep descent from Ill Bell, passing over the narrow ridge above Kentmere Reservoir. Froswick lies directly ahead, with deep valleys on either side. Another climb brings us to the summit at an altitude of 720 metres (2362 feet) ranked 97.

Its position close to the head of both the Kentmere and Troutbeck Valleys provides Froswick with an improved

view down both these long divides. The reservoir lies directly below, in the shadow of Ill Bell's fearsome and very dominant northern face.

Although nothing of consequence has changed in the general outlook since Ill Bell, Ullswater can be seen more clearly now beyond the col of Threshthwaite Mouth. In the same direction, a sweeping ridge rises up to Thornthwaite Crag, taking our path with it. This appears to be a relatively easy climb on the grassy fellside, but like many long, gentle gradients it seems uneventful and is therefore disproportionately tiring.

However, the effort is rewarded by reaching a point where the route curves over to the east and so passes along the very crest of the valley head. With steep crags and Kentmere's yawning chasm at our right hand side, the way is clear across to Mardale Ill Bell.

On The Way

With its position at grid reference 466078, Kentmere Pike is the easternmost peak of the Lakeland 100.

Having only a 10 metre height separation from High Street's summit plateau, Mardale Ill Bell cannot be included in the Lakeland 100. It is fortunate, then, that our route has to pass over it, for this 'peak' offers one of the Lake District's most popular viewpoints.

As the path descends towards the Nan Bield Pass, a classic combe is revealed beside us with Small Water nestled deep within the hollow. Beyond the tarn's outflow, Haweswater can be seen a further 200 metres below, overlooked by Harter Fell.

A large stone shelter marks the point where we pass over Nan Bield's old packhorse route, surrounded by shattered rock and crags. Climbing steeply over rock steps towards Harter Fell, the path emerges from this extremely rugged terrain, to level slightly and reveal a truly magnificent spectacle. To our rear in the north-west, the massive combes of both Small Water and Blea Water (King of the Tarns) are testament to the apocalyptic force of the ice ages. Indeed, before glaciers got to work hereabouts, the central axis of these mountains ran from Harter Fell in a line to the west, passing over Fairfield.

With Ill Bell and Froswick reaching for the sky to the left of the picture and a series of mountain ridges stacked one above the other ahead, for me, this view more than any other typifies the Lake District. Lakes, tarns, combes, ridges, valleys and mountains, all topped by Great Gable's sugar loaf far to the west.

Very soon after this, the path emerges on Harter Fell's expansive upper heights. A large cairn entangled by old iron fence posts marks the summit at an altitude of 778 metres (2552 ft). This is the highest point of the walk on peak number 61.

The southerly seascape and westerly mountain panorama previously enjoyed are still in evidence, with some changes now to the north and east. The peaks around Kidsty Pike are more widely separated, falling towards Haweswater and the Lowther Valley. Beyond Mardale Common, Branstree and the Shap Fells, the Pennines form a long background to a wide and far-reaching vista.

Usually, bringing a particular mountain or place to mind presents a clear mental image. But whenever I remember Harter Fell, a sense of distance and timelessness generated by the eastern view is evoked, rather than any picture. Curiously, this feeling is quite inappropriate, as a short detour to the north-east will put the bulk of Harter Fell behind you, unveiling a superb view of Haweswater and Mardale. These should serve as a pointed reminder to anyone of the march of time.

Any drought results in a white band of rock around Haweswater's shore – the fruit of Manchester Corporation's labours that transformed the lake into a reservoir. Also, a very long dry spell will reveal part of Mardale Green's sunken village, evident now only in boundary walls and tracks.

To the south, Kentmere Pike's uppermost tip can be seen from the summit cairn. Our way leads over a broad, grassy ridge with Ingleborough far to the south-east and Morecambe Bay ahead. A long easy descent is followed by the day's final climb.

The north-western prospect from Kentmere Pike's summit.

On the descent from Kentmere Pike, looking back up the valley.

Mercifully, this is short and reasonable in gradient.

Kentmere Pike is ranked as peak number 91, with a height of 730 metres (2395 ft). A long wall follows our route across the mountain, with a triangulation column on the east side of the wall. This does not mark the summit proper, as slightly higher ground lies on the wall's west side, next to the path.

This is a broad, rocky summit area without a great deal to recommend it. Very few walkers would ever visit here if it was not on the route to, or back from Harter Fell. However, a short detour to the east, across the wall, offers a view down Longsleddale and over the

jumble of far eastern fells. A more appealing aspect is to the west and north-west, where Ill Bell and Froswick form a foreground for the main bulk of Lakeland's fells. This looks very much like a 'sea' of peaks; each mountain a separate rolling wave. It is not necessary to detour to the west for a view of Kentmere, as the finest views of this celebrated valley come later, surprisingly on much lower ground.

It is downhill all the way back to the valley now, heading south-east. Initially the going is easy with the long, wide ridge stretching out ahead. Soon, our path breaks towards Kentmere Pike's steep western slopes, where the valley view opens up.

The farm houses at Hallow Bank and Beckstones come into sight below, as the path steepens but remains comfortable. As more height is lost, the route passes through dense ferns with a scattering of trees, and the view up the valley continues to improve.

The descent ends at Hallow Bank, where we follow High Lane. Here, the valley's long curve is seen at its best, reaching up to the distant peaks. Stepping off the lane, we cross a footbridge over the infant River Kent, then pass down other lanes and tracks, returning to the church. The Duke William and Eagle and Child are the nearest watering holes – both are found at Staveley.

The Eagles' Range

A route of national importance, for both wildlife and geology, that takes in six of the Lakeland 100 including High Street, king of the Eastern Fells.

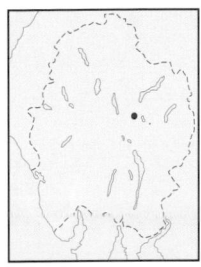

South of Ullswater, the long, verdant pastures of Patterdale stretch over 3½ miles to the northern foot of the Kirkstone Pass. The A592 travels along the valley, flanked throughout its course by high, pointed pinnacles and undulating fell tops.

Patterdale's small lake, Brothers Water, lies near the southern end of the valley, close to a minor road that branches eastward into the hamlet of Hartsop. Looking like an artist's impression of a Lakeland stone-built village rather than anything from reality, this sleepy settlement was in fact a busy mining centre during the 19th century.

There is a reasonably large and beautifully situated car park at the

A look backwards whilst on the approach to Stony Cove Pike.

eastern end of the hamlet, although this is likely to be full after mid-morning at weekends. If so, try the Cow Bridge car park on the A592. This is the place I usually choose anyway, because I can never shake off the feeling that visitors' cars are intruders in Hartsop. Nevertheless, the route description begins in the hamlet.

An 8½ mile walk from here takes in six of the top 100 peaks including the king of the eastern fells – High Street. Along the way, this route passes above areas of national importance for both wildlife and geology – areas where I have spent countless happy hours (and one of sheer misery!)

In the northern reaches of Patterdale there are hotels, inns and a post office/grocer's. If these cannot satisfy your needs, Glenridding is a short distance along the road. At the southern end of the valley, just beyond Brothers Water, there is the Brothers Water Inn and Sykeside – a campsite with everything (including its own licensed premises).

Some Lakeland visitors prefer the freedom of camping on the fells rather than on any recognised sites. Such adventurous types can find one of the Lake District's most delightful locations for an overnight stay in 'the wild' very close to this route.

Instead of descending back to Hartsop via Hayeswater (point 19 in the route directions) continue to the north-west over Satura Crag to Angle Tarn. This water's fascinating shoreline offers numerous comfortable camping locations. A return can be made from here either via Brock Crags or by following the major track over Boredale Hause back to Patterdale.

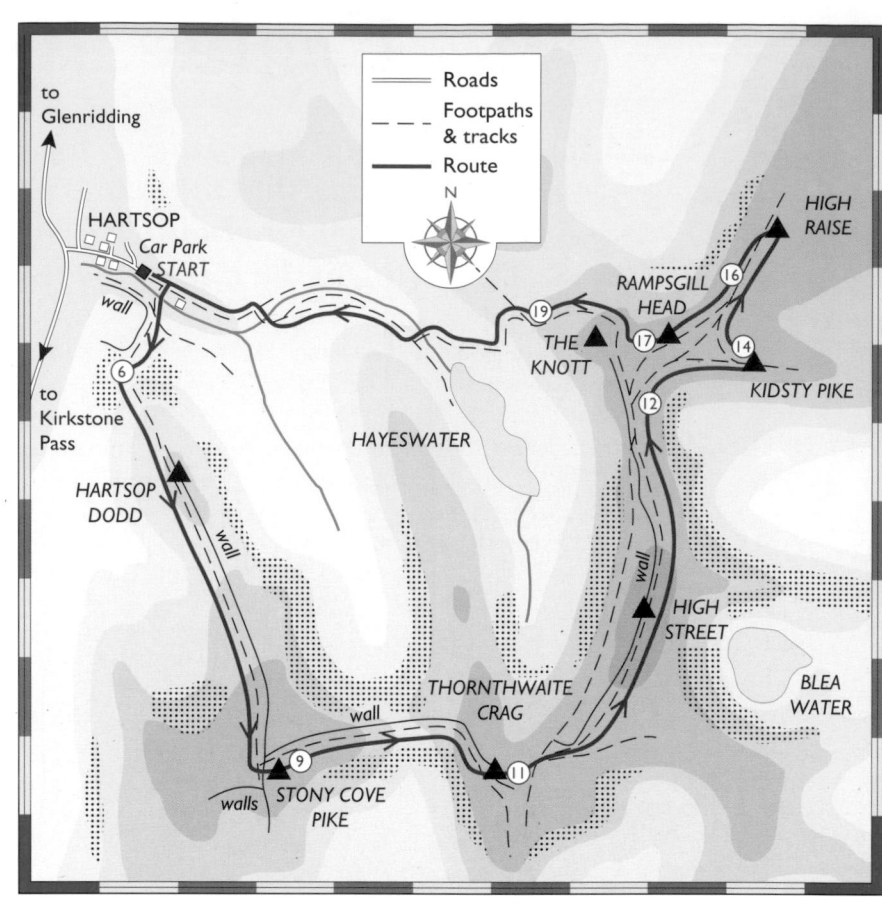

Peaks of top 100 on this route

35	*HIGH STREET*	828 metres (2716 ft)
42	*HIGH RAISE – EASTERN*	802 metres (2631 ft)
51	*RAMPSGILL HEAD*	792 metres (2598 ft)
56	*THORNTHWAITE CRAG*	784 metres (2572 ft)
58	*KIDSTY PIKE*	780 metres (2559 ft)
70	*STONY COVE PIKE*	763 metres (2503 ft)

Start/finish point: Hartsop car park, Patterdale (GR 410130)

Map: Ordnance Survey Outdoor Leisure Map 5 (1: 25 000)

Distance: Approx 8 ½ miles

Total ascent: Approx 1055 metres (3461 ft)

Difficulty: There is a very steep climb immediately on starting out (to Hartsop Dodd). From there, the section to Stony Cove Pike is very comfortable. The descent into Threshthwaite Mouth and the climb out to Thornthwaite Crag are very steep, with some scrambling required. After Thornthwaite Crag the route is relatively easy with just one steep descent towards Hayeswater.

Time: Allow 6 hours.

Route directions

1   Go through the car park gate, turning right following the sign 'Public footpath Pasture Beck'.

2   Cross the stream and carry on straight up, alongside the wall.

3   Bear right where the path forks, taking the fainter track after passing through some gateposts.

4   Follow the wall up to a stile.

5   Continue alongside the wall after the stile.

6   When the ascent reaches the crest of the ridge, bear left (south) away from the wall corner toward the summit of Hartsop Dodd.

7   On the approach to the summit, a wall can be seen that leads past the summit cairn all the way to Stony Cove Pike. A clear track runs along the wall's western side.

8   Stony Cove Pike's summit cairn appears on the opposite side of the wall.

9   Head due east from the summit. You will then be able to pick up the path that leads down to Threshthwaite Mouth.

10 Carry on across the narrow col and follow the track south-east up to Thornthwaite Crag.

11 North-east of Thornthwaite's column, a wall can be seen coming down from High Street. Go across to the wall and follow the path that runs along its eastern (far) side. This leads directly to the summit trig point.

12 Continue to follow the wallside path all the way down to the Straits of Riggindale. Shortly after the path begins to rise, watch for a branch to the right. Follow this around the rim of crags, heading to the east. Ignore any branches to the left (north).

13 The path becomes very faint on the final approach to Kidsty Pike, but the way is obvious over the short distance to the summit.

14 From here a path can be seen heading north towards High Raise. Follow this until it regains the course of the main ridge-top path (High Street once again).

15 This path passes about 100 yds to the left (west) of High Raise's highest ground. At this stage, a short detour is required in order

to visit the summit cairn.

16 Return along the path, heading south. Watch for a faint branch to the right (west) that follows close to the edge of the ridge. This leads to Rampsgill Head's summit cairns.

17 Head due west from here, down the grassy slope to The Knott. There is no path on the ground, but the distance is very short.

18 Turn right (north) on reaching the path that skirts around The Knott.

19 The path curves to the west and begins to descend more steeply. Watch for the cairn that marks a branch left down to Hayeswater.

20 Descend all the way to the footbridge at the tarn's outflow. Cross the bridge and then immediately turn right (north) on the track that descends above the gill.

21 Stay on the main track above the gill to the footbridge opposite Pasture Bottom.

22 Cross the bridge then turn left down to the car park.

The walk begins at Hartsop's car park where a well-beaten track leads up towards Hayeswater Reservoir. However, this comfortable path marks the course of our eventual return, not our outward leg. Be prepared for an extremely steep introduction to the journey, for the first objective is Hartsop Dodd which towers immediately above the car park.

A path branches across Hayeswater Gill, then begins the assault towards the mountain's narrow northern ridge.

The good news is that the rewards of this climb are proportional to the effort it requires. Very quickly, a bird's-eye view of Hartsop is gained, with its colourful background of Brock Crags. Patterdale stretches out ever further until Ullswater enters the scene.

On reaching the ridge proper, Brothers Water is unveiled below, together with arresting views of Deepdale and Dovedale. As the path climbs higher, St Sunday Crag, Fairfield and the Helvellyn Range present their most appealing faces. These lie to the right (west), with Patterdale and the lakes to the rear (south), and it is difficult to look away from their splendours. That is, until one realises that to the east, above Pasture Bottom's deep valley and Gray Crag's escarpment, the major peaks of the route are beginning to show themselves.

The steep ascent approaches what appears to be a cairn, but is in fact an end-on view of a wall. This dashes hopes of having arrived at the summit, but the remaining distance to this is short and much more comfortable.

Here, High Raise, Kidsty Pike and High Street are seen to the east, with Thornthwaite Crag and Stony Cove Pike ahead. Red Screes stands proudly in the south-west, separated from our route by the deep divide of the Kirkstone Pass.

The going becomes very easy now, with the path clearly seen stretching far ahead over the narrow summit ridge, following the course of the wall. The ridge widens on the approach to Stony Cove Pike, rising gently over the rounded, grassy slopes of the peak's north-western face.

These immediate surroundings give a false impression of the mountain, as all its other slopes are comprised of towering, broken crags and cliffs which are as yet unseen. The summit plateau becomes very broad and rather featureless, save for stony outcrops protruding through the general covering of turf and grasses.

The Kentmere peaks appear ahead and then the summit cairn can be seen

Below: Rest Dodd and The Nab viewed from The Knott.

Bottom: The southern prospect from Thornthwaite Crag's Column.

on the eastern side of the wall. The cairn stands at an altitude of 763 metres (2503 ft), qualifying Stony Cove Pike as peak number 70. Directly ahead, Windermere, Coniston Water and Morecambe Bay present a bright, airy scene, although this will improve immediately on leaving the summit.

On The Way

Once having gained Hartsop Dodd's summit, only a further 165 metres (541 ft) of ascent is required over a distance of 1.25 miles to Stony Cove Pike.

Beyond the now obscured Kirkstone Pass, a long, undulating landscape rises in the south-west at Coniston Old Man, then proceeds over the Scafell and Helvellyn ranges to the Dodds. To the rear (north), the far distant Eden Valley can be seen in the background as Rest Dodd introduces the long march of High Street's range. Thornthwaite Crag lies due east and close at hand, leading to the Kentmere chain of Froswick, Ill Bell and Yoke.

Stony Cove Pike's true rugged nature can be appreciated as the route heads for Thornthwaite Crag. An extremely steep ascent of the eastern ridge passes gingerly over broken rock into the deep col of Threshthwaite Mouth. This narrow, jagged edge provides a natural link with the High Street range, and offers a spectacular view down the Troutbeck Valley to Windermere and the coast. On the other side (north), Pasture Bottom lies far below, leading back to Patterdale.

Climbing out of the col, the steepest ascent of the day takes the path up and across Thornthwaite's western crags to the tall stone column.

This marks the summit of peak number 56 at an altitude of 784 metres (2572 ft). Now that the High Street massif has been gained, the remaining peaks of the route are easily conquered.

Thornthwaite Crag's most popular attraction is undoubtedly its superb vantage point near the head of the Troutbeck Valley, and the view of Windermere this allows. Immediately to the east of this scene, Froswick, Ill Bell and Yoke have closed almost into a single line running directly away to the south.

Kentmere Pike, Harter Fell and Mardale Ill Bell lead to the close and imposing bulk of High Street, which has temporarily obscured Kidsty Pike. Thornthwaite's own mass blocks the panorama to the north, after which Blencathra and its companions lead to the Dodds and all the long mountain chains previously described. Once again, Coniston Old Man is the last major peak in the south-west, after which the much closer upper heights of Wansfell Pike bisect the shores of Windermere.

The route turns northwards now, climbing gently alongside a wall over the grassy 'whale-back' of High Street. A triangulation column marks the summit at 828 metres (2716 ft). This is peak number 35, but the wide expanse of the summit plateau effectively removes any depth to the panorama. Practically all the previous mountain tops can still be seen however, and the Shap Fells have come into view along with a distant line of the Pennines in the east.

High Street is the highest point of an undulating mountain ridge that runs over 20 miles from south to north. The Romans took full advantage of this, constructing the highest road in England along its length. The road is

Making way for heavy traffic in Patterdale.

still used as a footpath, passing slightly to the west of the trig point and wall. As you might have gathered, the mountain was named after the road.

To fully appreciate High Street, it is necessary to wander extensively around the top. To the west, the Roman road offers a good view of Hayeswater and Gray Crag, but more importantly, a short detour to the east should not be missed by any visitor. After moving on from the trig point for a short distance, two tiny cairns can be seen branching away from the wall to the east. Follow in their direction to a large cairn that stands above the sharp spur of Long Stile, then feast your eyes on one of Lakeland's natural wonders.

A summer morning on High Street, overlooking Blea Water.

Approximately 1,100 ft below lies Blea Water in its magnificent combe, flanked by Riggindale Crag and Mardale Ill Bell. This is the deepest of all Lakeland's tarns and a site of special scientific interest.

Returning to the main path, the route continues its gentle descent as High Street's plateau grows ever narrower, eventually terminating on the Straits of Riggindale. Hayeswater (the tarn) lies beneath the left hand immediately to the west, but it is the breathtaking scene to the east that will captivate everyone's attention. Here, the crags fall approximately 1,300 ft into the great valley of Riggindale which leads almost 2 miles to Haweswater (the lake).

Kidsty Pike's pointed pinnacle soars above the valley's left (northern) flank, with the Riggindale Crag/Rough Crag ridge forming the southern rampart. An extremely keen pair of eyes might detect a flicker of movement or colour far down in the valley, around a wall and tiny box-like construction. This is an eagle hide, erected by the RSPB for the benefit of those who cannot resist the fascination of England's solitary nesting pair.

The birds have been here since 1969, but recently their chances of remaining seemed slim. The nest had failed to produce any young for three years, and that was an unprecedented period. The RSPB suspected that the male bird was too old to breed, and hoped that a younger male would be attracted from Southern Scotland. Also, it was possible that once vacated, the area could have been reinhabited by a completely new pair.

Scenic splendour not withstanding,

for myself and countless others, this area would have lost its magic if the worst had happened.

Fortunately, the spring of 1996 saw a healthy chick in the nest.

Thousands of people visit the eagle hide every year, but many leave without catching so much as a glimpse of the birds. Eagles are very active only when there are young or eggs in the eyrie. At other times much of their day will be spent simply sitting and watching. A sighting is very much a matter of being in the right place at the right time, neither of which are in any way predictable.

In this respect, I have been extremely fortunate over the years; I can remember only two occasions when I have been anywhere near Riggindale and not seen at least one of the pair.

Very early one July morning I was on Long Stile, coming over from Mardale Ill Bell where I had spent the night. My plan was to find a place above Riggindale where, if the birds appeared, I could perhaps take a photograph of them with the valley and Haweswater in the background. This would be unarguably a picture of the Riggindale eagles – a unique shot.

Approaching a point perhaps halfway down Long Stile, I moved a few paces to my left into a small grassy saddle overlooking the crags. Just as I thought that yes, this would be a very good spot, I was stunned by an explosion of crows escaping from the crags. Right there, no more than 20 yards from my feet, the female eagle (with seven-foot wingspan) was effortlessly gliding out from the rocks. She rose a few feet, saw me, then cruised back round for a better look, framing herself perfectly against the valley, fellside and lake. Moments later she was gone, lost to sight behind buttresses at the head of the valley. The camera, of course, was still deep inside my rucksack, but I did not feel any disappointment. I don't think anyone could.

The path begins to curve around to the east now, climbing gently over the short distance to Kidsty Pike. With its inspiring command over Riggindale and Haweswater, this is peak number 58 at a height of 780 metres (2559 ft).

On The Way

Despite rumours to the contrary, the Riggindale eyrie is unique to the whole of England, and perhaps more surprisingly, to Wales.

When viewed from east of Lakeland, Kidsty Pike's sharp point is an unmistakable landmark. I have often been drawn here by the silhouette that beckons one and all to eagle country. The bulk of High Street's range is the dominant feature from Low Raise in the north-east around to High Street itself in the south. Blencathra, the Helvellyn range, the Scafells and the Coniston Group can still be seen above this near landmass, but Kidsty Pike is not a peak from which to concentrate on distant views.

The yawning chasm of Riggindale and its immediate surroundings are all the reward anyone could wish for. Shap's sprawling fells lie beyond Haweswater, with Branstree and Harter Fell above Riggindale's rugged southern ridge. Both High Street's and the Straits of Riggindale's precipitous crags form the back wall of the valley, curving around to Kidsty Pike's own southern crags and screes that fall away immediately beneath one's feet.

It is almost certain that at any given time, there will be representatives of Martindale's wild deer herd down in Riggindale's basin. These tend to congregate deep within the valley below Kidsty Pike. It seems reasonable to assume that fully grown deer would be easy to spot in the empty grassy vastnesses, but that definitely is not the case. The true scale of Riggindale can only be appreciated when one realises that those minuscule specs below have moved slightly.

Heading north from Kidsty Pike, a short stroll and gentle ascent leads to peak number 42 on High Raise. At 802 metres (2631 ft) this rocky summit is second only to High Street in the long march of peaks that mark the course of the Roman road.

Due north, Red Crag, Wether Hill and Loadpot Hill can all be seen in line, where the 'road' continues toward distant Penrith and the Eden Valley. Ramps Gill's long, deep valley lies immediately below the steep western slopes of the mountain chain, with Haweswater to the east.

Very close in the north-east, the rounded hump of Low Raise introduces a background of the Pennines which lead to the Shap Fells. Branstree falls to the Gatescarth Pass, with Harter Fell between there and the Nan Bield Pass. All these constitute remarkably few landmarks given that they occupy the full eastern semi-circle from north to south. To the west though, the semi-circle is full of mountains, both near and far. However, the depth to this view is obscured by High Raise's western boundary and the panorama is much better appreciated by moving the short distance south-west onto Rampsgill Head.

It was on this ridge that I was caught out by the worst weather conditions I have ever encountered on the fells, on the first and last time that I will ever venture out without checking the weather forecast. A bright and peaceful June morning seemed to offer the opportunity for a long walk from Pooley Bridge at Ullswater's far northern tip, then along the Roman road as far south as Thornthwaite Crag. From there the

Walkers on the approach to Kidsty Pike.

On Kidsty Pike looking to the Straits of Riggindale.

plan was to return via Ullswater on a full-length lake cruise – very pleasant, thank you.

By Loadpot Hill dark clouds had rolled in, with a few drops of rain on a rising breeze. Just a shower of course; it would soon pass, wouldn't it? By Wether Hill I had to concede that my tee-shirt, shorts and sandals had not been a wise choice for the day, but my waterproofs surely would suffice. By Red Crag the rain was being driven horizontally into my face by a gale force wind. Cold water was penetrating every possible breach of my suit's defences, soaking me to the skin. I could not look into the rain – it was blinding. Looking in any direction was pointless anyway, as the rain cloud had cut visibility to less than 10 yds. I could not stand up at an angle anywhere near vertical at any time, and frequent gusts were knocking me flat. From then, things got worse.

I was convinced that this was not a case of extremely bad weather conditions – this was personal! The wind was a separate living entity; a screaming, demented banshee, and it was trying to kill me.

Eventually, knowing only that I was still somewhere on the ridge, I came to a place where the ground underfoot gave way to only cloud. I guessed that had to be Riggindale beneath me and turned to the west, hoping to find the path that would lead to The Knott and from there, down. Well, I had to get something right. Before long I was underneath the worst of the tempest, dropping steeply towards Hayeswater Tarn, and very relieved. Nothing was sailing on Ullswater that day.

Conversely, it was also in this area on another summer day that I

On High Raise, overlooking Ramps Gill.

discovered how pleasant walking in the rain can be. A gossamer-fine rain cloud in a dead calm was being effectively blocked by my sweater, which allowed my body heat to evaporate the rain at exactly the same rate that it was falling. All the way over Kidsty Pike and down Kidsty Howes, that wonderfully refreshing equilibrium was maintained. Even though I was approaching the end of a very long and somewhat difficult walk, I skipped down that hill like a lamb with two tails.

Rampsgill Head is peak number 51 with an altitude of 792 metres (2598 ft). It has a rounded, grassy dome that sports two cairns. The southerly one marks the summit, but the cairn a few yards north stands above some very impressive crags and buttresses, and provides the finest viewpoint. Immediately below, almost the full course of Ramps Gill's valley stretches away to the north, and the mountain ranges in the western semi-circle from north to south are seen at their best now.

A series of interlocking ridges and peaks rise one above the other. Beyond Ramps Gill and Martindale Forest two sections of Ullswater are visible, with a glimpse of Brothers Water sandwiched between the near fells. The Knott, Brock Crags, Angletarn Pikes, Rest Dodd and The Nab are the closest of these, with Beda Fell, Place Fell and Hallin Fell completing the cluster this side of Ullswater.

The background for all these is formed by Great and Little Mell Fells, Blencathra, Skiddaw and the Helvellyn range. From west to south-west, the Fairfield group and Red Screes lie before the Scafell massif and

The north-eastern outlook from Rampsgill Head.

Coniston group. Coming round to the south, Thornthwaite Crag and High Street are the prominent landmarks.

A comfortable descent of Rampsgill Head's grassy western arm leads very quickly to a path which skirts around The Knott. The graceful land curve between Rest Dodd and The Nab presents a fascinating spectacle as the rocky path continues to descend gradually.

With The Knott to the rear, a steep descent zigzags down to Hayeswater, where the valley head soars up to a tight curve formed by High Street, Thornthwaite Crag and Gray Crag.

Stepping over a footbridge at the tarn's outflow, the route follows a wide stony track above Hayeswater Gill's cascades. The track passes around Gray Crag's pointed northern ridge, after which Pasture Bottom is revealed between Gray Crag and Hartsop

Dodd. Some scattered remnants of the mining years can still be seen at the entrance to the valley, but like many Lakeland ruins, they complement rather than detract from the picture.

Another footbridge crosses the gill's beautifully clear waters, after which all that remains is a relaxed stroll down to the car park and the peaceful approaches to Patterdale.

Whenever I get carried away with a plan – trying to complete a walking schedule that conditions or time of day suggest should be aborted – I remind myself forcibly of an encounter I had on this exact spot some years ago.

Around a half-hour before dark on a day when the felltops had been consistently foggy, I was heading down past Pasture Bottom when I crossed paths with a young man in fell-running gear. He had a very defeated look and his movements were sluggish. I was

already puzzled by his direction up towards the mountains so late on a bad day, as he was not carrying any camping equipment. Then he asked for directions to Kentmere, and I was amazed that he could even consider the journey, although I did my best to conceal it. He explained that he had left his car at Kentmere to run the Kentmere horseshoe. Somewhere around Thornthwaite Crag he had become completely disorientated in the fog and had spent the next five hours running up and down countless fellsides and valleys, never knowing his true whereabouts. Later, he admitted to having passed the Thornthwaite column three times!

He checked my map for the correct bearings (which I am sure he was too confused to understand) and insisted that he would continue on his way. Definitely, here was a man whose pride was leading him into trouble. Taking great pains not to preach, I pointed out that it would be pitch black before he even reached the tops – the very same tops where he had lost his way in daylight. His chances of finding the correct route were zero. Eventually, he was persuaded down to Patterdale and a taxi ride.

On The Way

The area immediately south of Rest Dodd is the main grazing ground for a wild herd of red deer that numbers over 600.

He regained composure over a drink in the village, where it transpired that he was a very experienced fell runner and walker. When I left him, he was incredulous that he had almost talked himself into such a foolhardy exercise.

The Grisedale Round

Striding Edge and Helvellyn are just two of the many popular features encountered on this classic journey through an exhilarating Lakeland landscape.

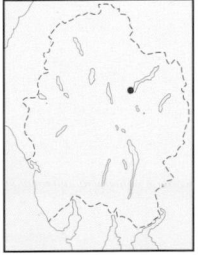

The picturesque village of Glenridding on Ullswater's south-western shore is the base for this 12 mile walk. Of the seven peaks within the route, one is a part of Lakeland's most popular feature (Striding Edge), with old favourites Helvellyn and St Sunday Crag also adding highlights on a classic journey.

Glenridding offers a variety of accommodation, with guest houses, hotels and an excellent campsite at Gillside Farm. For details of this, you can call Tourist Information on 017684 82414. Everything you might need by way of equipment and supplies is available in the village shops.

Summer colours above Glenridding and Ullswater.

Before starting out, prepare yourself mentally for the fact that Seat Sandal and St Sunday Crag are isolated from the main body of the route and from each other. As they are the last two peaks of the walk, they will appear daunting. This proves particularly true of St Sunday Crag, which requires a separate ascent of almost 1,000 ft. After all that precedes it, such a long climb will not be welcome, but bear in mind that the views from this mountain will be worth that extra effort.

A busy weekend on Striding Edge.

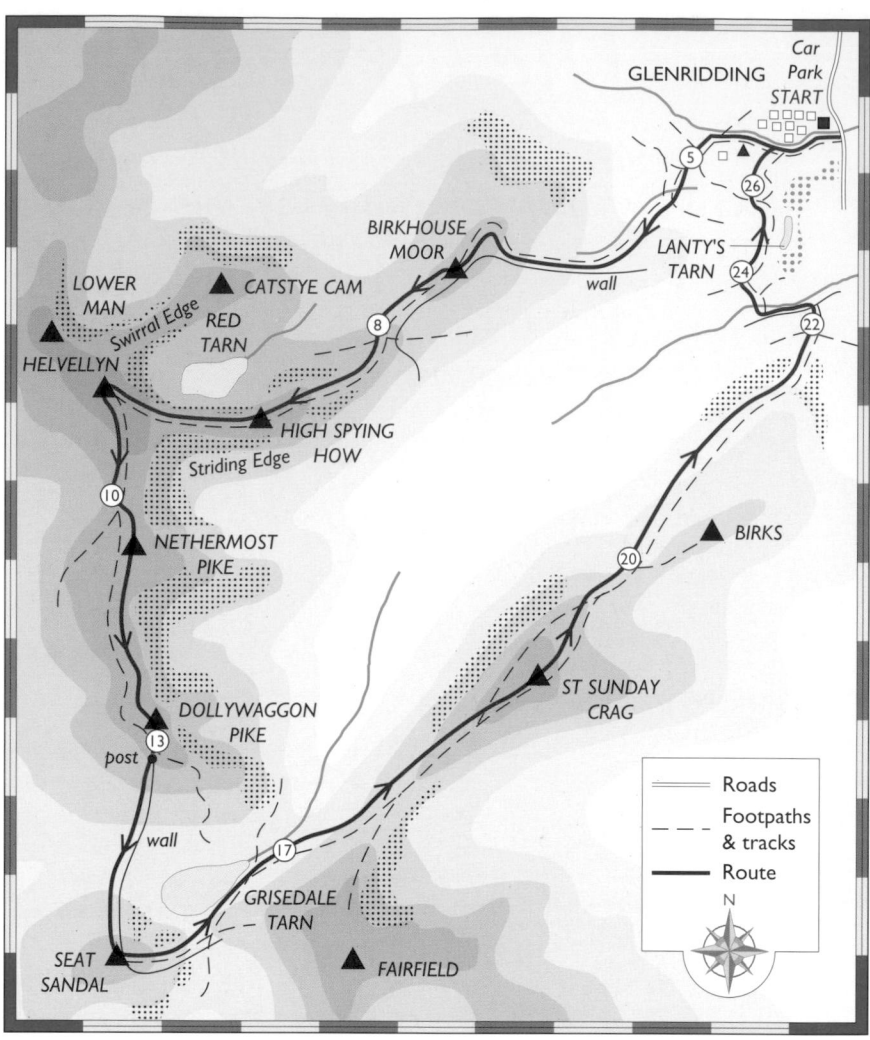

Peaks of top 100 on this route

4	*HELVELLYN*
	950 metres (3116 ft)
13	*NETHERMOST PIKE*
	891 metres (2923 ft)
22	*HIGH SPYING HOW*
	860 metres (2821 ft)
24	*DOLLYWAGGON PIKE*
	858 metres (2814 ft)
31	*ST SUNDAY CRAG*
	841 metres (2759 ft)
86	*SEAT SANDAL*
	736 metres (2414 ft)
99	*BIRKHOUSE MOOR*
	718 metres (2355 ft)

Start/finish point: Glenridding, Ullswater (GR 386169)

Map: Ordnance Survey Outdoor Leisure Map 5 (1: 25 000)

Distance: Approx 12 miles

Total ascent: Approx 1480 metres (4856 ft)

Difficulty: Long distances, steep climbs, very steep descents ... and Striding Edge. A challenging route.

Time: Allow 8 ½ hours.

Route directions

1 From the large, central car park in Glenridding, go back to the main road. Turn right, then right again after the bridge on the lane alongside the beck.

2 The lane becomes a track. Bear to the right (alongside the beck) where the track forks.

3 Go through the campsite, then turn left after the stone bridge, following the sign for 'Greenside'.

4 Follow the track that bears to the right, alongside the walls. At the first gate/stile, follow the sign 'Helvellyn via Mires Beck'.

5 A similar sign points to another gate/stile in a wall corner. Turn left after this, across the footbridge. Stay on the path as it climbs the right bank of Mires Beck then crosses to the left.

6 The way is clear now as the path climbs Birkhouse Moor. Approaching the top, the path is diverted to the right (away from the wall). Follow the posts as they come back round to the wall.

7 Follow the wall south-west on the ridge top, crossing the summit of Birkhouse Moor along the way.

8 Go straight across the path that bears to the right at the wall stile. Continue along the ridge over Striding Edge.

9 After the scramble up Helvellyn's adjoining slope, bear to the right to the obvious summit area.

10 From Helvellyn, head south on the main pathway. This leads into a saddle between Helvellyn and Nethermost Pike. From here, the obvious path skirts to the west of Nethermost's summit. Watch for the faint track that bears left to the summit cairn.

11 From Nethermost, return to the main path and continue southwards. The path skirts around High Crag, then passes to the right (west) of Dollywaggon Pike's highest point. A short detour is required to visit the summit cairn.

12 From Dollywaggon Pike, return to the main path and follow it to an iron post which stands slightly before a steep descent into Grisedale.

13 Leave the path at the iron post, heading due south across the grass. After a few paces into this descent, old fenceposts and a broken wall mark the way.

14 Follow to the right (west) of the wall, going straight across the saddle and up Seat Sandal.

15 From the summit, follow the left (northern) side of the wall; on the faint track down to Grisedale Hause.

16 At the crosspath on Grisedale Hause, bear left on the clear track down to the tarn.

17 Before crossing the tarn's outflow, watch for a faint path that branches to the right (north-east). This becomes much clearer, and can be seen leading to the depression in the ridge to your right (Deepdale Hause). NOTE: This path leads north-east. It is not the extremely steep track that climbs east to Cofa Pike and Fairfield.

18 On Deepdale Hause, follow the clear ridge-top path north-east to St Sunday Crag. Bear to the right on the upper dome to visit the summit.

19 Head north from the summit to regain the main pathway.

20 In the col between St Sunday Crag and Birks, take the left branch where the path forks.

21 Continue north-east along the ridge, then down a very steep descent to a crosspath at the northern end of the ridge. Go straight over this, across the stile and down to the road.

22 Turn left on the road, then right to the bridge over Grisedale Beck.

23 After the bridge, bear to the left (in effect straight on) where the main track turns to the right.

24 Climb across the field, then turn right (north-east) through the wall gate. Follow the main path as it rises away from the wall. This leads to Lanty's Tarn.

25 Follow the path along the western shore to a gate. Continue on the main path after the gate. This leads to another gate.

26 Do not go through this gate, but turn sharp right on the path that leads down to a stile.

27 Follow the path as it descends to another small gate and a tiny footbridge. Turn right after the footbridge, returning to the track alongside Glenridding Beck.

28 Turn right here (downstream) to the village.

Beginning from a car park at the Information Centre, the route follows Glenridding Beck through the campsite. The head of Glenridding lies above, flanked by Sheffield Pike's impressive crags and Birkhouse Moor – the eastern end of Striding Edge's ridge.

After the campsite, the path leads away from the valley, climbing alongside Mires Beck on Birkhouse Moor's steep eastern face. A wonderful view of the village and Ullswater opens to the rear, becoming ever more far reaching until the path arrives at a shallow saddle on the ridge top.

At this point, many visitors take a short detour to the north-eastern end of the ridge. Here, a cairn stands above Nab Crags, offering Birkhouse Moor's finest viewpoint over Glenridding and the lake.

Believing that there is nothing of further significance in the immediate location, walkers return to the main pathway, eager for the splendours that await on the opposite end of the ridge.

Having crossed the saddle, the path follows a wall that runs along the ridge crest, undulating over a series of knolls. The highest of these (with the wall passing directly over the top) is the true summit of Birkhouse Moor. Although there is a cairn to denote this point, I know that many people have passed this way oblivious of the fact they are on the summit of a peak classed 99th in the top 100.

Apart from the altitude of 718 metres (2355 ft), there is very little here that could cause anyone to linger, especially as a clear view of Striding Edge and Helvellyn beckons directly ahead.

Nevertheless, a cursory glance around the compass shows Swirral Edge linking Helvellyn with the most eye-catching pinnacle – Catstye Cam. White Side, Raise and the Dodds come round to the north-east, where the line of sight is back over Glenridding's void to Sheffield Pike. After Great and Little Mell Fells, Ullswater introduces Place Fell and

Angletarn Pikes which lie before the High Street range.

A wide gulf formed by Grisedale's unseen valley lies immediately on the opposite side of the wall. Above this, Birks and St Sunday Crag display the latter stages of our route, leading round to Fairfield. Seat Sandal's more isolated top represents the end of the route's outward leg, after which the eye returns to Helvellyn's greater ridge. Here, Dollywaggon Pike and Nethermost Pike display their eastern crags.

On The Way

Between Birkhouse Moor and Striding Edge, a new memorial that contains a particularly touching poem can be seen alongside the path.

The wall continues along the crest, then falls into Grisedale where another footpath comes up on Birkhouse Moor's eastern slopes. This is the point known as Hole-in-the-Wall, after which the path continues above Bleaberry Crags.

The ridge is still quite broad here, but becoming increasingly rocky. A line of cairns lead on to Low Spying How, after which the ridge narrows and climbs to High Spying How. As this jagged 'tooth' marks the beginning of Striding Edge, it is of course very well known. However, as in the case of Birkhouse Moor, few visitors are aware that it is classed as a separate peak. Perhaps even more surprising is the fact that over 140 metres in altitude have been gained since the route arrived on the ridge top, with High Spying How's proud silhouette standing at 860 metres (2821 ft).

This is peak number 22, but a

On Birkhouse Moor, looking towards Helvellyn and Catstye Cam.

description of the panorama is unnecessary – there is nothing that cannot be included in Helvellyn's description, and more importantly, nobody visiting this location will show the slightest interest in distant views. All eyes and attention will be riveted to a spot much closer to hand.

Some 470 ft below to the right, Red Tarn glows in its awesome combe, enclosed by the twin arêtes of Striding and Swirral Edges, and Helvellyn's towering eastern crags. Directly ahead, the course of our route crosses a jagged series of minor pinnacles on Striding Edge itself.

It is worth spending some time now watching the progress of other walkers as they make their way across to Helvellyn. Those who follow the paths slightly below the knife-edge make a considerably swifter passage than hardier souls who insist on taking a consistently uppermost route.

The sense of height is greatest when looking to the left (south). Here, the crags fall over 850 ft into Nethermost Cove, which sits another 1300 ft above Grisedale.

Probably the last thing anybody could wish to see on their maiden crossing of Striding Edge is the monument that stands a few feet below High Spying How's summit on the Nethermost side. This is in memory of a fox hunter who fell to his death here. One can avoid the poignant spectacle by keeping eyes fixed firmly forward as the path leads into Lakeland's most exhilarating one third of a mile.

Despite the previous (somewhat sombre) paragraph, this is not a dangerous crossing as long as it is treated with respect and is only attempted in calm, dry conditions. After many breathtaking, memorable moments, the path arrives on

High Spying How and the Dixon Memorial.

Helvellyn's steep eastern face where a scramble leads to the summit at 950 metres (3116 ft).

A surprisingly poor cairn marks the highest point, above a firmly constructed stone shelter and two more monuments. One is in memory of another fallen walker, the other commemorates the derring-do of two airmen who landed here in 1926. A trig point stands slightly beyond the summit, where the ground curves round toward Swirral Edge.

The top is long, broad and pounded by more boots than any other Lakeland mountain. Wordsworth was a regular visitor, and Sir John Dalton (accepted father of Atomic Theory in physics) is reported to have climbed Helvellyn every year over a forty-year period. Why then, is a peak ranked only at number 4 so popular?

The answer lies both in the location and formation of the entire Helvellyn ridge. Effectively, it forms the backbone of Lakeland, separating east from west. Therefore, the views have

considerable depth and incorporate most of the Lake District's mountains.

To the west, where rounded slopes fall towards Thirlmere, the depth is not so pronounced. However, the eastern side of the ridge consists of long, jagged spurs issuing from towering cliffs, and enclosing rocky combes. This precipitous, rugged character provides viewpoints rich in all the classical Lakeland features.

The most impressive combe of all lies immediately below Helvellyn's summit, where the eastern wall falls over 800 ft to Red Tarn. The famous twin arêtes lie on either side, with the tarn's outflow falling towards Ullswater's distant, meandering course. The Pennines form the background to this wonderful scene; a picture that would account for Helvellyn's popularity even without the benefit of the remaining, glorious panorama.

Above Striding Edge's serrated outline, Grisedale's opposite flank is visible from east to south south-east,

Red Tarn in blue, viewed from Helvellyn.

where Birks and St Sunday Crag lead on to Fairfield. Above these, the skyline is formed by the High Street range and the Kentmere peaks, which come round to Red Screes and Hart Crag.

To the south, the smooth hump of Helvellyn's great ridge rolls away over Nethermost Pike to Dollywaggon Pike, clearly displaying the next stage of our route. Windermere and Esthwaite Water can be seen beyond Dollywaggon, with a background of the sea.

All the way from south to north-west, Helvellyn's smooth slopes fall to reveal the most mountainous outlook, where a series of ridges interlock and climb to a complex skyline. Blea Rigg and Harrison Stickle lead on to High Raise and Ullscarf, then Borrowdale introduces Dale Head and Maiden Moor. Above all these, the Coniston Group and the Crinkle Crags/Bow Fell ridge lead on to the Scafells and the great cluster around Wasdale. The Buttermere Trio are next, before the sector is completed by the Derwent Fells.

In the north-west, Helvellyn's own bulk is prominent, with the trig point silhouetted against a hazy Solway Firth. From there, Swirral Edge forms the foreground as it connects with Catstye Cam's distinguished pinnacle. Above the edge, White Side and Raise fall towards Brown and Keppel Coves, and introduce the northerly march of the greater Helvellyn ridge. This continues over the Dodds to Clough Head, beneath a skyline of the Skiddaw group and Blencathra.

Finally, Green Side, Hart Side, Great Mell Fell and the distant Eden Valley lead back to Catstye Cam and the Ullswater picture.

A gentle descent leads southwards along the ridge to a shallow saddle between Helvellyn and Nethermost Pike. Along the way, a look backwards reveals the full length of Striding Edge, with a portion of Red Tarn peeping over the deepest part of the arête.

As the path begins an easy ascent of Nethermost, the top expands into a wide, flat plateau with no obvious summit. By leaving the path and staying close to the eastern crags, a small cairn is revealed where the top begins to curve eastward onto a rocky spur. This stands at 891 metres (2923 ft), qualifying Nethermost Pike as peak number 13. Exactly where the title 'Pike' comes from is a mystery, as there is an absence of anything remotely pinnacle-like on this desolate hump.

Fortunately, the crags offer spectacular views over Nethermost and Ruthwaite Coves into Grisedale, where sections of Ullswater are still visible, sandwiched between Birkhouse Moor and Place Fell.

Directly across Grisedale's deep chasm, Birks rises to the dominant feature of St Sunday Crag, and Fairfield stands above Dollywaggon Pike's eastern spur. This fascinating scene of daunting cliffs falling into the green valley is by far the most attractive outlook. Elsewhere, Helvellyn obscures more distant views in a wide northern arc, and the mountainous panorama from the Derwent Fells to the Coniston Group is robbed of any depth by Nethermost's broad plateau.

On The Way

In January 1996, an unaccompanied walker fell from Helvellyn all the way to the ice-covered tarn, yet still managed to return to Glenridding!

The route continues close to the ridge top, skirting round High Crag's summit then down to the saddle between High Crag and Dollywaggon Pike. Here, the path returns to the crest of the ridge, where a glance backwards will reveal a particularly rugged scene across the spurs, with

Hard Tarn's tiny pool nestled in its shelf high on Nethermost Crag.

Another comfortable and short ascent leads to the summit of Dollywaggon Pike at an altitude of 858 metres (2814 ft). This is undeniably a 'pike', and classed as peak number 24.

Again, the most arresting outlook is straight down Grisedale to Ullswater and Place Fell. Across the valley, St Sunday Crag looks particularly impressive now as it rears up from the depths.

Coniston Water is unveiled to the south, teaming up with Windermere and Esthwaite Water beyond Seat Sandal. The great mountains to the west have regained all their appeal, especially in the south-west where the Coniston and Scafell groups lie beyond an intricate array of peaks and ridges.

After our relatively easy passage since the ascent of Helvellyn, greater effort is required to complete the outward leg of the route. A steep descent leads to the col between Dollywaggon and Seat Sandal. Here, Grisedale Tarn lies below the left hand, perched imperiously at the head of the valley.

On a hot day, the water will be very tempting, and all kinds of excuses will be found to omit Seat Sandal from the itinerary. The imposing sight of St Sunday Crag, and the knowledge that it still has to be climbed within this route might even clinch the argument. But the ascent of Seat Sandal (although steep) will soon be over, and its views are certainly worth the effort. What's more, you can savour the thought that you are standing on a peak that few walkers take the trouble to visit.

At 736 metres (2414 ft) it comes in at peak number 86, sporting three cairns on its generally grassy dome. It

is necessary to wander back and forth around the top in order to enjoy all the fine viewpoints, but this is no great inconvenience.

A short detour north-east from the highest cairn overlooks the tarn. Its outflow points down to Ullswater,

flanked by the steep slopes of Dollywaggon and Fairfield in a charming scene.

From the summit proper, the western outlook is still superb over the mountains, and Thirlmere has entered the picture in the north-west. But Seat

Looking down Grisedale from Dollywaggon Pike.

Looking towards St Sunday Crag whilst on the approach to Nethermost Pike.

Sandal's major contribution to this walk is in the southern vista, where lowlands roll away to the sea, liberally decorated by forest, lakes and tarns.

Grasmere has joined Windermere, Coniston Water and Esthwaite Water among the lakes on display, with Blelham, Wise Een, Alcock and Easedale Tarns completing the aquatic offerings.

In the east, of course, the long Fairfield ridge is pre-eminent, leading round to St Sunday Crag.

After a steep descent to Grisedale Hause, a comfortable track leads down

The classic northern prospect from St Sunday Crag.

to the tarn's shore as the route begins its return leg. At this point, it is tempting to stay on the main track and descend into Grisedale. But allow the tarn's refreshing water to work its magic, and steel yourself for one more major ascent.

A faint path branches up the valley's eastern flank, heading for Deepdale Hause. This is a narrow col between Cofa Pike and St Sunday Crag, where the views into deep valleys on either side will banish any lingering desires for the lower path.

One further push up the broadening ridge leads to St Sunday's stony dome, where the most obvious path skirts to the left (west) of the

summit proper. Before making the short detour to the highest point, savour the greater depth of the present viewpoint across Grisedale, where Helvellyn, Striding Edge and all the crags of that great mountain ridge are on display.

Also, a look back over the left shoulder will reveal the finest possible view of Grisedale Tarn as it rests in a throne formed by Fairfield, Seat Sandal and Dollywaggon Pike.

Two cairns mark the summit of this, peak number 31, at a height of 841 metres (2759 ft). The view for which St Sunday is most renowned cannot be enjoyed just yet, but the eastern outlook is at its best from here.

Grisedale Tarn viewed from Seat Sandal.

Looking out over Deepdale, its eastern ridge curves up to Fairfield's daunting buttresses, before a background of the Kentmere peaks and Red Screes. The High Street range marches from north-east to south-east, with a sighting of Angle Tarn nestled peacefully above Patterdale.

In the south-west, a major cluster of peaks including Scafell Pike and Bow Fell can be seen beyond Seat Sandal and Dollywaggon.

Far to the north of Helvellyn's range, Blencathra, Bowscale Fell and Carrock Fell lie directly ahead as the route descends slightly to St Sunday's northern cairn. From here, a few more paces lead to an outcrop of sharp rocks

that introduce this mountain's finest outlook. It is all the reward any walker could require – an ideal location to rest and reflect on the day's proceedings.

St Sunday's precipitous crags generate a delightful sense of height to the entire scene. Immediately below, Grisedale's green pastures flow between the descending ridges of Birkhouse Moor and Birks to the southern reaches of Ullswater. The tranquil lake heads away to the north, then crooks sharply north-east around Birk Fell's distinctive pinnacle. Gowbarrow Fell stands above the far shore, before the eye is drawn to distant lowlands and the Pennines.

The route continues directly into

this wonderfully atmospheric picture, descending very steeply on St Sunday's northern ridge. A relatively level section skirts to the west of Birks' summit, where the view of Helvellyn's ridge is still a major attraction.

The lake is unveiled once more on another extremely steep descent as the path picks its way down the northernmost crags into Grisedale.

A minor road is followed above Grisedale Beck's wooded gorge before the route crosses a bridge deep within the valley basin. One more (slightly unwelcome) ascent leads to the forested hollow of Lanty's Tarn, then down to Glenridding Beck and the village.

Around Keppel and Brown Coves

Catstye Cam's pyramidal form dominates this short but rewarding route that includes a crossing of Swirral Edge.

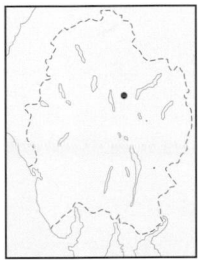

Once again, Glenridding becomes the base for this 6 mile walk. Despite the shortness and relative ease of the route, the peaks encountered are all high-ranking among the top 100. White Side is the lowest of those encountered, but even that comes in at number 21.

For the sake of convenience, the route is described as commencing from the top of Greenside Road above the village. Although the upper section of the road is classed as private, it is open to visitors of both the youth hostel and the lodges at Greenside mines. Others must first make their way to this point. In Glenridding the

Looking northwards to Skiddaw from White Side's summit cairn.

road is clearly signposted 'Gillside Farm' and 'Greenside'. Leading past rows of former miners' cottages above Glenridding Beck, the minor road degenerates yet remains passable up to the youth hostel. A few yards past this is an adequate parking area, just below Greenside's abandoned mines.

Immediately on stepping out of the car, mountain scenery and sounds invade the senses. Already one is high above the village, looking down through a steep-sided gorge with a crashing beck that falls towards the lake.

Conifer plantations adorn the gorge's lower flanks and their scent adds a little spice to the clean air. The precipitous heathered crags of Sheffield Pike lie on one side, with Birkhouse Moor's steep northern spur on the other. The road terminates at a group of renovated mine buildings, one of which is available for hire (Swirral Bothy, 01768 772803). The others are outdoor pursuit centres.

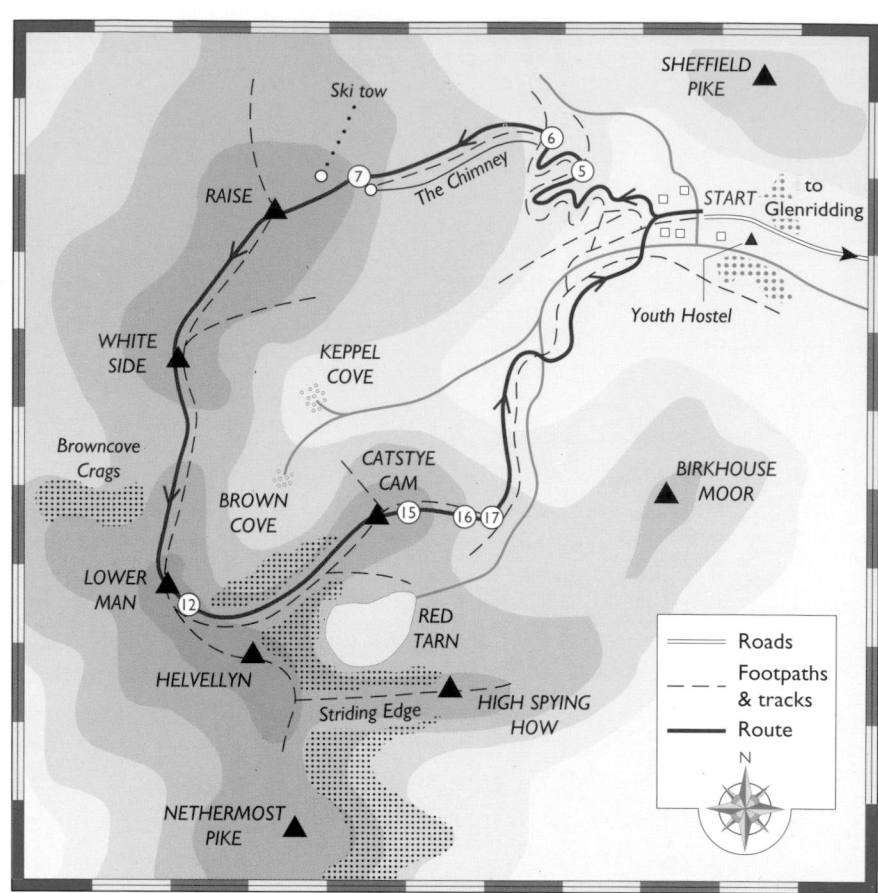

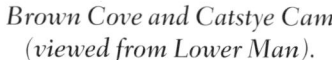

Brown Cove and Catstye Cam (viewed from Lower Man).

Peaks of top 100 on this route

8   *LOWER MAN*
    925 metres (3034 ft)

14   *CATSTYE CAM*
    890 metres (2919 ft)

16   *RAISE*
    883 metres (2896 ft)

21   *WHITE SIDE*
    863 metres (2831 ft)

Start/finish point: Glenridding Youth Hostel – parking spaces at top of Greenside Road (GR 366174)

Map: Ordnance Survey Outdoor Leisure Map 5 (1: 25 000)

Distance: Approx 6 miles

Total ascent: Approx 865 metres (2838 ft)

Difficulty: The climb to Raise is quite tiring, particularly over the latter stages where there is no recognisable footpath. Lower Man's ascent is steep, after which one must exercise caution on the crossing of Swirral Edge. The descent from Catstye Cam is very steep for a short distance, but once having joined the path alongside Red Tarn Beck, the going becomes much more comfortable.

Time: Allow 4 ½ hours.

Route directions

1   At the top of the road, go through the gate at the Outdoor Pursuit Centre.

2   A white-painted arrow and a sign for 'Sticks Pass' can be seen on the facing wall. Follow these to the right, after which the track curves sharply left.

3   Where the path forks, one sign points to 'Red Tarn, Helvellyn', and another to 'Brown Cove, Whiteside Bank and Sticks Pass'. Take the path to the right, for Brown Cove etc.

4   Another fork goes left to 'Brown Cove, Whiteside Bank' and right to 'Sticks Pass'. Go to the right, heading towards the pass.

5   The path's zigzagging course becomes steadily northerly, climbing toward Swart Beck's ravine. The mining areas are below to the right (west). Before reaching the ravine, there is a sign on the right of the path requesting walkers to stay on way marked paths. Three or four paces after this sign, look to your left and locate the path that goes up the hillside. This branches sharply away from the main track, almost doubling back.

6   After a few yards, this lesser path bends sharply to the right, continuing to climb. Three small cairns mark the path. One is before the right-hand bend, one is within it, and the third is

a few yards past. Perhaps 10 yds after the third cairn, some old pit props (railway sleepers) are embedded in the path. At this point, a stone ditch comes down to the path from the left (west). This is the Chimney. Follow the path that leads up alongside it.

7   Where the Chimney terminates, two tracks are seen to carry on. The more obvious one bears to the left (south-west), with the other going to the right (in effect straight on) to the west. Take the fainter, right branch.

8   This leads to a tiny square enclosure of corrugated sheeting. There are no further tracks to follow, but Raise is directly ahead (west). The summit area can be gained by whichever route one is comfortable with, but a direct approach is best.

9   Pass to the left (south) of the ski tow up to the summit.

10   On Raise, a clear path marked by cairns leads southward to White Side.

11   From White Side continue southwards along the ridge top path to Lower Man.

12   From Lower Man, the path drops gently toward Helvellyn on a south-easterly bearing. You will find the way marked by cairns. Where the ascent of Helvellyn begins, bear to the left of the

main path, staying closer to the ridge.

13   This leads to a small cairn directly above Swirral Edge, where a number of narrow tracks lead down and across. I find the easiest route is to stay on the track furthest to the right (nearest to the tarn).

14   After the steepest part of the descent, the path levels and comes to a major fork. The right branch leads down to Red Tarn, the left stays on the highest part of the ridge to Catstye Cam.

15   From Catstye Cam, take the path down the north-eastern ridge (continuing in the same direction as your ascent).

16   Initially, this path is very clear and marked by cairns. Where it peters out on the lower slopes, carry straight on to cut across the brown scar of Red Tarn Beck's obvious path.

17   Turn left (north) on the path, heading downhill.

18   The path crosses a footbridge over Red Tarn Beck, then continues down the valley on the southern side of Glenridding Beck.

19   Cross the bridge over Glenridding Beck, then turn right to return to the Outdoor Centre and the parking areas.

After passing through the buildings, a clear, stony track snakes up through the old mine workings. As the path zigzags from east to west, the view down Glenridding grows ever more impressive, appearing first over one shoulder then the other. On western headings, the line of sight is up towards the beck's source between Birkhouse Moor and Raise. There, Catstye Cam's sharp pinnacle reaches for the sky. Great Gable and Catstye Cam are perhaps the most instantly recognisable peaks in Lakeland. Gable's sugar loaf aspect can be lost from some angles, but Catstye's pyramidal form is always unmistakable.

A high, jagged ridge can be seen leading from Catstye towards Birkhouse Moor's smoother skyline; this is High Spying How, the eastern end of Striding Edge.

The path continues its steep ascent below Stang End's broken crags, on the easternmost arm of Raise. Slightly before reaching Swart Beck's ravine, the route turns westward, following what appears to be a stone channel. It is marked on OS maps as 'The Chimney', and that is exactly what it used to be. Over a kilometre in length, this ingenious construction rises about 200 metres in height as it climbs Raise's eastern ridge, terminating in a short, cairn-like stack.

After the closure of Greenside's mines, the chimney deteriorated into its present form. When in use, it effectively removed fumes from lead smelters to a safe distance. Occasionally, the smelters were shut down so that miners could ascend the chimney and collect deposits of pure lead from its walls.

From a path that follows the chimney's course, old quarry workings and spoil heaps can be seen below, in the shallow corrie of Sticks Gill. Nowadays, these are largely overgrown, rapidly becoming a 'sea' of rounded grassy humps. Of the tarn that used to nestle here, there is no sign other than reeds and a little marshy ground.

After a steep ascent the chimney's course flattens considerably over the last 200 yds. Sticks Pass (the highest in Lakeland) can be seen ahead to the north-west. Its title derives from wooden stakes that used to mark the way. Now that the route has travelled towards the west, the opposite side of Catstye Cam has come into view. Swirral Edge links Catstye and Helvellyn, while Lower Man and its tight curve of crags stand above a still-unseen Brown Cove. To the south-east above Birkhouse Moor and Bleaberry Crags, St Sunday Crag rises up beyond the great void of Grisedale.

To the north, Green Side and Stybarrow Dodd climb above Sticks Gill, with a very conspicuous chunk hewn out of Green Side by its quarry.

The upper heights of Raise are directly ahead from the chimney, and a steep ascent over grass is necessary now. Along the way a marvellous view of Ullswater opens to the rear above Green Side and Sheffield Pike, then Great Dodd appears beyond Stybarrow Dodd.

Raise's northern flank retains snow for longer than most other slopes in the area, which explains the unusual sight of a ski tow as the route climbs higher. On approaching the summit, a wide panorama is revealed ahead where the distant horizon of peaks arcs from south-west to north.

At 883 metres (2896 ft) Raise is ranked peak number 16. An abundance of strangely weathered rocks, like so many lumps of Swiss cheese, surround the cairns and summit outcrops. When viewed together with wide areas of sharp, shattered stones, the overall impression is that of a moonscape.

Raise is a part of a mountain chain that runs from north to south for over seven miles. Rising at Clough Head in the north, the chain contains nine

Evening shadows begin to lengthen on Raise.

Above Swirral Edge, overlooking Catstye Cam and Red Tarn.

recognised peaks of which Helvellyn is the highest. Dollywaggon Pike is the most southerly, after which the chain is effectively broken by Grisedale Tarn's deep bowl. From Clough Head down to Raise, the peaks are predominantly grassy and have a smooth, rounded appearance despite some steep slopes.

On the western side, this mostly gentle face continues even beyond Dollywaggon Pike, falling throughout its length towards Thirlmere. However, on the eastern side, Raise effectively marks the end of rolling slopes. From here, the chain continues in a series of towering crags, deep combes and sharp spurs.

This change of terrain is apparent now, as the flowing line of the Dodds comes over Raise from the north, then heads south for White Side. In that direction, across the deep hollows of Keppel and Brown Coves, are White Side and Helvellyn's eastern precipices. Complementing the rugged outlook are both Striding and Swirral Edges, one above the other.

A few paces to the west will reveal Thirlmere far below. Way beyond the lake, that captivating mountainous horizon from south-west to north includes some of Lakeland's most famous names: Crinkle Crags, Bow Fell and Esk Pike lead up to Scafell Pike, then Lingmell and Great Gable. Kirk Fell, Red Pike (Wasdale) and Pillar introduce the Buttermere trio, after which come the Derwent Fells.

The most eye-catching section is north-west to north, where Bassenthwaite Lake and Skiddaw come round to Blencathra.

In the arc from north to east, Ullswater steals the show, before High Street's long range reaches Stony Cove Pike, Ill Bell and Yoke. St Sunday Crag is seen in more detail now, then Fairfield completes the circle, peeping over Striding Edge between Catstye Cam and Helvellyn.

The route turns southwards now, following the mountain chain. Level ground precedes a shallow col between Raise and White Side as the path begins to skirt the rim of Keppel Cove. A comfortable climb leads to the summit of White Side at 863 metres

The path from White Side to Lower Man and Helvellyn.

(2831 ft). Despite its ranking as peak number 21, White Side is only a station along the way to Lower Man.

Grassy slopes fall gently from the large summit cairn. Initially this is true even of the eastern side above Keppel Cove. Of course, that kindly gradient swiftly becomes steep crags, but nevertheless White Side cannot offer our route's best view into the cove. That comes later on Swirral Edge and Catstye Cam.

The only noticeable change or addition to the outlook since Raise are the crags and cliffs on Lower Man's north-western spur. As previously stated, these are a rarity for the chain's western side. On OS maps they are named Browncove Crags, which is curious as Brown Cove is on the other side of the mountain.

A distinctly red, shale path leads down White Side towards Lower Man. Brown Cove is immediately below to the east now and Catstye Cam is becoming an ever more dominant feature across the hollow.

The ascent of Lower Man is steep and quite long, on a narrowing ridge. The stony top stands at 925 metres (3034 ft). Ranked at number 8, this is the lowest of Lakeland's 3000 ft peaks.

A small pool (hardly a tarn) can be seen in the basin of Brown Cove, where a thin stream trickles to join another from Keppel Cove. Both hollows contain a few relics of the mining years. These are evident in broken dams, but mostly in the large and most modern dam beneath Keppel Cove. This is not the one that burst on the infamous night that Glenridding village was swamped, but a later construction. As one can see, it was ineffective, and Keppel Cove's tarn exists only in the history books.

The westerly view of peaks is much more striking now, above a foreground formed by the spur of Browncove Crags. Thirlmere is still evident below, presenting a pleasant picture with woods climbing away from its far shore. Both Nethermost Pike and Dollywaggon Pike can be seen now above Helvellyn's upper western slope, while above Swirral Edge, the High Street skyline looks very impressive.

From here, the route follows the rim of Brown Cove. A comfortable ascent of Helvellyn's north-western ridge arrives directly above Swirral Edge, where a cluster of striated rocks introduce one of the finest scenes in the whole Lake District.

Approximately 750 ft below, Red Tarn lies cradled between the long encircling arms of Striding and Swirral Edges. Its smooth, shining surface is a perfect foil for the sharp, jagged teeth of the Edges and the pointed cone of Catstye Cam.

With Helvellyn's summit merely yards away, it is highly unlikely that anyone will come to this point above Swirral Edge without taking the short detour. Returning to the route, a very steep descent leads down the arête. For 200 ft or thereabouts, a little scrambling is required before the gradient eases.

Soon, the last climb of the day begins as a path branches toward Catstye Cam. Although quite a steep ascent, only a few minutes are needed to reach the summit at an altitude of 890 metres (2919 ft).

Standing here on the peak ranked number 14, it is easy to imagine oneself atop the spire of a cathedral. Very little intrudes into the immediate surroundings of empty space.

Most eyes will be drawn to the superb image of Ullswater as it snakes away to the north-east. For both distance and depth, the easterly outlook is by far the best now, with Sheffield Pike and Place Fell providing attractive flanks for the lake.

Angletarn Pikes and the tarn itself can be seen above Birkhouse Moor. Beyond all these is the magnificent line of High Street's range, and further

Above the clouds on Lower Man.

Catstye Cam viewed from above Greenside Mines.

still are the distant Pennines. In the north-east, vast green plains stretch out behind Great and Little Mell Fells.

Elsewhere, the massive bulk of Helvellyn with Striding Edge and the peaks of our early route are the dominant features.

Immediately below are Brown and Keppel Coves. Their infant becks quickly join forces to begin Glenridding Beck's long course down the valley. Raise, White Side and Lower Man tower above the coves but still allow glimpses of distant fells.

Helvellyn's great eastern wall fills the arc from west to south, plunging down to Red Tarn. Across the water, Nethermost Pike, Dollywaggon Pike, Fairfield and St Sunday Crag peer above Striding Edge.

Very steep paths descend Catstye Cam's north-western and north-eastern ridges, although neither are marked on OS maps. Perhaps it was from one of these that the mountain's title was derived. An amalgam of Old English and Old Norse, it means 'the ridge with a steep wild cat's path'.

Our route follows the north-eastern ridge over a clear path, marked with cairns. Initially, this path is so obvious that one is amazed at its omission from OS maps. However, it peters out on the grassy lower slopes, until the route cuts across Red Tarn Beck's major footpath.

Accompanied by a chorus from the beck's numerous cascades, the path descends steeply below Birkhouse Moor. A wooden walkway provides comfortable passage over one short section that must have suffered badly from erosion at some time.

Catstye Cam towers to the rear, with White Side and Raise above the coves. Their outflow joins Red Tarn Beck as the path drops deeper into the valley, approaching the broken workings of Greenside.

On The Way

Snow cornices can linger as late in the year as June on the upper rim between Swirral Edge and Helvellyn's summit.

After crossing Glenridding Beck's footbridge, the path passes a deep pool and weir then returns to the parking area.

Before reaching the village, the road passes the Traveller's Rest, which is very handily placed for the campsite. In Glenridding itself, both hotels have comfortable public bars.

The Dodds Range

The remote and grassy expanses of the Dodds form an excellent outing on a walk featuring views of Thirlmere and Ullswater.

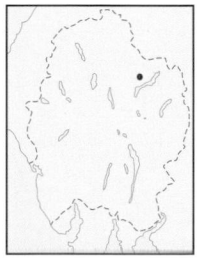

From south to north along Helvellyn's long range, the mountain ridge passes over Raise then falls to the Sticks Pass. From there, the ridge's character changes from rugged and broken, meandering over a series of rounded, grassy summits. These are Stybarrow Dodd, Watson's Dodd, Great Dodd and Little Dodd. Calfhow Pike's small pinnacle is the only pointed aspect of the ridge's smooth contours until the entire range reaches its northern terminus at Clough Head.

Another ridge flows east then north-east from Stybarrow Dodd, conveniently passing over Green Side and Hart Side before falling towards Watermillock Common. The small village of Dockray lies at the foot of the

Blencathra and Skiddaw viewed from Clough Head.

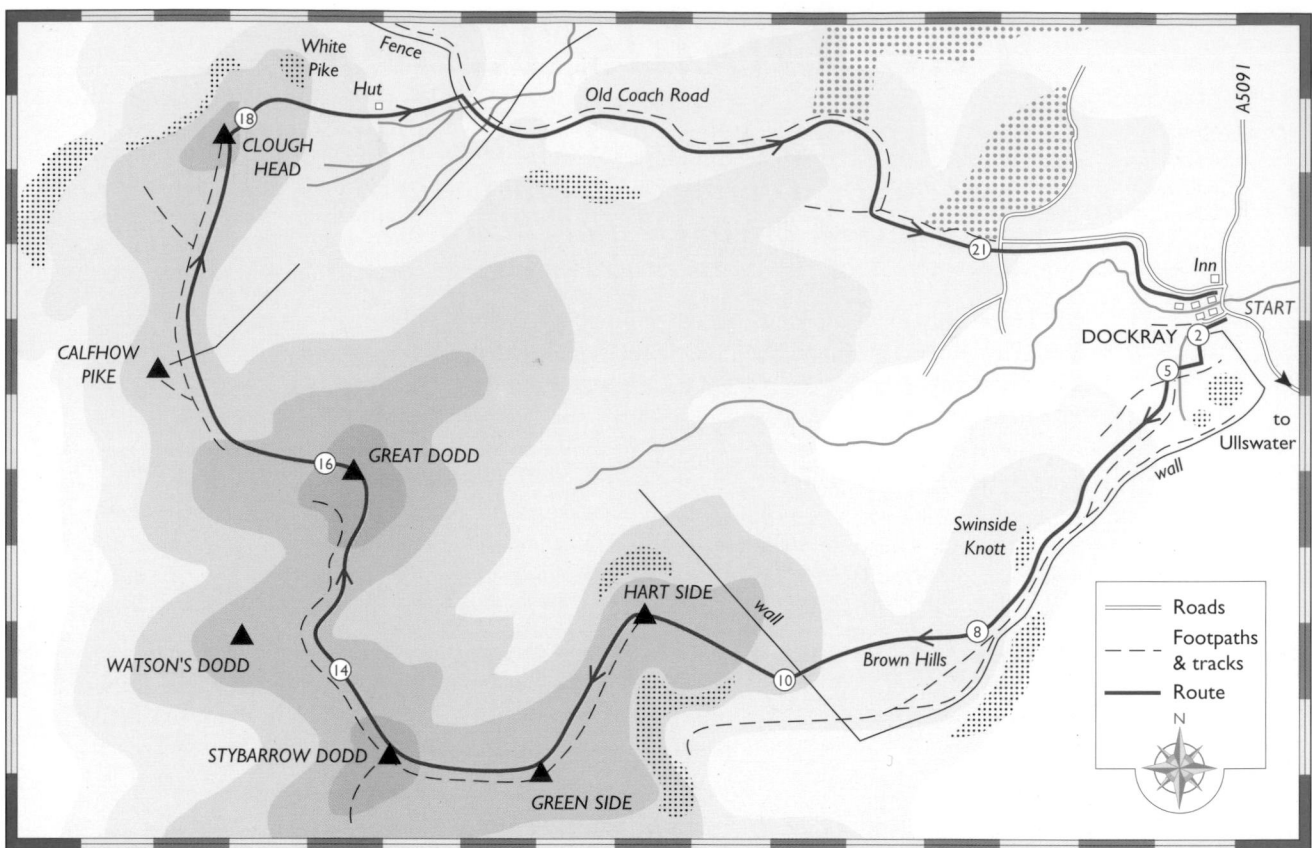

Common, providing a suitable starting location for this route.

The initial ascent of the walk is lengthy and quite steep, but this apart, the only difficulty of the route is its 11½ miles distance. Five of the Lakeland 100 will be visited along the way.

Apart from the view from Clough Head, and despite its generally high altitude, this route has a predominantly moorland atmosphere. It is more reminiscent of a Pennine walk than any other central Lakeland route, and can be recommended to walkers who wish to put a few miles under their belts without having to tackle any exposed or craggy paths.

Dockray's Royal Hotel and public bar are ideally situated at the end of

Peaks of top 100 on this route
25 *GREAT DODD*
     857 metres (2811 ft)
29 *STYBARROW DODD*
     843 metres (2765 ft)
49 *GREEN SIDE*
     795 metres (2608 ft)
74 *HART SIDE*
     756 metres (2480 ft)
93 *CLOUGH HEAD*
     726 metres (2381 ft)

the walk, but there is little else in the way of accommodation. The villages and campsites around Ullswater provide a more likely base, as the lake itself is only 1½ miles to the south on the A5091.

Start/finish point: Parking spaces at Dockray road bridge, near the Royal Hotel (GR 393215)

Map: Ordnance Survey Outdoor Leisure Map 5 (1:25 000)

Distance: Approx 11½ miles

Total ascent: Approx 845 metres (2772 ft)

Difficulty: No problem other than the distance

Time: Allow 7 hours.

In Dockray, a small parking area can be found on the southern side of the bridge over Aira Beck. On stepping across the road, a short lane gives access onto the moor leading to Watermillock Common.

Route directions

1 Opposite the parking spaces on the southern side of Dockray's road bridge, there is a telephone booth and a lane signposted 'Public footpath'. Follow the lane away from the road and the beck.

(2) This leads to a gate and a National Trust sign designating 'Watermillock Common'. Go through the gate then immediately turn left (south) alongside the wall that leads away from the main track.

3 OS maps mark a footpath here but it is not discernible on the ground. Where the wall turns sharply left (east), carry on south toward the pass that lies straight ahead between Bracken How and Common Fell.

4 On reaching the foot of Bracken How, a path skirts to the right (west) of the hill. Continue in this direction and go past the first minor branch to the left (south).

(5) Immediately after crossing a narrow stream (Pounder Sike), take the narrow track that branches left (south) alongside the stream.

6 Soon, the path angles away from the stream but becomes intermittent. If you should lose sight of it, head south-west until reaching the wall that comes up from the left (north-east). Here, the way becomes much clearer.

7 Follow the wall south-west. Eventually, the wall becomes a fence and passes immediately underneath a distinctive rocky pinnacle (Swinside Knott).

(8) After passing Swinside Knott, a faint track branches away from the fence heading for the next hillock along (Brown Hills). Take this branch, then turn off it when it skirts to the left (east) of Brown Hills' highest ground. Head west to the top of Brown Hills, then continue to the west along the ridge top.

9 A faint track runs along the ridge up to a wall. If you cannot locate the track simply continue westward to the wall.

(10) The wall climbs toward Birkett Fell, heading north-west. Go through the wall gap then head away from it at an angle of approximately 40 degrees, heading west and ascending the steep slope immediately ahead.

11 On reaching the top, Hart Side's true summit can be seen a little further to the north-west.

12 From Hart Side, a faint grassy track leads south south-west along the ridge top to Green Side. Head for the cairns on the skyline, remembering that Green Side is the first high point along the way.

13 From Green Side, head west along the ridge to the next high point. This is Stybarrow Dodd.

(14) Head north-west from Stybarrow Dodd, and bear right where the track forks, skirting to the east of Watson's Dodd's summit.

15 On the ascent of Great Dodd the track forks again. Ignore the branch to the left and continue up to the summit, heading north north-east.

(16) From Great Dodd's summit cairn (not the shelter), go down the ridge toward Little Dodd, initially heading south-west, then curving north-west as the ridge descends to Calfhow Pike's unmistakable rocky pinnacle. There is no easily discernible path on the ground until approaching Calfhow Pike.

17 The path skirts to the right (east) of the pike, then continues in a north north-easterly direction up to Clough Head. On the ascent, ignore the track that branches left (north-west).

(18) On Clough Head go north-east, descending gently toward the nearby rocky knoll of White Pike. Slightly before reaching the knoll, turn due east and descend with the knoll to your left and a long shallow gully to your right.

19 Pass to the right of a wooden hut, keeping left (north) of the gully stream. The Old Coach Road can be seen ahead and it is simply a matter of reaching it by whatever route you feel comfortable with.

20 Turn right (east) on the coach road, and follow it until reaching the motor roads at a crossroad.

(21) Go straight across the crossroad following the sign for 'Dockray 1, Ullswater 2'.

22 Turn right at the Royal Hotel to return once again to the parking spaces.

As the route climbs gently toward Common Fell, Matterdale's lowlands stretch out beyond Dockray to the rear. Peaks east of Ullswater appear through a col ahead, then the lake itself begins to unfold. As more height is gained, nothing obstructs a view straight down Ullswater's southern reaches into Patterdale, which is seen surrounded by a magnificent cluster of major peaks.

Our present position is opposite Silver Point – the southern crook of Ullswater's two major course changes. This allows a view over the lake's long central section, looking north-east almost as far as Pooley Bridge. Across the water, High Street's long range forms the skyline.

The route turns westward away from the lake, heading over the Brown Hills ridge and climbing toward Hart Side. Glencoyne lies below the left hand, but is mostly unseen as we continue above its northern crags. On reaching the skyline, Hart Side's true summit appears a little further ahead, to the left (west) of Birkett Fell.

Two more minutes along the rounded tops brings us to the summit of peak number 74 at a height of 756 metres (2480 ft). The generally grassy surface of the dome is broken by stones and boulders with three cairns.

Deepdale lies immediately below to the west, promptly rising to the long ridge of the Dodds. This obscures distant views in that direction, but as the eye passes southwards the panorama becomes dramatic. Looking over Green Side, both Lower Man and Helvellyn are separated from Fairfield by Catstye Cam's dominant pinnacle. Birkhouse Moor and St Sunday Crag lead south-east into the most attractive sector, where a multi-pointed cluster ranges from Red Screes and Stoney Cove Pike through the Kentmere peaks and the High Street range. Closer at hand in the same quadrant are Sheffield Pike and an impressive Place Fell.

Hart Side's own eastern bulk hides

Left: Winter landscape viewed from Green Side.

Below: On Hart Side looking toward the north-eastern lowlands.

Looking into Deepdale from Stybarrow Dodd.

most of Ullswater, although a small section can be seen in the north-east. Coming round further north, a wide and far-reaching view of moors leading to the Eden Valley is punctuated by Great and Little Mell Fells, with the large conifer plantations around Great Mell Fell adding more colour to the scene. Finally, from north to north-west, Carrock and Bowscale Fells lead round to Blencathra, with Skiddaw beyond Clough Head and Great Dodd.

Green Side is close by, separated from Hart Side by only a shallow declivity and a gentle ascent. This is another broad, grassy dome with protruding stones, adorned once again with three cairns. The summit stands at 795 metres (2608 ft) and is ranked as peak number 49.

So close to Hart Side, little has changed in the general outlook, although Raise has become a prominent feature immediately to the south-west. The ski tow on Raise's northern flank is on full display leading down toward Sticks' Gill and Cove. A detour is necessary from the summit if one wishes to look down into the cove or over Glencoyne and both views require the sacrifice of some height.

The plains are still visible to the north, while Catstye Cam remains pre-eminent beyond Raise. The course of Swirral Edge has become more pronounced, leading from Catstye Cam to the crags linking Helvellyn with Lower Man.

A very short distance and another comfortable ascent leads due west onto the Helvellyn/Dodds ridge on Stybarrow Dodd's summit. At 843 metres (2765 ft) this is peak number 29. With nothing to obstruct westward views now, a magnificent panorama of interlocking ridges and peaks is unveiled. A few paces in their direction will add greater depth to the

scene, and reveal Thirlmere way below. Above the lake's forested western flank, the Derwent Fells lead to a compact display of both the Buttermere and Newlands trios. Great Gable and its companions around Wasdale Head introduce Scafell Pike and the Bow Fell chain with Harrison Stickle and Pike O'Blisco leading to Grey Friar and Great Carrs.

To the south, of course, Raise and the Helvellyn range restrict any distant views, while the Fairfield and High Street groups are still dominant in the south-east. A few paces north-east will reveal a breathtaking view through Deepdale Crags to the valley unwinding below Green Side and Hart Side. The distant lowland views and the Pennines are still in evidence in this direction, while Bassenthwaite Lake is a newcomer in the north-west.

The ridge heads north-west towards Watson's Dodd then swings back to the north-east and Great Dodd. On the descent from Stybarrow, Watson's Dodd's cairn can be seen on the skyline, but this point lacks sufficient height separation to qualify as a subsidiary summit and the route therefore skirts around it to the right (east). The massive bulk of Great Dodd is clearly seen ahead and to the right, rising high above Deepdale.

On OS maps, the distance between Stybarrow and Watson's Dodd appears roughly similar to that between Watson's and Great Dodd. On the ground however, the steady plod up to Great Dodd seems disproportionately long and much steeper than the contour lines suggest. Perhaps this is owing to the featureless character of the grassy ridge, or it might be only a personal impression, but Great Dodd's summit is curiously elusive.

Eventually, the route arrives at a large stone shelter and then the cairn that stands on slightly higher ground. At 857 metres (2811 ft) this is peak number 25 and the apex of the walk. Our increased height and more northerly bearing has revealed Wetherlam and the Old Man of Coniston above Lower Man's ridge in the south. Also, there is slightly more depth to the mountainous panorama from south to west which is seen above the long Ullscarf/Bleaberry Fell ridge. The Derwent Fells are growing ever more impressive and remain so as the route continues.

Coming round to the north-west, Derwent Water, Bassenthwaite Lake and Keswick can be seen where the land falls to introduce the Skiddaw group and Blencathra. Below these, and much closer at hand, the ridge bends away to reveal Little Dodd, Calfhow Pike's odd little pinnacle and Clough Head.

The lowland panorama is seen to great effect now, occupying a wide arc from north to east, and it is when looking in this direction that one can fully appreciate Great Dodd's high ranking in the top 100.

A steep but comfortable descent leads to Calfhow Pike with a far-reaching view down Matterdale below the right hand. The day's final peak lies immediately ahead, and it is a long rather than steep ascent that arrives on Clough Head's summit at the trig point and small shelter. At 726 metres (2381 ft) this is peak number 93, and the finest viewpoint of the route.

By definition, any peak that forms the tip of a mountain range should be relatively isolated with uninterrupted views in at least one direction, and Clough Head is no exception. Only Great Dodd's bulk obscures more distant landmarks, although even this

allows glimpses of Watson's Dodd, Helvellyn and Raise. Also, Great Dodd's rounded lines are complementary to a wonderfully diverse panorama of otherwise rugged mountains, with placid lakes and sweeping lowlands.

Looking northwards, precipitous crags and screes fall from under one's toes into Threlkeld's deep valley which flows across the line of sight from west to east. Below the left hand (west) the vale comes to Derwent Water and Keswick, then continues north-west over completely flat and bright green fields that lead to the blue of Bassenthwaite Lake. Much closer in this direction, Tewet Tarn can be seen before the eye turns back towards the east.

Here of course, are the wide moors and woods that lead to Great and Little Mell Fell's stranded high points.

The grassy sweep of Great Dodd, viewed from Stybarrow Dodd.

The western prospect from Stybarrow Dodd.

Beyond lies Penrith, with the Eden Valley and vast lowlands rolling to the distant Pennines.

However, all these fascinating vales and waters are merely a foreground to the dominant feature of Clough Head's entire outlook. Directly across the valley, and viewed face-on are the dramatic southern ramparts of Blencathra. All its spurs and gullies are on display, with the mountain filling a wide arc from north to north-west. Where Blencathra's western arm falls over Blease Fell towards Keswick, Skiddaw's group takes up the gauntlet to emphasise the great mass of Lakeland's northernmost massif.

Elsewhere, Grisedale Pike marks the beginning of a mountain complex that almost precisely fills the arc from west to south. The pike is just one of the rugged profiles of the distant fells as they come round to the Buttermere trio and the cluster around Wasdale

Head. Scafell Pike leads on to Bow Fell's multi-faceted ridge before the Coniston Group ends at Wetherlam, completing this remarkably intricate quadrant.

After Great Dodd allows distant views to continue, the High Street range can be seen from its parent mountain up to Loadpot Hill. Gowbarrow Fell is closer in the east before the circle comes round to the lowlands. Finally, Souther, Carrock and Bowscale Fells rise out of the plains bringing us back to mighty Blencathra.

The route continues for a short distance along Clough Head's top towards a rocky knoll known as White Pike. Below in the east, a wide and clear track can be seen leading across the low moor. This is the Old Coach Road, and despite the lack of a path down to it, the descent is steep but comfortable over thick grasses.

On reaching the road, all the hard work is over. There is still a very gentle ascent after Mariel Bridge, but it is barely noticed as the route crosses the southern perimeter of the moor. Wolf Crags are immediately to the right (south), forming the lower ramparts of both Matterdale Common and ultimately Great Dodd. Great Mell Fell pierces the horizon ahead and to the left, above approaching conifer plantations. Across the far-reaching moor, Greystoke Forest's outline can be discerned on the north-eastern skyline. Blencathra and Skiddaw lead round to the rear where White Pike's high knoll completes a very restful scene.

As the coach track passes by the woods, High Street's range comes back into view ahead. Soon after this, the route emerges on a road that descends gently for a mile, returning to the Royal Hotel at Dockray.

Blencathra's Summit Ridge

An exciting journey that takes in the majestical Blencathra and involves crossing the most demanding ridge in the entire Lake District.

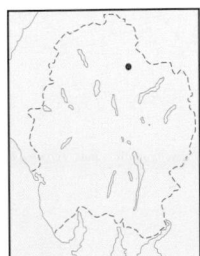

There is no other Lakeland mountain that presents such an appealing picture from a distance as Blencathra.

Standing in splendid isolation, it rears up from a wide valley and the A66 about 5 miles east of Keswick. Fortunately, it is the remarkable sculpture of its southern flank that faces the road, looking over the great bulk of the Lake District. The anonymous northern façade is smooth and rounded, facing the Caldbeck Fells, away from public gaze.

The main body of the mountain is around 3½ miles long. At each end (west and east) there are rounded slopes that rise up almost to summit level, where four combes cut deeply into the mountainside. Gully streams flow down through each combe, divided by three awesome, jagged

On Hallsfell Top – Blencathra's summit.

spurs or ridges. When added to the two of the east and west slopes, we have the five ridges with four deep ravines for which Blencathra is renowned. Summer and autumn enhance this spectacular scene, when the ridges are cloaked in vivid red-purple heather.

The sharp, broken aspect of the ridges and combes is a result of granite intrusions into the ancient slate that forms these northern fells. Glacial action and general weathering causes the intrusions to break into very large pieces, but erodes the softer slate into much smaller, finer forms. Hence the rounded shape of the mountain's main body.

Scales Tarn lies deep within a corrie, hidden from the valley and road, immediately to the north of the west ridge. Its craggy back wall rises up to the eminently visible Atkinson Pike, which is linked to Blencathra's central pinnacle by the highest section of the summit ridge. That central pinnacle is Hallsfell Top, the summit of Blencathra. The next pinnacle along the summit ridge is Gategill Fell Top and these three peaks are all within the Lakeland 100. Once the first has been conquered, it is merely a pleasant stroll over the other two.

Blease Fell (the western slope) fails by only 1 metre in height separation to qualify as the mountain's fourth peak. Otherwise, with an altitude of 804 metres (2258 ft), it would have qualified as peak number 41.

The connecting ground between Atkinson Pike and Hallsfell Top forms the distinct shape from which the mountain's nickname 'Saddleback' is derived. Its true title is widely held to derive from Celtic words meaning 'The Hill of the Devil'. Recently, however, I was persuaded that the derivation is from Old Welsh, and means 'Hill of

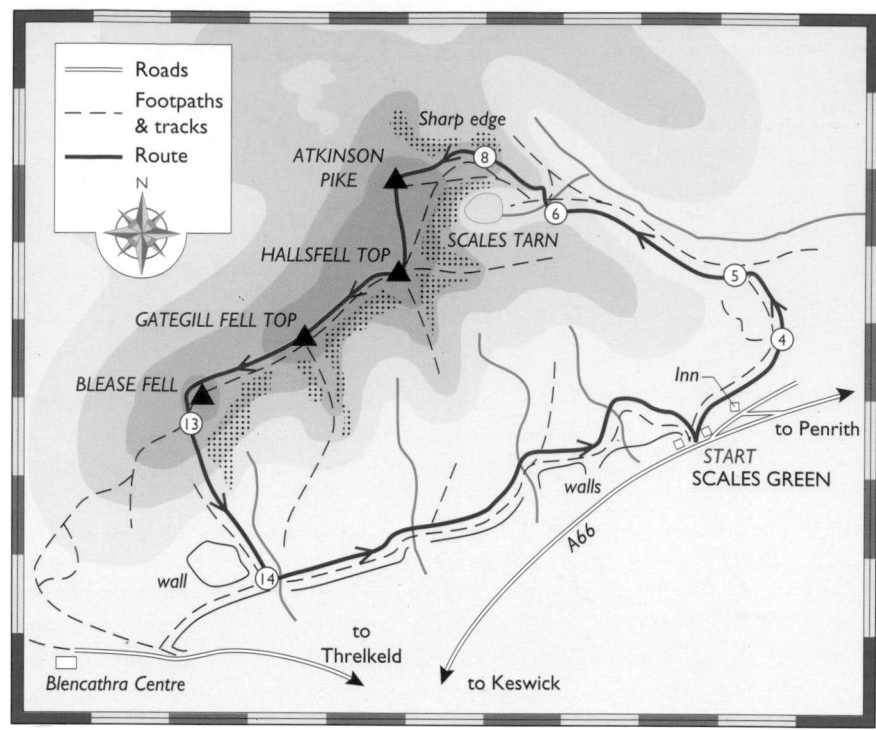

the Summit Chair' – this seems much more likely.

There are various campsites dotted around the A66 to the east of Blencathra, another one near Tewet Tarn to the west and many more around Keswick. The close proximity of this major Lakeland town ensures

that you will not struggle to find supplies or equipment. Hotels and guest houses are plentiful in town, with Threlkeld and Scales offering limited accommodation at the very foot of the mountain. At the end of your walk the White Horse Inn is two minutes away.

Peaks of top 100 on this route
18 *HALLSFELL TOP*
    868 metres (2847 ft)
27 *GATEGILL FELL TOP*
    851 metres (2791 ft)
28 *ATKINSON PIKE*
    845 metres (2772 ft)

Start/finish point: Parking spaces at Scales Green on the A66 (GR 340268)

Map: Ordnance Survey Outdoor Leisure Map 5 (1:25 000)

Distance: Approx 5½ miles

Total ascent: Approx 710 metres (2329 ft)

Difficulty: The crossing of Sharp Edge represents the limit of a fell walker's capabilities; do not underestimate this section. Steep descent from Blease Fell.

Time: Allow at least 4 hours.

Route directions

1 Between Doddick and Scales Farms on the A66 there are a number of small parking places. The most convenient is at Scales Green next to Toll Bar Cottage, on the northern side of the road. The most spacious is a little further west (towards Keswick).

2 There are two signs at Scales Green, a wooden one stating 'Public footpath', and a metal one declaring 'Public footpath Scales Fell 1 Scales Beck 2'.

3 Follow the path up to a gate, then go right (north-east), up to the main path, where again the way is to the right.

4 After about ½ a mile a grassy path bears left through the ferns. Stick to the more trodden earthen path that leads straight on.

5 This leads around the top of Mousthwaite Combe, up to the col. Stay on the main track here where another branches to the right. Your heading now is north-east, above the River Glenderamackin.

6 The long, level path leads to Scales Beck. Cross the beck then turn to the left (east), on the path that climbs alongside the beck.

7 Slightly before reaching Scales Tarn, the path branches to the right, up to the first rock outcrops on Sharp Edge.

8 At this point there is a choice of routes. The classical way is along the very crest of the ridge, clambering over various pinnacles with steep drops on either side. Not much advice can be offered here, other than to take your time on whichever course across the rocks you feel most comfortable with. Although it sounds unlikely, you might find it easier to climb over the top of the rocks rather than to edge around them. The other way is to the right (northern) side of the ridge, where a path traverses a few feet below the top. This also involves a scramble when it reaches the buttresses of Atkinson Pike but overall it is much the easier passage. Before reaching the buttresses, take a minute or two to decide exactly which way up them looks comfortable to you – the path diverges on them.

9 Both routes come together on Atkinson Pike. The main path branches left (south) here, above Scales Tarn. Look for the lesser path that leads west for a few paces to the summit.

10 From Atkinson Pike head south, following the cairns.

11 At the third cairn (or wherever you prefer) bear left and down to join the main path, continuing in a southerly direction. Blencathra's stone crosses can be seen ahead from the cairns, to the right (west) of the main footpath.

12 The path leads directly over Hallsfell Top and Gategill Fell Top to Knowe Crags on Blease Fell.

13 There is a choice of two routes from here. The steepest and quickest way is to keep the ridge of Knowe Crags a safe distance of about 50 yds to your left, descending due south. There is no path on the ground, but eventually you will see one below, cutting a clear route through ferns, running roughly parallel to Blease Gill. Simply work your way down to meet this path. Alternatively, follow the main path down from Blease Fell that leads to the south-west. After the very steep section, watch for where this path bears to the right. Do not take the one that leads straight on as it will soon disappear. Eventually the main path curves around to the left (south then south-west) above the Blencathra Centre. Bear to your left from there on the path that leads to Blease Gill.

14 The short route descends parallel to Blease Gill, meeting a major track that runs along the base of Blencathra from south-west to north-east. Turn left (north-east) here, crossing the beck.

15 After the beck you will see two gates. Ignore the small one, and go through the one to the left. After this gate a wall sign points to Gate Gill.

16 Stay on the track heading eastwards. This crosses Gate Gill, Doddick Gill and Scaley Beck, returning to Scales Green.

On stepping out of your car at Scales, there is already a wide view over the valley to Threlkeld Common and Clough Head, with Great Mell Fell prominent in the east. Initially the path climbs gently across Scales Fell, leading north-east through a mass of gorse bushes. The gradient becomes steeper to reveal Mousthwaite Combe below to the right (north-east). This deep hollow is the only break in Scales Fell's otherwise rounded contours. Passing around the lip of the combe, the path approaches a col linking Scales Fell with Souther Fell – mountain of the 'spectral army'. During the 18th century many local people witnessed apparitions of horses, carriages and men on Souther Fell, that could not and never have been explained.

Matterdale and the Helvellyn range lie to the south as we reach the grassy col top, when suddenly to the north-west, the eyes become riveted to an awesome spectacle.

Rising high beyond Scales Fell's northern flank is the precipitous, craggy eastern face of Atkinson Pike, displaying in no uncertain manner where the main body of Blencathra terminates. Coming down from the peak is the outline of Sharp Edge, falling in a series of needle-like pinnacles to Brunt Knott. The picture is all the more impressive because it marks the course of our route, and the path leading to it across Scales Fell can be seen stretching out all the way from the col.

The river Glenderamackin flows down below, at the foot of Bannerdale Crags, as the wide valley view disappears to the rear. A long, level section above the river leads to Scales Beck, and a steeper ascent towards the tarn. The tarn's towering back wall looms large with Sharp Edge reappearing, before Scales Tarn itself is unveiled immediately ahead.

This is a natural and popular resting place to gather one's strength and wits (certainly you will need the latter), before the ascent of Sharp Edge. Neither the famous Striding Edge nor Jack's Rake on Pavey Ark have such exposed positions as this one.

On The Way

Sharp Edge can be completely avoided by taking the path that climbs southwards from Scales Tarn up to Scales Fell ridge then Hallsfell Top.

A wide, eroded track leads up to the first outcrops of the edge, where long views over the north eastern plains unfold to the rear. Now comes the highlight of the walk: a painstaking traverse of Sharp Edge with Scales Tarn way below to the left, and steep crags falling down into a deep combe on the right. This crossing should not be attempted in strong winds or slippery conditions. At any time it is safer to take the lower path described in the route's directions.

Eventually, the edge arrives at a path that continues along the ridge top to the summit of Atkinson Pike. At an altitude of 845 metres (2772 ft), this is ranked peak number 28. Owing to its position at the northern tip of Blencathra, this peak lacks the full majesty of the views on offer from the summit proper, although a wide vista has been unveiled. Attention is drawn mainly in a northerly bearing, in an arc from west to east, looking out over the vast, rolling acres of Mungrisedale Common to the Caldbeck Fells. The eastern plains lie beyond Bannerdale Crags, topped by the distant Pennines, and the Solway Firth is in view now with the Scottish hills. However, there

Sharp Edge and Scales Tarn from Atkinson Pike.

Hallsfell Top and Ridge from Gategill Fell Top.

is nothing here that cannot be seen to better effect on Hallsfell Top.

Three stone crosses lie between Atkinson Pike and Hallsfell Top, higher and a little to the west of the path. The largest is constructed from white crystallised stones which were carried up here by the builder, a local fell runner. It is a monument to a friend of his, built alongside an earlier and much smaller cross of ordinary slate. The third can be seen further south, constructed from white stones 'borrowed' from the major cross for purposes unknown.

A short and comfortable ascent brings us to Hallsfell Top; peak number 18 at 868 metres (2847 ft). The separation of Blencathra from the main body of mountains renders this a unique viewpoint, high above Threlkeld Valley and Common. The sense of height is gloriously enhanced by the jagged spurs and deep combes as they fall directly beneath us.

Beyond the valley, the arc from east to west (looking southwards now), is jammed with almost every notable lakeland peak. From Penrith and the distant Pennines, the skyline undulates over the full High Street range and the Kentmere peaks across to St Sunday Crag and Helvellyn. The Coniston group lead onto the Scafells, and quite the most vivid display of the Buttermere and Derwent Fells one could wish for. All this is merely a background for Derwent Water, Borrowdale's fells, Castlerigg Stone Circle, Thirlmere, St John's in the Vale, Clough Head, Threlkeld Common, Mosedale and the plains. By far the most arresting sight is close at hand in the rugged spur of Gategill Fell, as it rises to its pointed summit, touching the south-western horizon.

Continuing through a full 360-degree panorama, the Irish Sea with

Enthusiastic youngsters on Knowe Crags.

the Isle of Man come round to neighbouring Skiddaw and its acolytes. Caldbeck's rolling fells are the foreground to Scotland and the Solway Firth, before the circle is completed by Bowscale Fell, Bannerdale Crags, the Eden Valley and Souther Fell.

To itemise the features in this way cannot possibly give the reader a full understanding of their effect. Hopefully, the story of an encounter I had will do justice to the scene. I am on record as stating that Blencathra is my favourite Lakeland mountain, and that is still the case. But my appreciation of the place is nothing compared to that of a gentleman from Durham I met here.

Before the dawn of a cold October day, I had set out to watch the sun rise over Scales Tarn from above Tarn Crags. Hard frosts and the first dusting of snow of the year had rendered ridge routes up the mountain inadvisable, especially in the dark. I opted for the route over Blease Fell, crossing the full length of Blencathra's heights.

Approaching Gategill Fell Top, in the half light there appeared to be an abandoned sack or long pile of rags ahead of me in the snow and ice. As I passed close by a head popped out, bidding me a cheery good morning. I returned the greeting, then carried on my way. An hour later, on the way back to Blease Fell I had time to chat.

Apart from his bivi and sleeping bags, this hardy soul had everything required for an extended stay. He was enthusing about Blencathra, a mountain he had not previously climbed. When I asked how long he would spend in the Lake District on his visit, he replied that he was here for four days. Then I enquired which other mountains were in his itinerary, and he looked surprised, saying, 'No, I mean that I am *here* for four days.'

A clear path leads on across the summit ridge to Gategill Fell Top. This is peak number 27 with an altitude of 851 metres (2791 ft). Being a part of the same mountain, nothing much has changed regarding the outlook here, although one can look back now to Hallsfell Top with its spur plunging to the valley. It is possible to descend by way of Gategill Fell, but a visit to Blencathra feels incomplete without the full crossing to Knowe Crags on Blease Fell. This forms the western rampart of the mountain, and looks out over Keswick to the marvellous jumble of the Derwent Fells.

There are two descents from here, the quickest route dropping steeply over thick grasses and a little scree, straight down Knowe Crags' southern flank. This reaches a path alongside Blease Gill, then joins the main track that runs along the complete southern base of the mountain.

We cross the stream here, below the first of four magnificent gullies that illuminate the homeward leg of the route. The going is relatively level now, and remains so for the rest of the journey.

Gate Gill's beck runs through the second gully we cross, between Gategill and Hall's Fell, where our line of sight up the gully leads to dizzying mountain heights. The old weir and hut here are relics of Threlkeld's lead mine. It is hard to believe when looking at these fragments, that during its boom years in the late 19th century, this mine employed a hundred people.

Green pastures lie immediately to the right now, with an increasing drone of traffic reminding us that the journey is almost complete. Doddick Gill comes next, followed by a scramble round Scaley Beck with its breathtaking glimpse of Tarn Crags and Sharp Edge.

Minutes later the path drops its last few feet, back to the road and car park.

The Skiddaw Group

Glorious views of lakes, woods, mountains and coastline – and soaring high above this panoramic route, the magnificent Skiddaw.

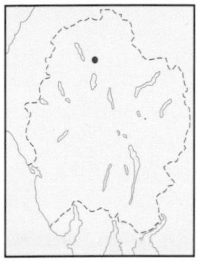

Rising straight out of the Vale of Keswick, Skiddaw completely dominates the town and its environs. In the busy streets and in the villages, locals and visitors alike are constantly aware of the classical alpine backdrop formed by the mountain's sprawling massif. On the roads and lanes around Keswick, Skiddaw's presence is felt even more forcefully, with its wooded lower slopes complementing a colourful, natural picture.

Only four separate Lakeland mountains top the 3000 ft mark, with Skiddaw ranked the fourth of them. When subsidiary tops are included, its ranking slips to seventh, but this peak is held in far greater affection than that number suggests.

A look backwards on the ascent of Carl Side.

For some reason, Skiddaw is sometimes reported as a 'boring mountain'. I find this impression totally unfathomable, unless certain people find glorious views of lakes, valleys, woods, mountains and coastlines boring.

Perhaps if one followed the long and uneventful tourist trail from near the base of Lonscale Fell, and returned by the same route, then yes, that could be tedious. Otherwise Skiddaw and its acolytes are stimulating, with rewards on a par with Lakeland's finest ranges.

Having said that, I should point out that the most uninspiring walk I have ever undertaken was along a section of the Cumbria Way, near Skiddaw House Youth Hostel. If you should ever feel in need of penance, this particular stretch will fully absolve the most unconscionable sins! Fortunately, our route goes nowhere near it.

A little under six miles of walking results in visits to Carl Side, Long Side, Skiddaw and Skiddaw Little Man. A steep ascent leads to Carl Side and Long Side, with a further 200-metre climb to Skiddaw. After that, Little Man presents no difficulty. The homeward descent is very steep (particularly over the final drop), but surprisingly short.

Keswick is the obvious base for those who enjoy creature comforts, while the campsite at Braithwaite is handily placed for others. Millbeck village is the starting point of the walk. To find it, take the A591 from Keswick, heading north-west toward Bothel and Carlisle. Turn right at the sign for Millbeck, then left at the T-junction in the village. About 100 yds up the road, a lane branches sharply to the right, signposted 'Skiddaw footpath'. Parking spaces can be found opposite, but for these you will have to arrive early.

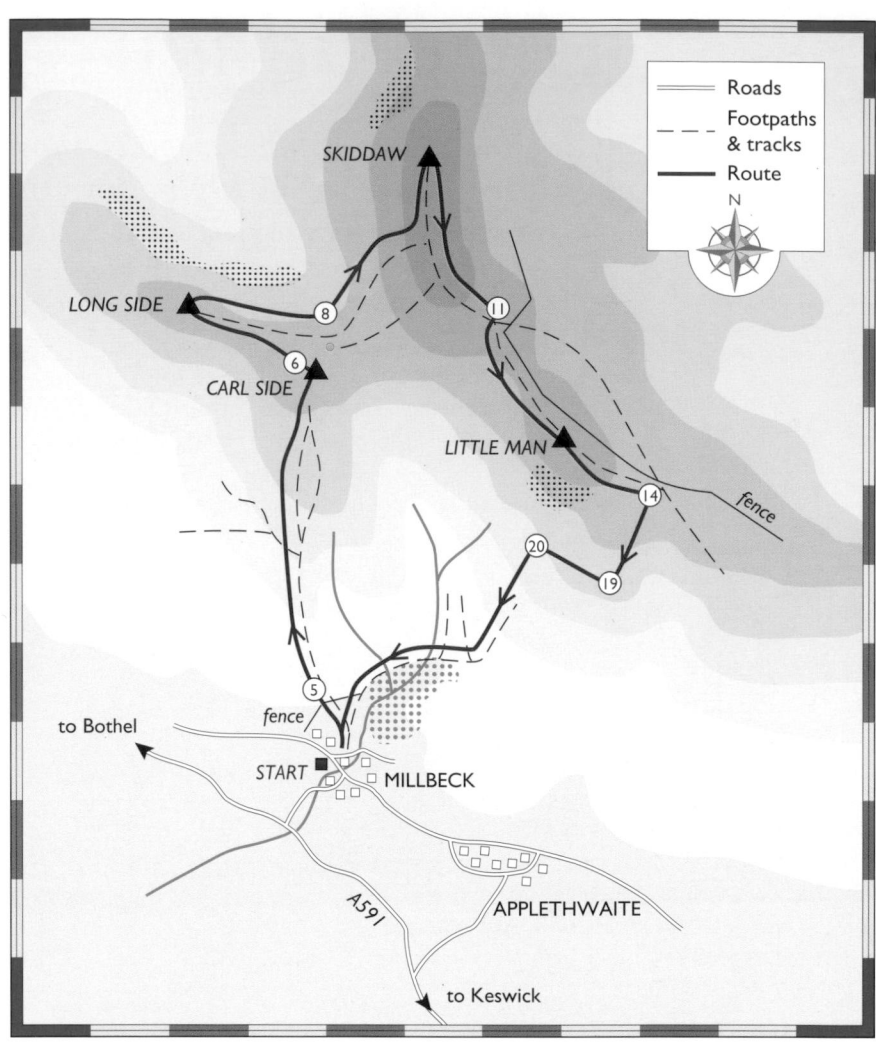

Peaks of top 100 on this route

7   *SKIDDAW*
    931 metres (3054 ft)
20 *SKIDDAW LITTLE MAN*
    865 metres (2837 ft)
78 *CARL SIDE*
    746 metres (2447 ft)
88 *LONG SIDE*
    734 metres (2408 ft)

Start/finish point: Roadside in Millbeck Village, due south of Skiddaw (GR 255262)

Map: Ordnance Survey Outdoor Leisure Map 4 (1:25 000)

Distance: Approx 6 miles

Total ascent: Approx 950 metres (3117 ft)

Difficulty: Having arrived (panting) on Carl Side and Long Side, be prepared mentally for the push up Skiddaw. After Little Man, care must be taken to follow the route directions closely in order to avoid damaging the fell's heather covering.

Time: Allow at least 4½ hours.

Route directions

1 Head up the lane, following the 'Skiddaw footpath' sign.

2 Go past the first gate on the left, up to a second Skiddaw sign at the next gate.

3 Go through the gate, where the path leads up between a wall and a line of trees.

4 After another gate, a grass track bears to the left, leading up to a fence and stile.

5 A clear path leads up from here, slightly to the right (east) of Carl Side's ridge. Stay on this all the way to the summit, ignoring the path that branches to the left (west).

6 From Carl Side, bear to the left (north-west) to pick up Long Side's ridge-top path.

7 From Long Side, return along the ridge path, passing slightly north of Carl Side.

8 Two paths climb Skiddaw from Carlside Tarn. Take the one on the left (across Skiddaw's western face).

9 On Skiddaw's summit ridge turn left to the north top.

10 Return along the summit ridge and continue toward the south top, where the path descends to the south-east.

11 Follow the path as it leads down toward a gate and stile. Slightly before reaching these, take the path that branches to the right leading to the fence corner. Follow the path on the western side of the fence, up to Little Man.

12 From the summit carry on in the same direction to the lower cairn, then down to where the path meets Skiddaw's main track.

13 In very poor visibility, follow the track all the way back to the road, then turn right (west) back to Millbeck. In clear conditions, head away from the track at this point where the track crosses a stile. Using the stile as a pointer, head south-west. There is no path in this direction, but the going is comfortable over grass.

14 When Derwent Water's north-western tip appears ahead, head straight towards it.

15 Continue in this direction until reaching the heather line. Follow this to the right (north-west) to the point where the line drops deeper, then curves back upwards.

16 Go to the deepest part of this curve, where you will see a faint track heading straight down through the heather. If this is not immediately apparent, look to the bottom of the slope where you will see a wall running parallel with the mountain.

17 Line yourself up about halfway between the gap in the wall and the line of trees that runs directly away from the wall. The wall gap is to the right (west) of the line of trees. You should be able to locate the track now.

18 This leads down to the edge of a large area of ferns.

19 At this point a sheep trod bears sharply to the right (north-west) following the contour of the hillside. Other trods branch off this, but stay on the higher one across the hillside until you approach Mill Beck's gorge.

20 When you see a clear grass avenue leading up through the heather and ferns, follow it down to your left.

21 Exactly at the point where this grassy path becomes an earthy track, branch off it to the left on the grass clearing that leads steeply down to Mill Beck.

22 The easiest crossing can be found about 30 yds upstream. Having crossed, go downstream to pick up a clear path.

23 This leads back to the gates at the foot of Carl Side, the lane, and the road.

The path leads very quickly onto the grassy lower slope of Carl Side. Heather covered fellsides lie ahead and above, with Skiddaw Little Man most prominent.

Steep climbing begins almost immediately, on a grass track leading up to the heather line. A vast network of fields around the River Derwent and Keswick opens to the rear, with Derwent Water itself appearing before a wide horizon of peaks. All this is visible within five minutes of starting out, simply by taking a look backwards at the first fence!

As the route continues to climb over a steep clear path, this southerly outlook grows ever more detailed and far reaching. A long ascent finally approaches the summit plateau, where Skiddaw and Little Man tower above.

Their powerful overbearing serves as a reminder that Carl Side is merely a foot soldier in the company of generals. Nevertheless, its summit cairn stands at 746 metres (2447 ft), qualifying Carl Side as peak number 78.

Skiddaw and Little Man effectively block the north and east, and Carl Side's own plateau obscures immediate valley views to the west. All of which does not matter in the least, for the southerly aspect is quite simply beautiful.

The rooftops of Keswick lie far below, a quaint toy town foreground to natural treasures. Slades Beck's deep, wide gorge separates Carl Side from Little Man, with steep slopes falling away from Carl Side by our left hand. Looking over its course to the south-east, the line of sight goes north of the town then passes over St John's in the Vale to Clough Head.

Marching southwards from there in an unbroken line are the Dodds and Helvellyn's range to Seat Sandal. Far to the south, the Coniston group with Pike of Stickle and Pike O'Blisco lead round to Crinkle Crags, Bow Fell and Esk Pike.

The middle ground of this southern arc holds the most eye-catching features of the view. Here, Derwent Water is enclosed by the High Spy/ Cat Bells ridge on its western side and Bleaberry Fell with High Seat to the east. Beyond the lake, the Jaws of Borrowdale and Castle Crag are a

On Carl Side's summit.

Ullock Pike and the coastal plains from Long Side.

gateway to Glaramara.

The Scafells take up the horizon as it leads south-west, passing over Great Gable and Kirk Fell. Pillar, Steeple and High Stile complete the distant arc. Closer at hand in the south-west are the Derwent Fells with their intricate sculpture seen to great effect.

A short, westward stroll across the plateau from the summit reveals yet more delights, in Bassenthwaite Lake and Dodd Wood.

On the easy passage to Long Side, the north-western view comes into its own. One's eyes are transfixed by almost infinite green flatlands and hazy coastlines.

As Long Side's summit lies on a much narrower ridge than Carl Side's,

there is little to interrupt the views now from south to north.

The summit stands at 734 metres (2408 ft). Lacking a separate mass of its own, Long Side is actually the highest point of a ridge between Carl Side and Ullock Pike. However, with sufficient height separation, it is ranked as peak number 88.

Only Clough Head is obscured by Carl Side from the previously described mountain views, but now attention is drawn to the arc from west to north. Close at hand, the ridge continues to Ullock Pike, then curls gently around to the north, displaying precipitous crags.

Bassenthwaite Lake and Dodd Wood lie below to the west, where the

distant Irish Sea and Cumbrian Coast come into view. The initial thin strip of the coastal plain grows deeper as the Solway Firth and southern Scotland take over the horizon. Coming round towards the north, the flatlands and plains reach out for mile after mile to the Solway. Around 25 miles to the north, four white towers of Annan's Power Station are amazingly clear on the Scottish coast. Of course, good weather is necessary if one is to be witness to all this, but on a clear day (most often to be had in winter), Long Side's coastal views are nothing less than hypnotic. Now that the foothills have been dealt with, the walk and views become even better!

Heading back towards Carl Side,

Mountain rescue team practise on Skiddaw.

the route passes close by a tiny pool, flattered by the title 'Carlside Tarn'. Turning to the north-east the path traverses Skiddaw's steep western face. I remember trudging up this in deep snow one winter's day. Every step seemed to result in an equal slide backwards, which was my desert for failing to bring either an ice axe or even a walking stick.

Before very long, the path emerges on Skiddaw's long and stony summit ridge, at a stone shelter. This rests on the central of three distinct humps

A crisp November day on Carl Side.

On the descent from Skiddaw, heading for Little Man.

along the ridge. From here, the path continues to the far northern cairn and triangulation column, at 931 metres (3054 ft).

The view from north to east is completely open now, providing Skiddaw with a considerable advantage over our earlier peaks. Here, there is a marked contrast between the plains and seascape on one side, and a succession of rolling hills and ridges on the other. The eye passes back and forth from west to east, marvelling at the sudden changes.

The land falls down Skiddaw's eastern flank to Skiddaw Forest (denuded of trees), then up to Little and Great Calva. Above their steep outline are the rolling hills of Caldbeck's more distant fells highlighted by Carrock Fell and High Pike. Topping the scene and far away are the Pennines.

Caldew Valley divides this group of unfrequented hills from the rounded features of nearby Sale How and Mungrisedale Common. Then Lonscale Fell rises up through Jenkin Hill to Little Man: wave after wave of hills, rich in heather. Above these are Bowscale Fell and Blencathra, coming round to High Street's long ridge, and the earlier mountain skyline.

Skiddaw has always played a major part in Lakeland's history and culture. It was an important beacon station of the old national network, although the long summit ridge required a beacon at each end.

Northern England's most celebrated huntsman, John Peel, ran his hounds over these fells, and it was on this mountain that Wordsworth and Southey chose to celebrate the victory at Waterloo. By all accounts this was quite a lavish affair, with a bonfire, guests and unrestricted merry making.

Skiddaw even had its own hermit, one George Smith, who lived in a hut on the lower slopes during the 19th century. Reputed to have been an accomplished portrait painter, he managed quite nicely until his home was wrecked by a group of townsfolk (all good conservatives, no doubt).

The route turns back southward now, crossing almost the full length of

At Little Man's untidy summit cairn.

the summit ridge. A comfortable descent leads to a fence that points the way to Little Man.

I was here early one morning, after a night of blizzards had screamed over the Lake District. Where the fence crosses the deepest part of a depression between Skiddaw and Little Man, for a section of about 100 yds an astonishing ice formation had adhered to the fence wire.

The wire is shaped in squares, something like four inches per side. The ice had formed in squares identical to the fence measurements, but extended at least six inches away from it. Each square was a perfect box shape, with every compartment formed by an ice shelf and side of

exactly the same girth as the wire. The entire construction terminated with laser-like precision.

I stood and stared at this in utter disbelief. Even the most skilful craftsman could not fashion anything so exquisite from the same material.

The fence climbs Little Man's gentle slope, taking our path with it. At 865 metres (2837 ft), Little Man is peak number 20. The summit cairn is an unsightly pile of stones spiked with iron bars but there is nothing tawdry about the view.

Dodd Wood and the Derwent Fells are particularly beguiling beneath a distant seascape that comes around to the great mass of Skiddaw. In the east, Blencathra and Bowscale Fell have

grown more detailed, while the lonely Caldbeck Fells are still much in evidence. Most attention will be given to the reopened southern panorama and the distant line of hills marking the course of High Street's roman road.

It is downhill all the way back to Millbeck from here. Initially, the path leads to Little Man's south-eastern cairn, then drops to Jenkin Hill. From there, the route heads south-west, dropping steeply, then traverses Little Man's heathered southern flank. Another steep descent leads to Mill Beck's gully where the stream is crossed. After crossing another stream above a small wood, the path returns to the lane and road.

The Coledale Round

The first of three routes over the colourful Derwent Fells with easy access to five peaks and superb valley scenery.

A compact group of mountains rises to the west of Derwent Water and east of the long Crummock Water/Buttermere divide. Known collectively as the Derwent Fells, this group is a magnet for walkers, its popularity boosted by easy access from Keswick.

Along with steep-sided peaks offering superb mountain and valley views, the Derwent Fells have the added attraction of a comprehensive heather covering.

No fewer than twelve of Lakeland's top 100 peaks can be found here, five of which are visited on the Coledale round. This 8½ mile walk entails a long and steep first ascent (to Grisedale Pike), but once that has been achieved the going is relatively easy.

Looking down on Braithwaite at the beginning of the walk.

Owing to the tightly knit nature of the fells, Coledale Hause serves as a fulcrum for both this walk and another in the series of three Derwent routes. However, the ground shared by these two routes amounts to only half a mile.

Braithwaite village lies 2½ miles west of Keswick, just off the A66. Accommodation is limited, although there is a good hotel (Ivy House). Coledale Inn also offers accomodation. One of the Lake District's finest campsites is here, complete with a site shop, but do not expect to have the place to yourself – this site serves the whole Keswick area. At the end of your walk (or the beginning in the case of some of my colleagues!) the Coledale Inn and Royal Oak are waiting for you.

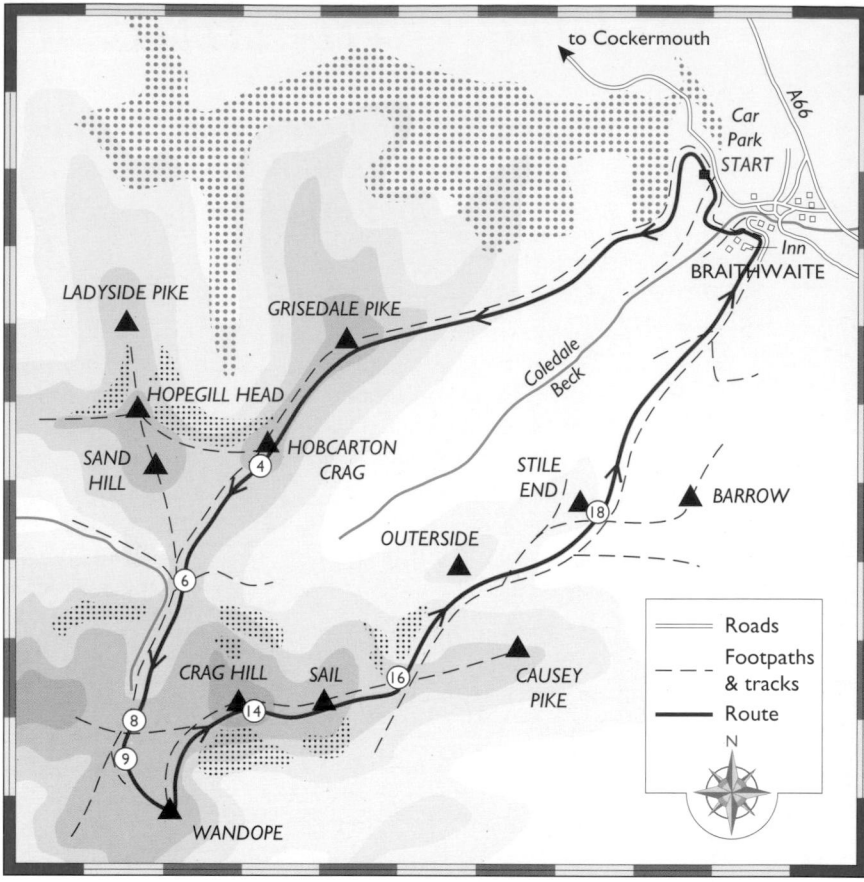

Perched on Grisedale Pike above Coledale.

Peaks of top 100 on this route

32 *CRAG HILL*
    839 metres (2752 ft)
52 *GRISEDALE PIKE*
    791 metres (2595 ft)
65 *SAIL*
    773 metres (2536 ft)
66 *WANDOPE*
    772 metres (2532 ft)
83 *HOBCARTON CRAG*
    739 metres (2424 ft)

Start/finish point: Car park on B5292 west of Braithwaite Village, near Keswick (GR 227238)

Map: Ordnance Survey Outdoor Leisure Map 4 (1:25 000)

Distance: Approx 8½ miles

Total ascent: Approx 995 metres (3264 ft)

Difficulty: A long and somewhat tiring ascent to the first peak of the route (Grisedale Pike) is followed by a much easier passage to the next three. A steep but very short descent and climb lies between Crag Hill and Sail. The return leg is long but very easy, descending for the most part over gentle contours all the way back to Braithwaite (approx 2536 ft).

Time: Allow at least 5½ hours.

Route directions

1 From the car park follow the sign 'Footpath to Grisedale Pike'.

2 Initially, this heads north then comes around to the south. Where another faint track joins from the left (east), the path turns westward and remains clear all the way to Grisedale Pike.

3 Continue on the same ridge-top path to Hobcarton Crag (the next minor pinnacle along).

(4) After the Crag, the path comes to a cairn where it forks. Take the left (south-west) branch here, away from the ridge, and down.

5 On Coledale Hause, the path is joined by another coming down from Sand Hill. Continue to the south here.

(6) Three paths lead upwards. The central one will save a few yards, but any can be taken (the aim is to head south alongside the stream).

7 A path from Coledale joins from the left, after which the way is clear by the stream.

(8) After a few hundred yards, at the top of the Hause, you will arrive at a clear crosspath. Go straight across it.

(9) Thirty/forty yds further, a path branches away to the left (south-east). Take this, heading towards the grassy hump of Wandope.

10 Quite soon, this path fades. Carry straight on in the same direction, cutting across the next path you see.

11 Continue south-east up the hillside to Wandope's summit (this is further than it appears).

12 From Wandope take the path that can be seen on the edge of the cliffs heading north then curving north-west.

13 On the ascent of Crag Hill, leave the rim where you see cairns a few yards to your left (north and west). From these, follow the main path to the summit.

(14) The path down to Sail is to the east, along a steep, narrow ridge.

15 From Sail continue easterly down to a crosspath in the deepest part of the col between Sail and Scar Crags.

(16) Turn left here (north-east).

17 This path leads across a steep slope, arriving eventually at a cairn on Outerside. A grassy track branches to the left here, heading for Stile End around a slightly higher contour than the main path. Either can be taken but the higher one is slightly easier.

(18) On the main path, go left (north-east) where the path forks, passing round the eastern side of Stile End.

19 If you have taken the higher path, stay on it until it meets the major track, then turn sharp left (north).

20 Stay on the main track all the way to Braithwaite, passing through the gate and onto the road.

21 Follow the road as it bends to the left (westerly).

22 After the Coledale Inn, the road curves sharply to the right. Branch off it here, alongside Holghyll House.

23 Turn left after this, then quickly right to cross the footbridge.

24 This path leads to the B5292. Turn left, up to the car park.

The route begins at a small parking area slightly west of Braithwaite. To find this follow the B5292 through the village heading towards 'Cockermouth via Whinlatter Pass'. As the road curves around to the north uphill, a blue parking sign '½ mile' will be seen on the left. Note that the car park is here, and not further on.

Almost immediately on starting out, Bassenthwaite Lake and Skiddaw lie ahead, then the path curves around to display Keswick, an impressive Great Mell Fell and the Dodds.

Derwent Water opens out over the left shoulder, with the long, wide valley stretching eastwards beyond Keswick. After a clear view of Braithwaite, the grassy track heads up with Coledale far below. Across the valley lies Outerside's ridge on which we will return eventually, with Causey Pike a little further afield. Grasmoor and Crag Hill stand above the valley head as Bassenthwaite Lake disappears to

Right: Looking back to Grisedale Pike from Hobcarton Crag.

the rear. Grisedale Pike demands attention now, looming ever larger.

At the top of the first of three steep ascents towards the summit, Thornthwaite Forest is unveiled immediately to the north, with the course of our route stretching out clearly ahead.

A shallow descent leads to the second climb, where a mass of ferns breaks the dominance of the heather. After a level section, the third ascent leads over rocks and heather to the summit. At 791 metres (2595 ft) Grisedale Pike is ranked peak number 52, offering a 360-degree panorama rich in contrasting colour and texture.

Immediately below, from north-west to north-east are the large plantations of the Whinlatter/ Thornthwaite Forest with Dodd Wood across Bassenthwaite Lake. The

The north-eastern prospect from Grisedale Pike.

horizon in this quadrant is formed by a long section of coastline, with the Solway Firth and southern Scotland leading to Skiddaw in the north-east.

Keswick's long valley and Derwent Water are topped by Blencathra and the Pennines, which lead in turn to a skyline of Clough Head, the Dodds and the full Helvellyn range. Continuing to the south, Ullscarf and the Langdale Pikes come round to Glaramara and the Scafells. Beneath this long, rugged horizon lies an intricate array of the Derwent Fells around Borrowdale and Newlands.

To the south-west, Crag Hill and Grasmoor appear much closer now, above Coledale Hause. Perhaps the most impressive feature, however, is close at hand from south-west to west, where Hobcarton Crag leads up to the sharp point of Hopegill Head and on to Ladyside Pike. From there, in an arc back to where we are, is a precipitous curve of cliffs and crags falling straight down to Hobcarton Valley.

It is a short stroll down to the subsidiary summit of Hobcarton Crag, with a view of cliffs and forests the dominant features. So close to its parent body of Grisedale Pike, the crag has nothing new to offer, save a clearer sight of our route across Coledale Hause. Nevertheless, with sufficient height separation and an altitude of 739 metres (2424 ft), it is ranked as peak number 83.

Most long-distance views are obscured temporarily as the path descends into the 'moorish' area of Coledale Hause, although a sighting of Loweswater is made through the deep V-shaped valley between Whiteside and Grasmoor.

The Hause leads up alongside a stream between Crag Hill and Grasmoor, to emerge on open ground where Wandope appears ahead and to the left (south-east). As yet, the summit is unseen beyond the grassy hump of its western face. The approach begins mundanely, but then presents what I find to be the highlight of this walk.

An intricate display of light and shadow viewed from Wandope.

A distant horizon formed by the Helvellyn range comes into view, then the Bleaberry Fell/High Seat ridge below it. A few more paces reveals the Maiden Moor/High Spy ridge then the long ridges of Dale Head, Hindscarth and Robinson, topped by the Langdales. Finally, Knott Rigg and Ard Crags are unveiled, with a deep chasm immediately below.

Whilst all this has captivated one's attention directly ahead, a glance to the south will show that the Scafell group is on full display, along with Buttermere, High Crag, High Stile, Red Pike and Pillar.

At the trig point on Crag Hill.

On The Way

The three peaks of Wandope, Crag Hill and Sail are separated by only 1 mile in distance and a total ascent of just 122 metres (400 ft).

The suddenness and then the constant unfolding of the picture is absolutely breathtaking. This effect is enhanced, no doubt, by the uninspiring section from Coledale Hause that preceded it. Wandope offers entertainment far greater than could be expected from a relatively 'unsung' peak. The summit stands at 772 metres (2532 ft), qualifying Wandope as peak number 66.

Crag Hill is close by to the north, and our path approaches along the rim of Addacomb Hole. A further, short ascent comes out on the wide, stony top where a triangulation column stands at 839 metres (2752 ft). This is peak number 32.

The breadth of the summit area restricts the main part of a north to south arc to a view only of mountain tops, lacking any depth to the scene.

The Buttermere Trio and Pillar are still prominent there, but it is in other areas that Crag Hill offers its reward.

Standing at the head of Coledale, the mountain's precipitous north-eastern crags overlook the full length of the valley between Grisedale Pike and Outerside. Our line of sight in that direction continues over Keswick to Skiddaw and Blencathra. Far to the north, Cockermouth and the coastal plain lead on to views of southern Scotland.

Once again, there is a stunning display from east to south of interlocking ridges and peaks climbing ever higher to a jagged horizon. The pick of these are the Scafells, showing a clear distinction between Ill Crag, Broad Crag and their parent mountain Scafell Pike.

There is a small and rather useless stone shelter on Crag Hill, looking out over Coledale and Skiddaw. One cold October afternoon with a wind chill factor of an Arctic scale, I was huddled behind it, wondering how I could do this sort of thing for fun! I believed myself to be alone – there had certainly been no-one else on the expansive top for some time.

I do not know what alerted me, but turning, I saw three men standing silently no more than 10 yards away. Moments later another look revealed a fourth man had appeared, astonishingly quickly and again in silence. Without a word, he stripped to the waist, replacing his clothing from a rucksack carried by one of the other three. This done, one of the three said 'Right, you can run back now', whereupon he set off down the mountain, heading north at a reckless pace. The three then calmly walked away.

I have no idea who they were or what they were doing, but I do not think 'fun' had anything to do with it.

A steep but short descent from

Spotlight on Sail, viewed from Crag Hill.

Crag Hill leads towards Sail, which requires only a couple of minutes to climb. At 773 metres (2563 ft) Sail is ranked peak number 65, one metre higher than Wandope.

The summit cairn lies away from the path to the north along Sail's heathery and grassy dome. There is nothing new to see there, apart from Crag Hill's imposing bulk cutting out the westward view. The most pleasing aspect is the view to the south, at our right hand along the path. Here, steep crags fall down to the long impressive valley between Knott Rigg and Whiteless Pike.

The valley comes to an end at High Snockrigg, which falls to reveal Buttermere. Above High Snockrigg, the Buttermere trio and Pillar are still in sight.

On the homeward leg now, the path descends Sail's eastern ridge then turns north-east towards Coledale on a narrow ledge traversing Scar Crags' precipitous north-western flank. On the southern side of Scar Crags, away from our view, a small patch of woodland is all that survives in the immediate area of the ancient forest that was cut down to fuel smelters.

Coledale lies far below, with the old Force Crag Mine clearly visible. This was the last working mine in the National Park, where zinc and barytes were worked as recently as 1991.

Another old mine can be found on Sail's north face.

Griesdale Pike towers above, before the descent starts between Outerside and Causey Pike. Skirting around Stile End, a clear and well-trodden path leads away from the heathered slopes towards Barrow Gill's cascading gully stream. Bracken is much in evidence once more, as a very long, gentle descent leads through a particularly peaceful scene, graced by a narrow wood across the gully.

Eventually the route arrives back in Braithwaite – lo and behold – at the Coledale Inn's front door. There is still a short distance to the car park, but that can wait.

The Newlands Trio

Another route over the Derwent Fells to Robinson, Hindscarth and Dale Head, from where one of the finest views in the Lake District can be admired.

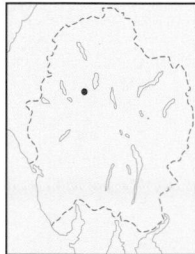

This second route over the Derwent Fells is an 8½ mile walk to Robinson, Hindscarth and Dale Head, the so-called Newlands Trio. On Dale Head, standing by the elegant cairn, one is treated to perhaps the finest Lakeland view that can be seen from an exact summit point.

The walk begins near Little Town in Newlands Valley – the 'new lands' created by the monks of Furness who drained a tarn near Uzzicar Farm. A narrow country road leads south from Braithwaite for about 3½ miles, where it crosses Chapel Bridge, then curves sharply to the north-east. After the bend, and slightly before reaching Little Town, parking spaces can be found by the roadside. Although accommodation is available at Little Town, and indeed dotted throughout the Newlands area, Braithwaite is the logical base for this route. Supplies will

Looking back over High Snab Bank from Robinson.

Peaks of top 100 on this route
77 *DALE HEAD*
   753 metres (2470 ft)
84 *ROBINSON*
   737 metres (2417 ft)
92 *HINDSCARTH*
   727 metres (2385 ft)

Start/finish point: Parking spaces at Chapel Bridge about 400 yds south-west of Little Town, Newlands Valley (GR 232194)

Maps: Ordnance Survey Outdoor Leisure Map 4 (1:25 000)

Distance: Approx 8½ miles

Total ascent: Approx 860 metres (2821 ft)

Difficulty: Care must be taken on the descent from Dale Head.

Time: Allow at least 5½ hours.

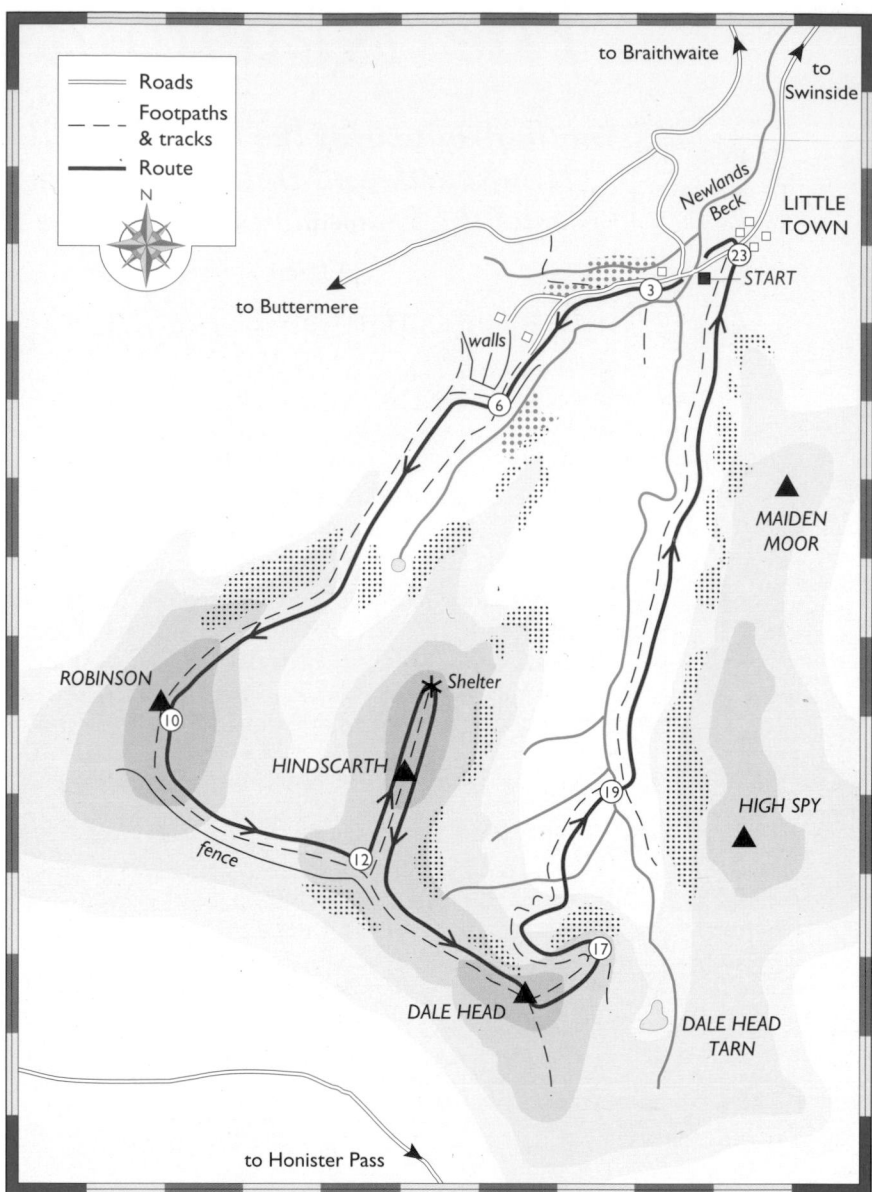

have to be gathered there before starting out. At the end of your day, the nearest inn is at Swinside, a couple of miles north of Little Town (you have to pass through Little Town to find it).

On arrival, it is difficult to believe that the rustic backwater of Newlands was formerly one of England's foremost centres of industry. In the 16th century, miners from Germany effectively took control of the existing Goldscope Mines ('Goldscope' is a corruption of German words meaning 'God's Gift'.), and began full-scale production of lead and copper. Profits were boosted by the discovery of a little gold and silver, with the smelting works at Copperheap Bay on Derwent Water becoming Europe's largest. All this was fine for the miners and for the Crown's taxes, but not so good for the landowner, the Earl of Northumberland.

He received little or nothing from the enterprise, and was irritated by the impact of serious mining on the land. Furthermore, the area's native male population took exception to the 'over-paid and over-here' Germans' habit of borrowing their womenfolk.

Eventually, many of the miners were integrated into the population, but not before a series of attacks had left at least one of them dead. As for the Earl, after trying litigation and even armed rebellion, his hash was settled by the Crown Executioner's axe.

The opening of Coniston's mines saw a decrease in Goldscope's viability until 1852, when a new, immensely rich lead vein was discovered. Around a decade of its most profitable years followed.

Route directions

1   From the parking area, re-cross Chapel Bridge.

2   Turn left (south-west) along the line signposted 'Newlands Church'.

③   Continue along the tarmac lane where a track branches left.

4   Go past the first 'Public footpath' sign on your right, then past the gate for High Snab Farm, and continue up the lane.

5   After passing through a gate and past a cottage, go through a second gate.

⑥   The track beyond the gate leads between two walls. At the right-hand wall corner, a path branches steeply up through ferns. Take this to High Snab Bank.

7   Ignore two minor paths that cut across and carry on to the ridge-top. At the top path turn left (south-west).

8   On the steep (scrambling section) of the ridge towards Robinson, the path splits occasionally. Stay on the most trodden path.

9   Approaching Robinson's summit, the path becomes unclear. Follow the line of cairns now.

⑩   From Robinson's summit head south, where a path quickly becomes clear, heading down towards a fence.

11   Follow the fence path down to the col then up to Hindscarth.

⑫   At the top of the rise, leave the fence and turn sharp left (north), along the ridge to Hindscarth summit.

13   From the summit cairn, continue north to the stone shelter for the best view.

14   Double back to the fence, then turn left (south-east) up to Dale Head. The path leads straight to the summit cairn.

15   Continue to the east from the cairn, where the path snakes down close to the crags.

16   Carry on down to a grassy spur that marks the end of the first part of the descent. The path can be seen veering round to the right after this, but do not follow it any further.

⑰   Look to your left at the spur and you will see a tiny cairn. This marks the beginning of a path that traverses the mountain face. Take it – this is much easier than it looks!

18   The path comes down to some ruins and a cairn. Watch for where it bends around to the right (back towards the cliffs). Some sharp zigzags follow, until the path heads northwards again, crossing Far Tongue Gill's stream.

⑲   Approaching the valley's main stream, another (Near Tongue Gill) comes down from the left (west). Do not cross it, but carry on down alongside it to Newlands Beck. Cross the beck wherever you feel comfortable.

20   On the eastern bank now, slightly ahead of you (north), a clear path can be seen rising up through a patch of ferns. Take this, it marks the beginning of a clear track through the valley.

21   Where the path forks, bear left (staying close to the beck).

22   The path widens into a major track, eventually leading to a gate, then the road.

㉓   Turn sharp left (south-west) on the road, to return to the car park.

Surrounded by peaks and ridges deep in the rural heart of Newlands, the route begins on a leafy lane climbing gently alongside Keskadale Beck. Causey Pike's distinctive pinnacle rises to the north, while ahead (to the south), Hindscarth's long ridge comes down to meet us. Continuing up the lane past trees and cottages, a view of Keswick and Skiddaw opens to the rear. The lane becomes a track which leads out onto the open fellside, where Robinson commands attention directly ahead.

Scope Beck can be seen crashing down from Little Dale's combe, at the head of the valley between Robinson and Hindscarth. The route turns away from the valley, climbing to join High Snab Bank's ridge path.

On reaching the ridge, a view opens over Keskadale and the Knott Rigg/Ard Crags ridge to the imposing bulk of Grasmoor, Crag Hill and their neighbours. The tiny wood on Ard Crags is known as the Keskadale Oaks

– another of Lakeland's surviving pockets of ancient forest.

In the opposite direction, a very attractive picture is formed by the Hindscarth, Maiden Moor and Cat Bells' ridges where they terminate in valleys sneaking up between them.

Our extremely enjoyable path leads southwards along a narrow ridge, with deep valleys on either side. To the right (west), the road up to Newlands Hause points towards Red Pike, giving a hint of what is to come. To the left (east), a tiny reservoir comes into view far below, within Scope Beck. This is another relic of the mining years.

A little scrambling is necessary over rock steps and knolls as the way becomes steeper. Robinson Crags fall away immediately to the west, then the path emerges on the broad top. A line of cairns marks the way over the considerable distance to the summit cairn at a height of 737 metres (2417 ft). Robinson is ranked peak number 84.

Previously known as Robinson's

Fell, the mountain was named after one Richard Robinson who bought various estates following the dissolution of the monasteries.

Beginning with the main bulk of the Derwent Fells, where Grasmoor is especially prominent beyond Newlands Hause, an arc from north-west to south-east has the most attractive features. The lakes of Crummock Water and Loweswater point towards the coastal plains and southern Scotland. Red Pike, High Stile and High Crag form an impressive picture beyond the Buttermere gap, together with Haystacks and Fleetwith Pike. The road over Honister Pass is very eye-catching on the col between Fleetwith Pike and Dale Head.

Further afield but still within this arc are all the giants of the Scafell range with one notable exception, Scafell Pike, which is hidden behind Great Gable. Esk Pike and Bow Fell lead on to Wetherlam and Glaramara, with the arc completed by Harrison Stickle and High Raise.

The proximity of Dale Head and Hindscarth, together with Robinson's own bulk, excludes any depth in the remaining panorama, but it is still worthy of attention. Helvellyn's long range is visible of course, leading toward the northern cluster dominated by Blencathra and Skiddaw.

Considerable height is lost on the descent to the depression on Littledale Edge – the connecting, narrow ridge between Robinson and Hindscarth. A fence runs down the edge, alongside our path, marking a distinct boundary between Little Dale's grassy slope and a rich heather carpet on the Buttermere side.

A short ascent leads to Hindscarth, where as yet the path is still on a ridge above the Honister Pass, linking

Crummock Water and Loweswater from Robinson.

At Dale Head's summit overlooking the Newlands Valley.

Robinson, Hindscarth and Dale Head. Both Robinson and Hindscarth's long spurs stretch away from this ridge, falling parallel with each other to the north-east. In order to visit Hindscarth's summit, one must walk along the spur, away from the connecting ridge. Later, our route to Dale Head entails returning to the ridge path, therefore Hindscarth's summit represents a detour, but a worthwhile one.

The summit has a height of 727 metres (2385 ft), qualifying Hindscarth as peak number 92. Apart from 'bagging' the ranking, any ascent of Hindscarth would be pointless without a visit to the large stone shelter a little further north from the summit. Here, the wide, grassy top falls away sharply to reveal a truly enchanting view.

I will not go into great detail, because this scene is almost identical to Dale Head's finest outlook, yet has a magical, almost fairytale quality of its own.

Robinson's long spur falls down on the left (north-west), with Keskadale and Ard Crags curving around behind it. Scope Beck's valley is immediately to the left, with Hindscarth's spur falling ahead from underfoot. Newlands' deep divide is to the right (east), flanked by the long High Spy/Maiden Moor ridge.

All these flow down to the wide, green Vale of Keswick, which appears for all the world like a sea. This impression is heightened by the small, conical form of Swinside rising straight up from the fields, its wooded slopes in marked contrast with the flat surroundings. Finally, the 'sea's' northern shore laps against the feet of Skiddaw.

Returning to the connecting ridge, Hindscarth Edge takes the path down

At Hindscarth's north shelter.

from there, then up the last climb of the day to Dale Head. Along the way, a fine view of Buttermere unfolds to the rear, and a strong sense of height is gained by peering down at the Honister Road.

From as far back as the ascent of Robinson, Dale Head's summit cairn has been a prominent feature. The path approaches it now, to arrive at the apex of this walk. The sense of height experienced on Hindscarth Edge pales in comparison to the airy vantage point enjoyed by this beautifully constructed slate cairn. At 753 metres (2470 ft), Dale Head is ranked peak number 77.

With over 1000 ft of practically sheer crags directly below, and around another 700 ft of rapidly descending ground after that, the gaze inevitably is drawn to the north. Here, the dizzying heights fall down to Newland's green channel as it flows for 5 miles to the Vale of Keswick.

Flanked again to the east by the dark, rugged crags of High Spy and Maiden Moor's ridge, the western flank is formed now by Hindscarth's similarly forbidding crags.

From Grasmoor in the north-west over to the distant Pennines in the north-east, a jagged skyline caps this spectacular view. Most prominent in the arc are Crag Hill, Grisedale Pike and Causey Pike with Skiddaw, Little Man and Blencathra coming round to Clough Head.

It is extremely difficult to tear one's eyes away from all this, but the remaining panorama should not be forgotten. From east through south to the west, Dale Head's upper heights obstruct nearby valley views, but Helvellyn's range can be seen leading on to the fully separated Langdale Pikes.

Bow Fell and Esk Pike lead to the Scafell massif, where Scafell Pike has emerged from behind Great Gable. Kirk Fell with the Black Sail Pass lead up to Wasdale's Red Pike, then Pillar introduces the Buttermere trio. Lastly,

Robinson can still be seen behind Hindscarth.

Having gorged yourself on the view from above Dalehead Crags, now you have the added stimulation of traversing across them!

The path from the summit heads down to the east, offering a tantalising glimpse of Borrowdale through the col above Dalehead Tarn. Shortly after this there is a choice of routes, either across the crags, or down to the unseen tarn. It has to be the crags – every time.

This path is steep and narrow, with Newlands down below the right shoulder, and the crags growing ever higher over the left. More steep crags (marked on OS maps as Great Gable) lie beneath the path, and you might hear crashing sounds of water rising up from them, where there should not be any water.

After the steepest part of the descent, the path enters ruins of an old mine building, from where it becomes grassy and zigzags downwards. This is an old 'sledgate' on which the miners hauled loads of slate. Temporarily now, the heading is back towards the crags, where the source of the water sounds becomes apparent.

Issuing from a narrow fissure in the rock face, a stream cascades down between Dalehead and Great Gable crags, falling perhaps 200 ft where it disappears beneath screes. It is not marked on OS maps, possibly owing to its short course.

Later, the route crosses Newlands Beck to emerge on an old mine's track that runs the length of the valley. There still remains a considerable distance to walk, but this is nothing more than a pleasant stroll past various mine workings, with peaks towering above on both sides. The beck remains more or less alongside, all the way back to Chapel Bridge.

The Sty Head Round

An upland area of widely contrasting features, and a route that completes a circuit of eight peaks over a distance of 10½ miles.

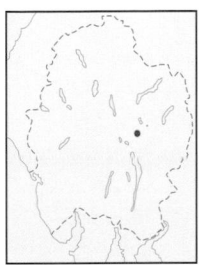

From Keswick, the B5289 heads south along the eastern shore of Derwent Water, then follows the River Derwent past the picture postcard village of Grange. Entering woodland, the road passes through a narrow gorge between high crags – the Jaws of Borrowdale – then exits into the green pastures of Borrowdale proper, the most celebrated of all Lakeland valleys.

A little further, after Rosthwaite Village, the valley splits to both east and west, bisected by the great bulk of Glaramara. This takes the form of a long, sprawling ridge that rises to join with the Scafell massif at Esk Hause – the pivotal point of

The northern outlook from Glaramara.

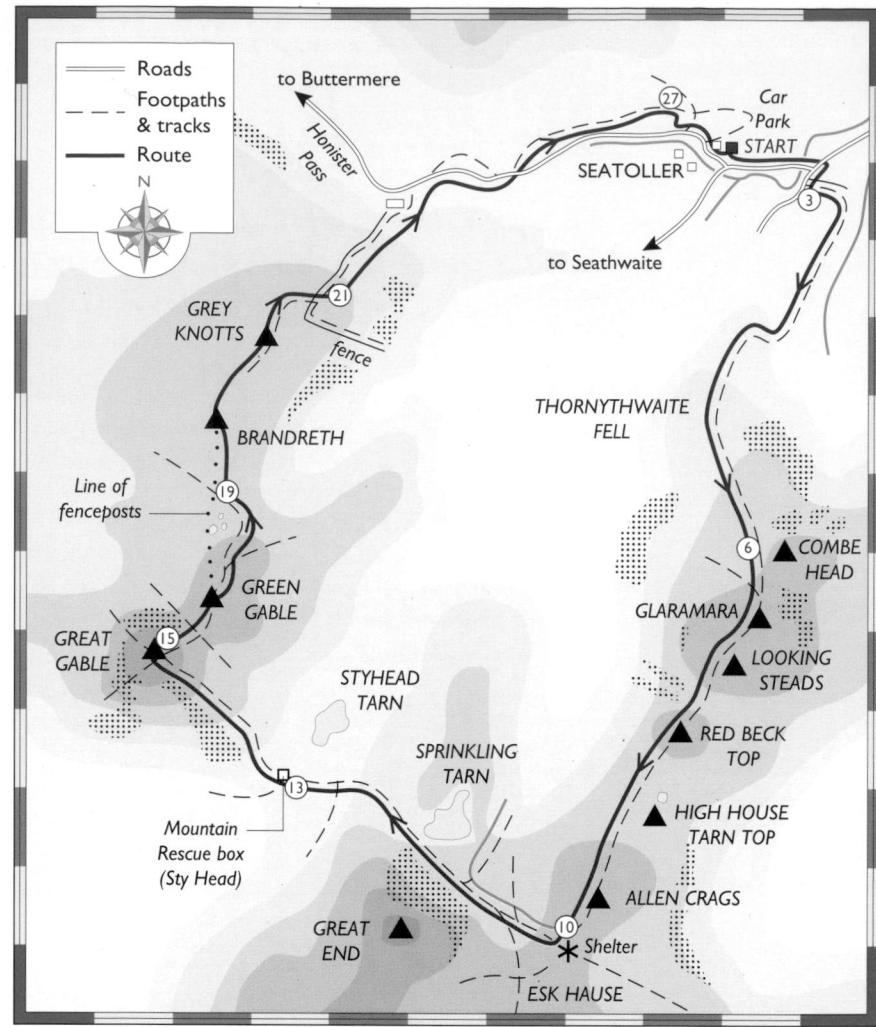

Peaks of top 100 on this route

11 *GREAT GABLE*
    899 metres (2949 ft)
45 *GREEN GABLE*
    801 metres (2727 ft)
54 *ALLEN CRAGS*
    785 metres (2575 ft)
57 *GLARAMARA*
    783 metres (2568 ft)
63 *LOOKING STEADS*
    775 metres (2542 ft)
87 *COMBE HEAD*
    735 metres (2411 ft)
96 *RED BECK TOP*
    721 metres (2365 ft)
100 *BRANDRETH*
    715 metres (2345 ft)

Start/finish point: Car park at Seatoller, Borrowdale (GR 245138)

Maps: Ordnance Survey Outdoor Leisure Maps 4 and 6 (1:25 000)

Distance: Approx 10½ miles

Total ascent: Approx 1455 metres (4777 ft)

Difficulty: Be prepared mentally for Great Gable's ascent followed by the scramble down to Windy Gap.

Time: Allow at least 8 hours.

Lakeland's main mountain ridges.

Where Glaramara's northern tip rises from Borrowdale, glacial action has scoured a deep combe from the mountainside. This has produced two lesser ridges to either side, Rosthwaite Fell and Thornythwaite Fell, which lead on to the summit ridge of the mountain. Along this undulating top there are no fewer than five separate peaks, four of which belong to Lakeland's top 100.

Our walk passes over these four and Allen Crags, then moves on to Great Gable, Green Gable and Brandreth, to complete a circuit of eight peaks over a distance of 10½ miles.

The starting point is the large National Trust car park at Seatoller, which lies on the B5289 at the foot of Honister Pass. Seatoller itself is only a tiny hamlet, but its important location merits a tourist information office (01768 72645). There are hotels and guest houses scattered throughout Borrowdale, but they are few and far between owing to the isolated, rustic nature of the area. Check the information centre for details. Basic tent pitching ground is offered at Seathwaite and Seatoller, with two good campsites at Stonethwaite. Groceries are available at Rosthwaite, but other supplies and equipment will have to be gathered before leaving Keswick.

At the termination of the outward leg of this route, a great deal of height must be sacrificed before the ascent of Great Gable. This particular section will prove testing even for experienced walkers, but once the summit has been gained the remainder of the route will seem easy.

Route directions

1 From the National Trust car park at Seatoller, turn left on the road, then left again to follow the road sign for 'Keswick 8 miles'. This leads down to a road bridge.

2 Leave the road at the bridge, turning right to follow the lane across the beck signposted 'Public footpath Seathwaite'.

3 After perhaps 200 yds down the lane (where the wall on your left becomes a fence), cross the stile on your left (east).

4 Follow the path and bear to the right with it to stay on the main track, on the west of the stream and gully.

5 This leads up Thornythwaite Fell onto Glaramara.

6 On approaching the summit, the path skirts to the right (west) of the first major pinnacle. This is Combe Head. Take the short detour to your left to visit this peak (a sheep trod marks the easiest way).

7 Return to the path and continue towards the summit crag (a short scramble is necessary here).

8 The ridge path continues to the south over Looking Steads (summit slightly to the east), then over Red Beck Top.

9 Carry straight on over another rise (High House Tarn Top) and past the tarns, up to Allen Crags.

10 Continue down in the same direction (south south-east) to the crosspath below Allen Crags. Turn right on this crosspath where you can see a star-shaped shelter ahead and to your left.

11 Soon after this the major track from Esk Hause will join your path from the left (south-west).

12 Stay on this track past Sprinkling Tarn all the way down to Sty Head. Do not turn left on the corridor route, and ignore any faint tracks you might see branching down to Styhead Tarn.

13 The track arrives at a major crosstrack at a mountain rescue box. Go straight on here on the stone built path up Great Gable. (Ensure that you are on the steep south-eastern ridge path, not the track that traverses Great Gable's southern face.)

14 Where the way up becomes very rocky follow the cairns.

15 To leave Great Gable head north-east along the plateau, following the major line of cairns.

16 A very steep descent leads to a crosspath in the col between Great and Green Gables. Go straight on up the red, eroded path to Green Gable.

17 On Green Gable head north, following the major path marked by a string of cairns. Go past the path that branches to the right (east).

18 On Ordnance Survey maps there appear to be two footpaths heading down towards Brandreth. The one on the left (west) is only the line of an old fence. Take the obvious path, following cairns to the right (east) of the small tarns at the foot of Brandreth.

19 Where the path meets the line of old iron fence posts on the ascent of Brandreth, leave the path (turning from north-west to north) and follow the fence posts up to the summit.

20 From Brandreth continue to follow the fence posts, heading north-east over Grey Knotts.

21 After the tarns on Grey Knotts, the faint path descends to a fence. Cross the fence stile (there are two – either is correct), and continue down with the fence on your left.

22 This path leads down to Honister Hause, into the car park behind the youth hostel.

23 Turn right, up to the road.

24 Turn right (east) on the road.

25 The old quarry track branches to the left. It is not worth taking this first branch as it quickly returns to the road.

26 Take the track's second branch on your left (north).

27 After a gate and stile, a grassy path comes down from the left (north) to meet our track, where there are small cairns on either side of the track. Look to the right here for the path that drops steeply down to the road.

28 Turn left on the road, back to Seatoller.

The walk begins on the road then enters fields at the head of Borrowdale, completely surrounded by high peaks. The jagged skyline of Rosthwaite Fell lies immediately to the left (east), as the path rises alongside the gully of Combe Gill. To the rear, Skiddaw appears beyond the Jaws of Borrowdale, before we arrive at a gate with a sign that warns of the dangerous condition of Dovenest Crag Caves. These are over on the far side of the facing combe, beneath Rosthwaite Fell. The largest natural caves in the area, they were uncovered when a crag broke away from the mountain side to reveal a network of underground cavities. Few people ever enter the combe, but those who do are usually tempted to explore by the sign that is supposed to deter them!

As the path climbs higher on Thornythwaite Fell, the V-shaped combe lies ahead, and slightly to our left. It comes to an abrupt end in the towering walls of Raven Crags, above which lies the first peak on our itinerary.

To the west, the hanging valley above Seathwaite comes into view, flanked by Base Brown and Grey Knotts, but it is to the rear that the finest panorama continues to unfold.

Here, Borrowdale's green carpet rolls up to the forested crags of the Jaws, with Derwent Water gleaming brightly before Skiddaw. Before long, Blencathra enhances the same northern view.

To the west, the sharp point of Honister Crag on Fleetwith Pike forms an impressive picture, with a glimpse of Buttermere's peaks beyond.

So far, the northern and western views have taken the eye, but now the east takes a bow, introducing the Helvellyn range. At the point when one becomes slightly awe-struck, wondering just how good this outlook can become, it then begins in earnest.

Great and Green Gables from Combe Head.

The Long Helvellyn Chain viewed from Looking Steads.

Suddenly, ahead and to the west, Great Gable rears up on the skyline, quickly followed by Green Gable, Brandreth and Haystacks. Directly ahead, Lingmell, Great End, Bow Fell and Esk Pike provide the massive southern arc to a circle of mountains around Glaramara that breaks only to the north above Borrowdale.

From here all the way across to Allen Crags, the walker is on a sprawling fortress of a mountain, which is separated from encircling peaks by deep valleys, and castellated by a multitude of pinnacles, rock outcrops and knolls. The path undulates over and around these, heading for its link with the dominant Scafell massif. Owing to this fortunate

central location, Glaramara provides its visitors with a sensation of being at the heart of things that no other mountain can match. Here, you will feel as though you have truly arrived.

The main summit lies ahead as our path skirts around Combe Head. This is the first peak of the day and requires a slight detour to the left (east). At 735 metres (2411 ft), it is ranked as peak number 87. The mountain skyline is best described from the main summit, but Combe Head's northerly position provides the finest view in that direction. With the Skiddaw range and Blencathra, this is the scene incorporating Borrowdale's graceful curve, the woodlands and Derwent Water. Without doubt, it is the most

enjoyable outlook of the entire Glaramara ridge. Also, the crags below this point were the inspiration for the mountain's name. Despite the distinctly Celtic lilt of 'Glaramara', it is in fact an amalgam of old Norse words that refer to the bulk of the mountain above the cliffs.

Moving on, a short scramble takes us to the main summit at 783 metres (2568 ft). This is ranked number 57. A full 360-degree skyline of mountains will keep you very busy should you wish to identify each one. Skiddaw and its companions are to the north, where the distant Caldbeck Fells lead round to Blencathra. From the north-east to east south-east, an unbroken chain marches from Clough Head over the

The south-western prospect from Red Beck Top.

Dodds, then across the Helvellyn range to Fairfield. Next comes High Street with Kentmere's peaks and then High Raise, the last link of the chain.

To the south-east are the unmistakable form of the Langdale Pikes and the far distant Pennines. The Coniston Group with Pike O'Blisco are next, before the imposing bulk of Bow Fell, Esk Pike, and Great End.

Between Lingmell and Great Gable lies the sea, after which a broad arc sweeps from west to north over such notables as Red Pike, Pillar, Brandreth, High Stile and a vast array of the Derwent Fells.

A couple of minutes is all that is needed to bring us to our third peak on Glaramara. This is Looking Steads; with an altitude of 775 metres (2542 ft) it is ranked at number 63. So close to the main summit, nothing has been added to the views. However, on the descent to the depression between here and Red Beck Top, the impression of the depth of Grains Gill's Valley to the right (west) increases greatly.

Red Beck Top is ranked 96, with an altitude of 721 metres (2365 ft). Again, there is nothing much to add, although Glaramara's fifth peak, High House Tarn Top, can be seen now. At

684 metres, this does not qualify for the top 100, but it lies on the route to Allen Crags.

Before reaching the fifth top, the path passes by a cluster of small tarns. The largest of these is High House Tarn, which provides a delightful foreground for a view over to the Langdale Pikes. Windermere enters the picture beyond these on the approach to Allen Crags, where a moderately steep climb brings us to the summit at 785 metres (2575 ft). This is peak number 54.

Now, apart from the unusual and spectacular aspect of the Langdales, the gaze inevitably is drawn down to the newcomer in the picture, Sprinkling Tarn. It rests with a number of other much smaller tarns on the ridge of Seathwaite Fell, beneath the towering walls of Great End. Along the same line of sight lies Great Gable, which is becoming extremely impressive. The bulk of Great End is the dominating feature here, challenged only by Bow Fell and Esk Pike. Slight Side and Ill Crag of the Scafells are visible, but not the highest summits – intervening ground obscures them as yet. The northern vista is greatly appealing once again, with the eastern chain still vying for attention.

A long descent that leads eventually to Sty Head begins now, as the path leaves this most memorable mountain ridge. We drop down towards a star-shaped shelter some way beneath Esk Hause, then turn to the north-west, continuing to descend in the shadow of Great End.

Great Gable grows inexorably in stature as the path leads down directly towards it. The deep gully and rich, red earth of Ruddy Gill lies immediately to the right (north) of the path, before breaking northwards on its way to Borrowdale. Very soon after this the path levels onto the shelf of Seathwaite Fell, arriving at the south-

western corner of Sprinkling Tarn. This large body of clean, refreshing mountain water is perhaps the best spot for a lunch break during hot weather. It might seem more logical to continue the descent to Sty Head, then to rest near the foot of Great Gable at Styhead Tarn. However, taking advantage of that particular water entails a short but unwelcome detour.

Another steep descent leads around the northern spur of Great End, to reveal the precipitous crags on the north-western flanks of Scafell's massif. The famous Corridor Route trail can be seen leading across them,

Looking at the Langdale Pikes whilst on the approach to Allen Crags.

Styhead Tarn from Great Gable's lower slopes.

below some deep, forbidding rock fissures. By far the most impressive of these is Piers Gill, between Lingmell and Scafell Pike.

Soon our route cuts across the ancient thoroughfare at Sty Head that links Wasdale with Borrowdale. A mountain rescue box sits at the head of the pass, exactly where the climb up Great Gable begins. I would advise you not to stop here for any length of time, as that could foster second thoughts. Gird your loins, and begin the assault of one of Lakeland's most prestigious mountains.

Much of the way is over a firmly built path, with the view to the rear becoming inspiring. Great End, of course, is the dominant factor in this. Then the Helvellyn range with the proudly marching Dodds form the skyline. Scafell Pike summit is revealed, then Sca Fell. The Langdales reappear beyond Allen Crags and Glaramara as our path deteriorates on the stony upper reaches of the mountain.

The summit plateau (peak number 11) is topped by rocks and cairns at an altitude of 899 metres (2949 ft). Set into one of the summit rocks is a war memorial to members of the Fell and Rock Climbing Club. A service has been held here on Remembrance Sunday every year since 1924, attended by hundreds regardless of the weather.

Great Gable is recognised as the birth place of British rock climbing. Its tall, broken southern crags are adorned with impressive rock sculptures such as Napes Needle and Sphinx Rock together with numerous gullies and walls. Nowadays, there are very few periods when climbers and the more adventurous walkers cannot be seen here, attempting to emulate the pioneers. The feats of these earlier visitors are well documented by photographs displayed around the Wasdale Head Inn.

A short walk from the summit, directly above the southern crags, stands a large cairn built by the brothers Westmorland in 1879. They believed the view from this point to be the finest from Great Gable, possibly the best in the entire Lake District. Looking out from here over jagged rocks into the fertile head of Wasdale, it is difficult to disagree. Beyond the fields lies Wast Water flanked by steep mountains with a background of the Irish Sea, where a clear day will reveal the Isle of Man.

Looking from the summit cairns (quickly skipping over the modern intrusion of Sellafield), Yewbarrow tumbles down to the lake and leads on to Kirk Fell. Further afield the skyline is formed by Seatallan, Red Pike, Scoat Fell with Steeple, and mighty Pillar.

Ennerdale's deep valley is flanked by the long Great Borne to High Crag ridge, after which comes Crummock Water's northern reaches, topped by a seascape and the hills of southern Scotland. The Derwent Fells lead on to Skiddaw's Group and Blencathra, then over the Dodds and Helvellyn range to High Street. The Kentmere Group are next, then the Langdales and Windermere. Beneath lies the early part of our route from Borrowdale over Glaramara.

Far away above Esk Hause are the Pennines, with Ingleborough surprisingly prominent. The Scafell massif in its full splendour is the most imposing spectacle, with the high breaking wave of Sca Fell seen to great effect. From there the land rolls down to Burnmoor Tarn and Illgill Head.

On some maps, a path traversing Great Gable's western slopes is marked as 'Moses' Trod'. This was named after Moses Rigg, one of the men who worked at Dubbs and Honister quarries on Fleetwith Pike. The path is part of the old 'sledgate' on which the quarry men would haul their loads of slate. Worthy labourer that he undoubtedly was, Moses' fame was not a result of his day job, however. One of Lakeland's better known

Wasdale and Wast Water from Great Gable.

The north-western outlook from Green Gable.

manufacturers of illicit whiskey, he is reputed to have had a still in Dubbs Quarry. At night he would smuggle his wares across the sledgate down to Wasdale and on to the coast. Sometimes he exchanged this for contraband brandy. Possibly his most lucrative sideline came from the storage and distribution of graphite or 'wad', stolen from Seathwaite wad mine.

During the 18th century, wad was an extremely valuable commodity with a variety of uses. I am told that a slight rise in temperature or pressure during the geological upheavals that formed graphite could have created diamonds.

The miners were thoroughly searched after each shift, with armed guards posted at night. Therefore, only very small quantities could be 'liberated' at any one time. A little below Great Gable's summit on the treacherous northern crags, the remains of a hut can be found. Almost impossible to locate from below and well hidden from above, obviously it was constructed for privacy, not convenience. This is generally believed to be Moses' secret place, where the wad and other goods could be stored until there was sufficient quantity for a trip to the coast.

A stony track leads across the summit plateau and then down a steep scramble to Windy Gap, the saddle between Great and Green Gables. On the descent, our path up Green Gable is clearly visible opposite in a red scar on the mountain side.

Styhead Tarn reappears way below the saddle to the right (south-east), before the short but steep ascent to peak number 45 on Green Gable's summit, at 801 metres (2727 ft). The origin of the mountain's title is apparent in its thin coat of vegetation.

The northern crags of Great Gable are by far the dominant feature here, towering above Stone Cove. Seatallan rises above the col between Great Gable and Kirk Fell, a foreground for the sea and Isle of Man. Pillar with Pillar Rock sweeps down to Ennerdale Forest and the River Liza.

To the north-west, the far (northern) tip of Buttermere can be seen, with Blackbeck and Innominate tarns on Haystacks. It is this rapidly unfolding quadrant that commands most attention now, with the Derwent Fells impressive and Grasmoor appearing quite enormous. Elsewhere, the outlook is relatively unchanged.

The route down to Brandreth and Grey Knotts' rolling massif stretches out ahead, clearly marked by a string of cairns. It leads in the general direction of Borrowdale, which is becoming clearer. From this position Grey Knotts appears to be higher than Brandreth, but this is an illusion.

On The Way

Across Sty Head, Wasdale and Borrowdale are linked by a footpath approximately 4½ miles long. To link both places by car involves a journey of about 50 miles.

Three small tarns nestle in the deepest part of the col between Green Gable and Brandreth, on Gillercomb Head. From there, a comfortable ascent leads onto the wide and rocky summit of Brandreth. This is peak 100, scraping home at an altitude of 715 metres (2345 ft).

The view to the north-west is wide open now with Ennerdale Water in the

Buttermere and Crummock Water from Brandreth.

picture, and Buttermere figuring much more prominently. The expansive nature of the summit requires a short detour in order to fully appreciate this scene. There is a peculiarly detached feel about Brandreth, as though it is an observer of the encircling mountains but not a part of them. Although Grey Knotts lies on the route, Brandreth is the last major peak of the journey, and a restful place to stay awhile and reflect on the day's proceedings. During high summer, a good day will see the sun arc down towards the view of lakes and tarns, the horizon ablaze with the reflected glow from the sea.

The path leads past a cluster of bright, airy tarns on Grey Knotts before starting the steep descent to Honister.

The road over Honister Pass quickly comes into view beneath Dale Head, and from this vantage point it appears remarkably level – a false impression as it happens. The quarries are unveiled far beneath us, with the old Drum House and tramway on the fellside to the left (west).

It was here at the Honister Pass that a particularly vicious skirmish took place between locals and the Border Reivers – Scottish raiders with a penchant for Lakeland cattle. The rustlers set a trap for their indignant pursuers at the head of the pass, but the plan backfired and they were routed. The grave of one of their leaders is somewhere on Honister Crag.

A youth hostel takes pride of place in the refurbished quarry buildings, which we pass by before stepping onto the road. It is much more enjoyable (and somewhat safer) to follow the old quarry track on the descent to Seatoller than to follow the road. Borrowdale grows ever larger ahead as High Stile Wood on Seatoller Fell comes into view. Then our path leaves the track, dropping steeply to join the main road in the wooded ravine, alongside a swiftly flowing stream. A few, final weary paces down the road bring us back to Seatoller, passing by the Yew Tree restaurant and public bar. If this is too crowded, seek out the Langstrath Hotel at Stonethwaite or the Riverside Bar in Rosthwaite.

The Buttermere Trio

High Crag, High Stile and Red Pike form the inspirational skyline for this popular route that encompasses some of the best views in the Lake District.

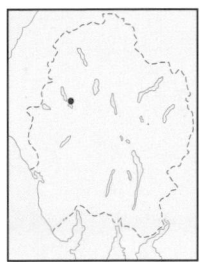

The Buttermere trio of High Crag, High Stile and Red Pike run in a line of the same length as the lake of the same name, and parallel to it. Over a lateral distance, considerably less than a mile, the craggy heights fall down to Buttermere's western shore by as much as 2300 ft.

This magnificent scene is completed where the line continues southwards over Haystacks' serrated summit, then curves northwards to Fleetwith Pike. The pike's tall conical form stands at the valley head where, but for the Honister Pass, it would seal off the entire Buttermere/Crummock Water vale from the east.

Looking toward Fleetwith Pike and High Crag from Buttermere's shore.

The B5289 runs along Buttermere's eastern shoreline for roughly 1¼ miles. Along the way passers-by are treated to the full impact of the trio's picture across the lake, complete with long, crashing becks and deep combes. Two hotels (with public bars), self-catering accommodation, and a campsite can all be found within Buttermere's tiny village. Along the lakeside road are a youth hostel, and another campsite at Dalegarth Guest House.

Unfortunately, provisions are a problem for those who stay at the campsites. Depending on one's avenue of approach to Buttermere, all supplies and equipment should be brought from Cockermouth or Borrowdale and Keswick; then nothing can detract from the pleasures of Buttermere. Without doubt, this area is as delightful as its evocative title suggests.

The trio's 6½ mile circuit is straightforward and very popular. Many fell walkers believe that Red Pike's views are the best in the Lake District, and most of them make that particular peak the first objective on the route. However, I find the walk is more enjoyable if the best is saved until last. Also, to ascend the ridge by way of High Crag is a little easier on legs and lungs.

Walkers who prefer lengthier excursions can extend the route to include Fleetwith Pike and the ever popular Haystacks. The most enjoyable way of doing this is to follow the footpath along Buttermere's opposite (northern) shore, then to follow the road for a short distance to where a footpath can be seen ascending Fleetwith Pike's sharp western ridge. Paths lead from there round to Haystacks and High Crag.

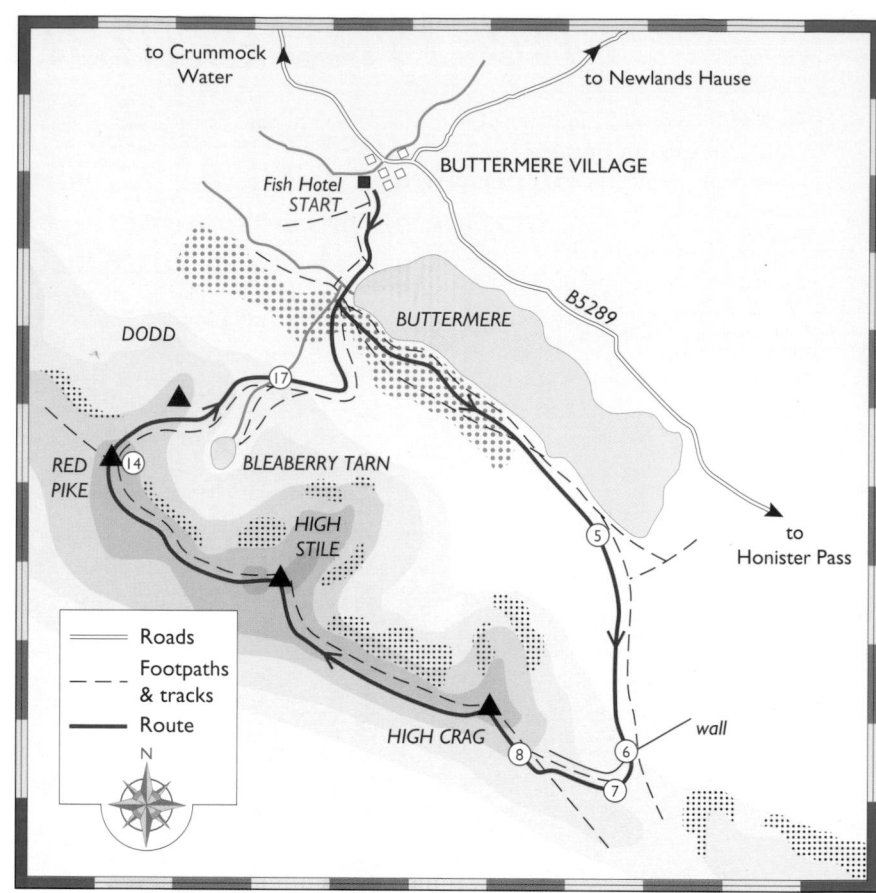

Peaks of top 100 on this route
40 *HIGH STILE*
   807 metres (2647 ft)
76 *RED PIKE*
   755 metres (2477 ft)
80 *HIGH CRAG*
   744 metres (2440 ft)

Start/finish point: Buttermere Village car park (GR 173169)

Map: Ordnance Survey Outdoor Leisure Map 4 (1:25 000)

Distance: Approx 6½ miles

Total ascent: Approx 775 metres (2543 ft)

Difficulty: The ascent to High Crag is very steep over the later stages, but once its summit has been gained, both High Stile and Red Pike are easily reached. The descent from Red Pike to Bleaberry Tarn is extremely steep over sand and shale initially, but then reaches a stone path where the going is much more comfortable. From the tarn, take care to avoid descending via Sourmilk Gill.

Time: Allow at least 4½ hours.

Route directions

1   At the Fish Hotel follow the sign 'Public bridleway. Buttermere Lake, Scale Bridge, private road'.

2   Stay on the main track where another branches right.

3   Turn right (south-west) on the path that runs parallel with the lake shore, about 100 yds from the water. This leads to a footbridge.

4   Turn left (south-east) after the bridge, to follow the track along Buttermere's shore.

5   At the far end of the lake, bear to the right (uphill), and continue upwards on the bridleway towards Scarth Gap. The heading now is due south.

6   About halfway between the lake and skyline, the path passes through a wall gap. Go through the gap, then follow the wall upwards. The route leaves the main path at this point.

7   Where the wall turns sharply to the right (west) continue to follow it. A faint path becomes visible now alongside the wall.

8   Follow the wall all the way up to the saddle between Seat and High Crag, where a major path heads north-west to High Crag's summit.

9   From High Crag, continue north-west along the ridge top path.

10   On approaching High Stile, the path forks. Bear right, following the line of cairns up to High Stile's eastern spur for the best view of Bleaberry Combe.

11   Turn left (west) along the spur top, returning to the main ridge top path. The most prominent cairn here marks the summit.

12   From High Stile continue north-west, following the line of fence posts.

13   Where the path and a string of cairns branch away from the fence posts, follow the path to Red Pike's summit.

14   From Red Pike, take the steep descent north-east, heading down toward Bleaberry Tarn.

15   Close to the tarn, take the left branch where the path forks.

16   The path follows Sourmilk Gill, then crosses it.

17   Cross the stream, then stay on the main track that leads away from it. Ignore the faint path that follows the stream.

18   The path leads down to a gate, then down through Burtness Wood to the lake's western tip.

19   Now, simply retrace the earliest part of the route back to the Fish Hotel.

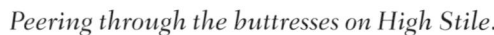

Peering through the buttresses on High Stile.

Beginning at the Fish Hotel, the route crosses a narrow alluvial strip between Buttermere and Crummock Water. Directly ahead, Burtness Wood decorates the trio's lower slopes, where Sourmilk Gill cascades down from a high combe between Red Pike and High Stile.

On arriving at Buttermere's north-western tip, the path crosses a brook that connects the two lakes. From there, a wide, level track leads through the woods with the lake shore immediately by the left hand and steep slopes on the right.

Having followed the full length of Buttermere, the route heads south up toward the skyline. Red Pike quickly passes out of sight on the ascent, but lofty peaks are all around. High Crag looks forbidding ahead, where the line of peaks passes over Haystacks' multi-pinnacled top and around to the dominant feature of Fleetwith Pike. In the hollow below them is the narrow valley and stream of Warnscale Bottom.

Over the right shoulder, Grasmoor is prominent among the colourful Derwent fells beyond the lake.

The going is steep over a clear, stony path heading toward Scarth Gap's pass. About half way between the lake and pass, our route heads west for the trio. Continuing to climb over rock and shale, the path approaches a shallow saddle between High Crag and Seat. Here, summits of mountains beyond Ennerdale Forest appear over the saddle, then reveal themselves more fully. Pillar is the most imposing form, accompanied by Scoat Fell and Little Gowder Crag's pointed silhouette. Having emerged on the ridge, the way now is north-west, following the top path.

Looking across Buttermere on the ascent of High Crag.

On the lakeside path at Buttermere.

Making sure of the way below High Crag.

I saw this path under repair in the early winter of 1995. National Trust workers with some army personnel were strung in a line all the way up to High Crag. Until that day I had no idea of how firmly and skilfully these stone paths are built, although if I had ever given the subject any thought it should have been obvious. Once in place, they must withstand pounding by countless boots, erosion by rainfall, and attack by frost and ice. They are much more than simple carpets of rocks: embedded drystone walls would be a more accurate description.

This particular one has been sorely needed for some time. The steep ascent to High Crag over stone and shale is badly scarred by numerous eroded tracks, becoming shabbier each year. The builders estimated that the path would be completed by February 1996 (it wasn't).

On the ascent, Ennerdale Water and its forest's upper western reaches come into view, leading on to the coastal plains. Above the scree-covered slope, High Crag's summit cairn stands at 744 metres (2,440 ft). This is peak number 80 but feels much higher. Its position at the eastern end of the trio's ridge commands an aerial view over Ennerdale Head, with the forest far below immediately to the south. Although there is quite a wide horizon on show, High Crag's finest outlook is over the southern void to Lakeland's premier peaks and due east over Fleetwith Pike.

Rising up beyond Ennerdale's great divide are Green and Great Gables, with Kirk Fell topped by the more distant Scafells. A few steps in their direction unveils that breathtaking view of the forest, where River Liza flows her long course down to the lake.

In the east, Fleetwith Pike introduces the distant line of the Dodds and Helvellyn range, which leads in turn to High Street, Fairfield, Great Rigg and finally Red Screes. In

Looking down on Bleaberry Tarn from High Stile.

the south-east and much closer are the Langdales and Glaramara.

A short detour to the north, where High Crag's grassy spur ends above buttresses, will unveil a comprehensive view of Buttermere. Nevertheless, all remaining segments of the panorama are better from the other two peaks of our route.

Now follows a truly exhilarating section of the route. The ridge becomes very narrow on the approach to High Stile, passing over rocks and boulders. Immediately below the right hand, a succession of buttresses and crags open and close to reveal spectacular images of Burtness Combe and the lake. Capping the scene are Robinson, Skiddaw and the Derwent Fells, where Grasmoor is becoming ever more prominent.

The last major buttress along this section is named Eagle Crag, although eagles have not nested here since the 18th century. Because of their absence, few people pay close attention when large birds are above the ridge or gliding around the combes. Even when they do, the sighting is almost invariably that of a buzzard, of which the Buttermere area has more than its fair share. But if the watcher is very lucky, that 'buzzard' might merit a second look, followed by a sharp intake of breath.

Every summer, second-year eagles fly south from Scotland over the Lake District, then return by way of the Pennines. They are drawn here in search of suitable nesting sites, their phenomenal powers of vision easily detecting the mountainside.

The crags above Buttermere must be especially attractive to them, with local sightings of these magnificent creatures rare, but not impossible. In July 1994 over a period of six days, I saw one here on three separate occasions. Of these, a sighting from Fleetwith Pike was the most fascinating. I noticed the bird as soon as it appeared from behind Red Pike, fully three miles away. From there, it floated across the crags down to Haystacks. Having circled above Warnscale Bottom, it returned northwards, disappearing somewhere on the crags above Bleaberry Tarn.

A comfortable ascent leads to High Stile's long north-eastern spur, emerging near the triangulation column. This does not mark the summit or even the highest point of the spur, but it is from this spur that High Stile's most renowned viewpoint is seen at its best.

On The Way

A total ascent of approximately 150 metres (492 ft) over a distance of 1¾ miles is all that is necessary on the crossing from High Crag over High Stile to Red Pike.

Immediately beneath one's feet, a deep combe falls over 1000 ft, where Bleaberry Tarn nestles below Red Pike and its junior partner, Dodd. The tarn's outflow disappears over the crest of the combe, falling another 1,300 ft toward Buttermere village and Crummock Water.

High Stile's summit is a short stroll across a jumble of rocks and boulders from our present position, on the mountain ridge itself. At 807 metres (2647 ft), this is the highest point of the ridge and is ranked as peak number 40. A full 360-degree panorama is visible from here, but Red Pike lies to the

The northern outlook from Red Pike.

north-west and much of the outlook is better from there. Before heading in that direction, take a last look at Glaramara, the Langdales, the Gables and Great End. Once on Red Pike, these will disappear behind High Stile.

The ridge route continues above Chapel Crags, where once again clefts appear between buttresses to reveal aerial views into a combe. In this one of course, there is the bonus of the tarn.

Our last ascent of the day is short and easy, leading onto Red Pike's summit at 755 metres (2477 ft). This is peak number 76.

Diversity is the key word in the description of Red Pike's views: soft rounded hills, stark soaring crags, long valleys, wide plains, and a seascape. Plus bare rock, heather carpets,

tarns, towns, forest and no fewer than five lakes.

Ennerdale Water leads to the west with Crummock Water pointing north to the Vale of Lorton and Cockermouth. The background of this arc is formed by an enormous patchwork of lowlands and coastal plains, leading to the Solway Firth and southern Scotland. In the middle and foreground between the lakes is the wide, grassy ridge of Great Borne and Starling Dodd. In the same segment similar soft features are seen in Mellbreak, Burnbank Fell and Loweswater, Hen Comb, Blake Fell and Gavel Fell. This wide land mass narrows to the east between Buttermere and Ennerdale's valleys. Where it reaches Red Pike's easting,

the landscape changes dramatically into higher, broken ground with deep, craggy combes and broken spires.

Rising from Crummock Water's eastern shore are the steep slopes of Grasmoor, which dominates the undulating mass of the Derwent Fells.

Far to the north-east, Skiddaw and Blencathra are a background for Keswick, Derwent Water and Newlands. Robinson rises from Buttermere's far shore, introducing a skyline that rolls from Clough Head over Helvellyn's range as far as Red Screes. Beneath these are Robinson's companions, Hindscarth and Dale Head. Immediately below in this quadrant are Bleaberry Tarn and Combe, from where Chapel Crags soar to High Pike's bulky summit.

The Scafells peep over High Stile's western shoulder, with Pillar, Scoat Fell, Haycock and Little Gowder Crag much closer in the south. Once again, the view softens in the south-west, where rolling hills come back round to Ennerdale Water.

A very steep descent leads towards Bleaberry Tarn. Before arriving in the grassy combe, the way alternates between badly eroded sandstone scars and a stone path. The origin of Red Pike's title is apparent in the barren scars, and this eastern face is in need of urgent attention by path builders.

After passing close by the tarn, the route follows Sourmilk Gill's heathered gully then heads eastward beneath the combe. A clear track becomes a stone path once more, leading down toward the lake and into the tree line.

Losing height rapidly in the woods, the path re-emerges at Buttermere's north-western tip. All that remains is a short walk across the alluvial strip, retracing earlier steps back to the Fish Hotel.

The Gasgale Round

With its spectacular ridges, fine peaks and high deserted valleys, this is hill walking terrain of the highest quality.

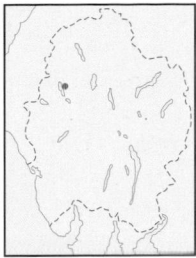

The third and final route over the Derwent Fells covers only 5 ½ miles but includes Grasmoor, the area's highest mountain. Only one climb worthy of the title is required for the first four peaks, with another separate ascent on Grasmoor.

Whiteside, Whiteside East Top, Hopegill Head and Sand Hill are the other peaks of the route, with only Whiteside failing to make the top 100. The Whiteside/Hopegill Head ridge (weather permitting) offers Lakeland's finest viewpoints over the Cumbria coastal plain to the Solway and Scotland.

The major part of this view, and much more, can be enjoyed again on the walk's final section, where it descends Grasmoor's exciting western ridge.

Approaching the Whiteside Ridge.

A car park at Lanthwaite Green Farm provides the start point, close by Crummock Water's north-eastern tip. Self catering apartments are handily placed at the car park (01768 770252), but otherwise the most convenient base is Buttermere Village.

If you do not wish to return to Buttermere after the walk, try the Loweswater Hotel, or carry on northwards to High Lorton. Equipment and supplies should be brought over from Keswick. If approaching from the north, bring them from Cockermouth.

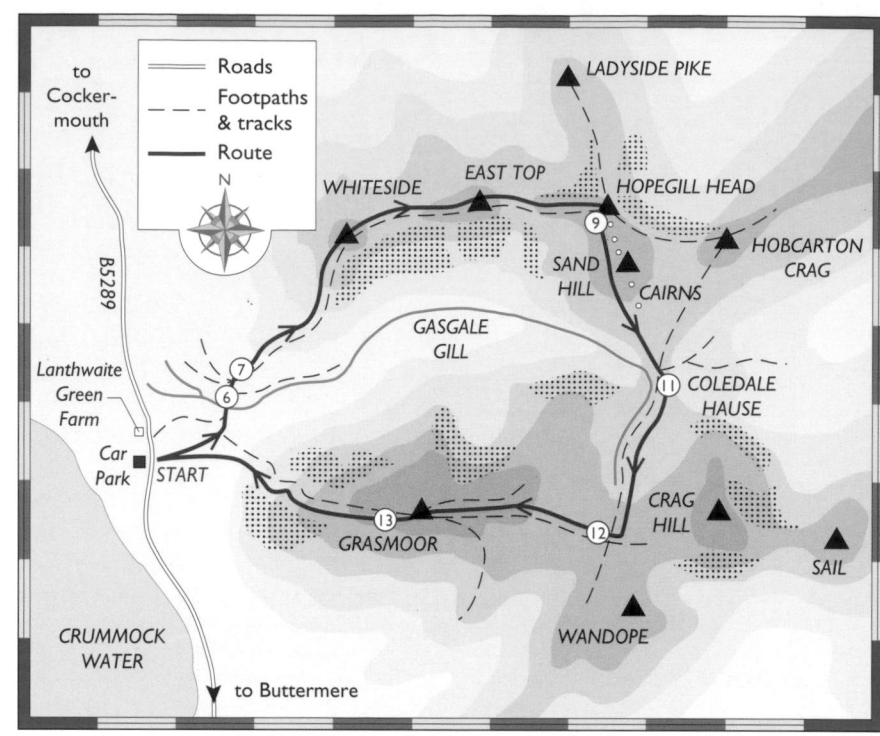

On Grasmoor's north-western ridge.

Peaks of top 100 on this route

26 *GRASMOOR*
    852 metres (2795 ft)
68 *HOPEGILL HEAD*
    770 metres (2526 ft)
75 *SAND HILL*
    756 metres (2480 ft)
98 *WHITESIDE (EAST TOP)*
    719 metres (2358 ft)

Start/finish point: Car park on the B5289 near Lanthwaite Green Farm, Crummock Water (GR 159208)

Map: Ordnance Survey Outdoor Leisure Map 4 (1:25 000)

Distance: Approx 5½ miles

Total ascent: Approx 910 metres (2986 ft)

Difficulty: The first climb of the route (to Whiteside) is steep but, once having gained the summit, an easy and visually spectacular walk leads across East Top to Hopegill Head. The descent from Sand Hill is uncomfortably steep but over safe, smooth ground to Coledale Hause. The ascent of Grasmoor is remarkably easy, but the descent of its north-western ridge is very exposed and requires a good deal of scrambling. Inexperienced walkers should descend Grasmoor by the alternative route described in the route directions.

Time: Allow at least 4½ hours.

Route directions

1 A telephone booth marks the most convenient car park for the route, slightly to the south of Lanthwaite Green Farm.

2 Head north on the road for a few paces until reaching a small, wooden 'Public footpath' sign on the right (east).

3 There is no path on the ground but head eastward towards the gully.

4 A clear path can be seen branching to the right (south-east) up the slope of Grasmoor. Go past this to the left, continuing towards the gully.

5 The path becomes clear now, dropping down to a footbridge.

6 After the bridge, go straight uphill to cut across the ridge path, then bear to the right on it (north-east).

7 On the lower slope, the path is unclear. Remember that the route follows the ridge. As it climbs higher, two paths branch to the right (east), into Gasgale. Bear to the left at both of these, staying on the ridge.

8 The path becomes obvious, and remains so all the way across the ridge top over Whiteside to Hopegill Head.

9 On Hopegill Head, the route follows a major track heading southward. This is broad, well-trodden and marked by cairns. Also, it leads away from other ridge-top paths.

10 Follow the cairns over Sand Hill and continue down to Coledale Hause.

11 Carry on to the south straight across the hause, then continue up between Crag Hill and Grasmoor.

12 On arrival at the crosspath, turn sharp right (west), to begin the ascent of Grasmoor.

13 Assuming that conditions are favourable, confident and experienced walkers can descend Grasmoor by passing over the full length of the summit area down to the westernmost cairn, then by way of the sharp north-western ridge. If you are in any way apprehensive about this particular section, simply retrace your steps along the path for approximately 200 yds from the summit shelter and cairn. A path branches southwards from here, descending by way of Lad Hows back towards Crummock Water. Turn right on the road to return to Lanthwaite Green.

14 Those who prefer the challenge of the ridge descent will find that the path forks at the westernmost cairn. Bear to the right (north-west) here, and a track can be seen leading onto and down the ridge.

15 Make sure you stay on the actual path – it is easy to confuse this with various little scree runs, all of which have the same colouring as the path. If in doubt, the correct way is usually to the right.

16 A rock outcrop stands within the path, clearly marking the beginning of another steep descent. The path appears to split both ways around it, but in fact the only viable descent is to the right. This leads into a gully of scree and shale.

17 Descend the gully for about 100 feet. After the deepest part – where the gully walls start to open out – look to the left for a view of Loweswater. As soon as the lake appears, turn to your left out of the gully (a small cairn marks the spot).

18 Pick up the narrow path here, then continue to descend the ridge.

19 There are numerous off-shoots along the way. Stay on the easiest path, keep looking to the right and remember to stay on the edge of the ridge.

20 Eventually the way comes down to steep scree. Below these a clear, grassy path can be seen on the lower slopes. Head down toward it, either on the scree (uncomfortable) or on the faint paths that fall on either side of it.

21 Once on the grassy lower slopes, open ground leads back to Lanthwaite Green.

Whiteside is the first objective, its high, pointed ridge coming down almost to the roadside. Gasgale Gill escapes through a narrow gully between Whiteside and Grasmoor, with our path climbing steeply up the northern side.

Crummock Water is clear to the rear, with Loweswater appearing across the valley to the west. Initially the way is through grass and ferns, then enters a vast heather carpet. Gasgale opens wide below, as the path continues along the ridge. Soon, it arrives at the rim, looking up to the ridge pinnacles and the point of Hopegill Head.

This line of sight is across Gasgale Crags – the southern ramparts of Whiteside. Here, a succession of sharp spurs plunge down towards the gill. They provide a fascinating and quite unique spectacle: razor edges running across a sequence of narrow troughs bedecked in heather.

More height is gained above the crags as the path begins to curve eastwards along the ridge top. Approaching Whiteside's first summit, a superb coast and seascape is revealed to the left and ahead (north-west to north), with Cockermouth immediately apparent down in the plains.

Whiteside's true summit (East Top) is unmistakable, and lies further along the undulating ridge at an altitude of 719 metres (2358 ft). This is peak number 98.

Undoubtedly, it is the coastal view that will most take the eye all along Whiteside's ridge. Also Gasgale's deep recess and Grasmoor's soaring heights are very impressive, with a look back through the mountain cleft towards Crummock Water. The high pass of Coledale Hause can be seen at the valley head, linking Hopegill Head with Grasmoor. These two giants mostly interrupt distant mountain views although Helvellyn's range and Skiddaw stake their claim (as ever).

Whiteside is reputed to be the epicentre of unusual seismic vibrations that occurred in 1908. Over a period of about one month, deep

Looking along Hopegill Head's northern ridge.

rumblings shook the ground, and smoke was often seen issuing from the crags. Speculation over possible volcanic activity seems fanciful, but nevertheless, the cause remains a mystery.

A third pinnacle and two depressions are crossed along the ridge top before Hopegill Head's summit is gained, at an altitude of 770 metres (2526 ft).

As peak number 68, Hopegill Head stands proudly at the hub of four connecting ridges. Apart from our route from Whiteside in the west, others come from Ladyside Pike in the north and Grisedale Pike in the east, with a stunted ridge leading south over Sand Hill. From there, it falls to Coledale Hause.

In keeping with so much of the Derwent Fells, the most impressive features around Hopegill Head are those of the immediate surroundings – or more accurately, the swift absence of them. Hobcarton Crags fall away between Grisedale Pike and Ladyside Pike's ridges. Hope Gill cuts a deep channel between the Ladyside and Whiteside ridges, with the abyss of Gasgale between there and Grasmoor. Elsewhere, there is a more earthly base running down toward Sand Hill.

Gasgale and a portion of Crummock Water viewed from Sand Hill.

On The Way

There are a total of 15 separate peaks over 2000 ft comfortably within a 2 mile radius of Coledale Hause. Of these, 9 belong to the Top 100.

Further afield, the view has expanded to include Sca Fell and Great Gable. Also, Glaramara and Pike of Stickle have appeared, leading round to a more finely detailed Helvellyn Range. Blencathra has teamed up with Skiddaw in the north-east, and of course, a wonderful seascape is still apparent. Coming round toward the south, a cluster of peaks with Mellbreak and Great Borne lie beyond Crummock Water. Grasmoor still cuts out a sizeable arc, allowing only High Crag of the Buttermere trio to be seen.

From Hopegill Head the route swings south, on the beginning of a wide circle around Gasgale back to Lanthwaite Green. A short descent leads to Sand Hill at 756 metres (2480 ft). This is peak number 75 – its only saving grace. 'Sand Hill' describes the form adequately: a shale and sand hump that is only ever visited on the way to somewhere else.

The view down Gasgale and across its spurs is still magnificent, but no better than before. In the opposite direction, Grisedale Pike and Outerside flank Coledale's long run down to the Vale of Keswick. Nevertheless, one's attention is held by Crag Hill and Grasmoor which lie ahead and to either side of the Coledale Hause divide.

After partaking once more of Loweswater's appearance in the west, we are back on the hause section shared with the Coledale Round. This can be shortened by bearing away from the path over Grasmoor's north-eastern ridge, along the right of way on OS maps. Unfortunately there is no clear path on the lower slope, and the going is very uncomfortable. Eventually, this way leads to a path above Dove Crags on Grasmoor's northern face, but overall it is much simpler to continue along the main avenue.

Here the route climbs gently to the top of the pass, then turns sharply to the west. A steep ascent leads to a false summit, then to an expansive view of Crummock Water. From here a gentle ascent over the narrowing ridge comes up to the summit at 852 metres (2795 ft).

Grasmoor is peak number 26, with a long and stony top sporting a most

Looking toward the distant Scafells from Grasmoor.

unusual stone shelter. This appears to be eccentrically arranged, but is cleverly designed to provide protection from every angle.

Crummock Water lies far below, occupying the base of an arc from west to south. Above its western shore, Mellbreak with the soft contours of Great Borne and Starling Dodd sweep round towards Buttermere. Now Red Pike and High Stile have joined High Crag, together with Haystacks and Fleetwith Pike. Above all these, a long, smooth line of hills flows from distant Lank Rigg to Caw Fell. The line becomes a little rougher over Haycock, Scoat Fell and Pillar, then breaks chaotically over the Scafells, Bow Fell and Wetherlam.

Grasmoor's dome creeps ever higher from south to east, but fails to interrupt the skyline. Glaramara, the Langdales and High Raise lead round to Red Screes, Fairfield and, of course, the Helvellyn range. The Dodds and Clough Head just manage to clear the foreground, before Blencathra and Skiddaw come round to closer peaks including Hopegill Head.

The remaining panorama is composed of that dreamy seascape, over the hills and far away. A string of cairns leads that way, following a path along the top to the far western cairn of Grasmoor. OS maps do not show any path continuing from there, but fortunately one does.

It heads straight for the sea, the plains and Loweswater, arriving at a stunning view above Grasmoor's sharp western ridge. There is a definite point where the ridge path begins to fall sharply from Grasmoor's heights. Even the most insensitive of souls could not fail to become a little breathless here, and to stay awhile amongst the rocks and heather.

At any time of year, this outlook is at its best late in the day, glowing brightly under the sinking sun. It is wise not to let it sink too low before you leave, as some daylight should be saved for the ridge descent.

A degree of concentration is required now, otherwise one's attention will stray constantly from the path to the airy fathoms all around. An extremely stimulating descent passes over a variety of scrambles and rock steps. The final section drops even more steeply, either over or alongside scree, arriving on the grassy approaches to Lanthwaite Green.

Above The Ennerdale Coves

A peaceful trek can be enjoyed here, in one of the more remote regions of Lakeland, beside forest plantations and lakeshores, through rugged rock terrain and heather-clad slopes.

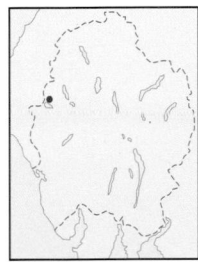

Probably the only difficulty one will encounter on this route is in locating the start point. If approaching through Ennerdale Bridge, ignore the first roadsigns for the lake and continue via Whins and Routen Farm to Bowness car park on the northern shore. The only other approach is through Croasdale,

then following the same directions.

This is an extremely remote area, barely inside the National Park's western boundary. There are some isolated farms and cottages in the vicinity offering B&B accomodation, but realistically, this walk represents a one-day detour from bases elsewhere within the Lake District.

Autumn evening light illuminates the southern prospect from Haycock.

No matter where I am in the Lake District, whenever I see the high ridge of this route, I am reminded of an incident that occurred below Haycock in the area described from its southern cairn. One bright November morning, a hunting party and their hounds were tunnelling enthusiastically into the side of a large pile of boulders. As I approached them, I saw a large 'dog' that I had not noticed previously. The animal was edging slowly away from the party on the opposite side of the boulders.

Its casual manner deceived me for perhaps a minute, when the realisation dawned that I was looking at an exceptionally large fox. Only when it was almost around a knoll – just feet away from being out of sight of the party – did it break into a run. The tension of that moment was absolutely electrifying.

It would have escaped (and the hunters would have carried on digging for a non-existent quarry), but for one man who happened to look up at the last second. His shout of alarm sent the hounds off in pursuit.

Some ten minutes later, the simply magnificent, beautifully proportioned fox ghosted right by me. It was moving now in completely the opposite direction to its initial flight, without a hound in sight. But sure enough, after the fox had disappeared over the horizon, a group of hounds came bounding past on its trail.

About a month later, a friend told me he had heard a report that the second largest fox ever caught in Britain had been killed the same weekend I saw the chase. However, he could not remember the location. I could have made enquiries, but I'm not sure that I really want to know.

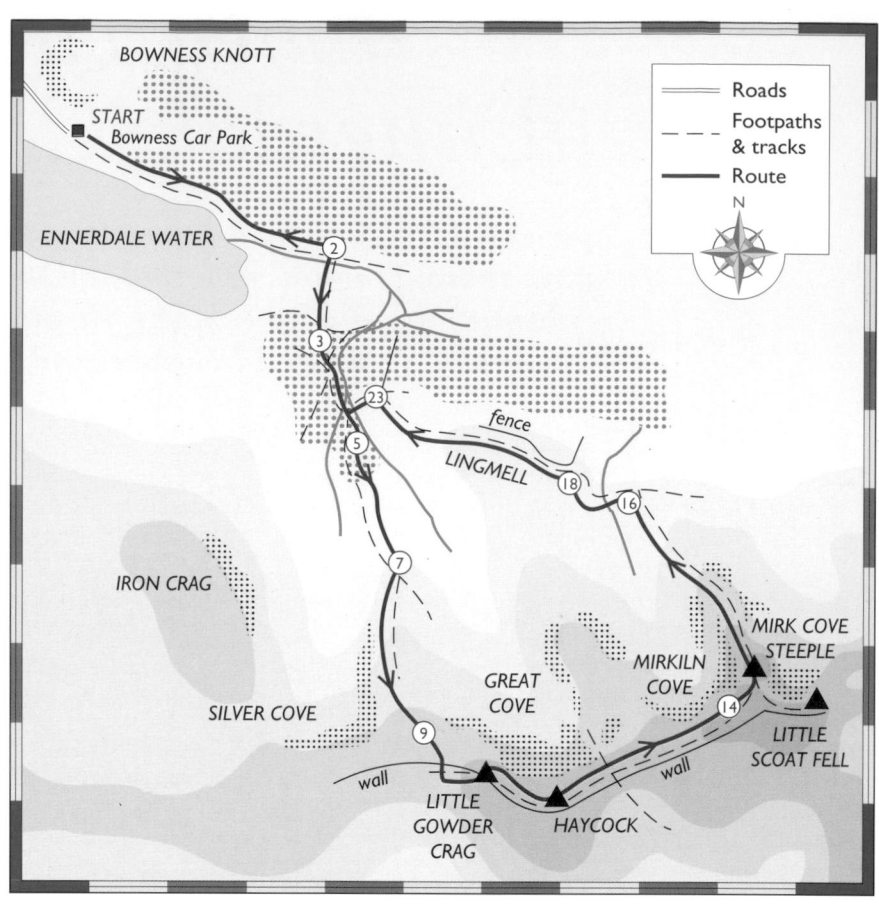

Peaks of top 100 on this route
38 *STEEPLE*
    819 metres (2686 ft)
47 *HAYCOCK*
    797 metres (2614 ft)
89 *LITTLE GOWDER CRAG*
    733 metres (2404 ft)

Start/finish point: Bowness car park, Ennerdale Water (GR 109153)

Map: Ordnance Survey Outdoor Leisure Map 4 (1:25 000)

Distance: Approx 9½ miles

Total ascent: Approx 885 metres (2904 ft)

Difficulty: After a very pleasent lakeside stroll, the ascent to Little Gowder Crag is long and steep, but not exhausting. From there, Haycock is easily reached, followed by a slightly more taxing climb to Little Scoat Fell. Care must be taken on the sharp ridge leading to Steeple. A steep descent to Lingmell (a hill of that name – not the mountain) is followed by an extremely steep but safe descent back to the valley.

Time: Allow 6 hours.

Route Directions

1 From Bowness car park, head south-east on the road alongside the lake. Ignore the route-marked trails that lead off into the woods.

2 After passing the eastern end of the lake, take the first track that branches to the right (south) on the bridge across Char Dub.

3 The track crosses fields then comes to a gate. After the gate, take the path that branches to the right (south), away from the main track. (This path is not marked on OS maps.)

4 Bear to the left (above and alongside the beck) where the path enters a clearing which appears to form a T-junction of pathways. (Blue-tipped posts mark the way.)

5 The path follows a wooded gorge then drops to a footbridge. Having crossed the bridge, and before reaching a second bridge, turn sharp right (south) on the faint path that climbs the narrow, wooded ridge.

6 On emerging from the trees, cross the stile and continue upwards on the clear path through the heather.

7 Where the path forks, bear right. This leads to a series of cairns.

8 Approaching the ridge top, the path becomes very faint then practically disappears. Follow

the high course of the ridge as it swings round to the left (east).

9 A wall ahead runs from west to east. Follow this eastward to Little Gowder Crag.

10 For the easiest ascent, go through the breach in the wall at the foot of the crag then follow the faint track up to the summit.

11 From Little Gowder follow the wall south-east. This leads directly to Haycock's summit.

12 Continue to follow the wall from Haycock on its left (northern) side. Go straight across the crosspath in the saddle between Haycock and Great Scoat Fell.

13 Approaching the top of Great Scoat Fell, follow the track that bears to the left, away from the wall. Continue above the rim of crags until reaching a line of small cairns and a clear track that leads north along the narrow ridge to Steeple.

14 From Steeple, descend north north-east along the ridge top. The path is intermittent but reasonably easy to follow.

15 Once down in the heather, the path becomes very clear. Turn left (west) when another path cuts across the way.

16 This leads down to a beck which is easily forded by moving ten yards upstream.

17 Follow the track on the western

side of the beck as it leads downstream, then cut across to the fence that leads westward on Lingmell. Now, simply follow the fence.

18 After a lengthy crossing of Lingmell, the path comes to a gate where another fence joins from the left (south). Go through the gate then continue to follow the original fence.

19 You will notice that the surroundings are not as they appear on OS maps (the forest boundary appears to have changed since the maps were last printed). Stay alongside the fence as it drops steeply.

20 Eventually, you will arrive at a wall that cuts across the way. Go through the wall gap then continue down to a gate. Continue to descend after the gate to a second gate.

21 Bear left after the second gate. (Blue-tipped posts mark the way once more.)

22 The path descends through the woods to a wide forest track. Go straight across this, following the posts to two footbridges.

23 Cross both bridges then follow the path down above the gorge.

24 Remember to bear right where the path appears to fork in the clearing, then simply retrace your earlier steps across the fields and alongside the lake.

From Bowness car park, Ennerdale Forest stretches almost six miles up to the Black Sail Pass. A wide track follows the forest boundary along the lakeshore, then continues through the plantations towards the pass. However, this track is for use by forestry vehicles only, resulting in a lengthy walk along the valley before our route branches up into the fells.

On starting out, both the crags of Bowness Knott and the forest obscure the long mountain chain that runs along the valley's northern flank. The lake is by the right hand, with Crag and Ennerdale Fells rising high on the far side of the water.

After a short distance along the track, all the peaks of the route can be seen ahead on the distant skyline. Little Gowder Crag, Haycock and Scoat Fell lead on to Steeple's distinctive silhouette, with the whole ridge dominated by Pillar's great bulk. Once clear of Bowness Knott, steep, forested slopes immediately to the left rise to Great Borne and Starling Dodd, with Red Pike glimpsed intermittently through the trees.

The lakeshore is followed for slightly over a mile to its easternmost reaches, where the route heads south across Char Dub and a network of fields. From here, the Buttermere Trio are revealed above the left shoulder until the route enters plantations on the southern side of the valley.

Moving toward the fells, the track degenerates into a narrow path in a deeply atmospheric and aromatic section within a wooded gorge. Little Gowder and Haycock can be seen directly ahead, with Lingmell's lower slopes rising on the far side of

Looking across Mirkiln Cove to Little Gowder Crag.

Steeple glows in late autumn sunshine.

the gorge and its cascading beck.

From here, a narrow, forested ridge rises between two becks. The greens and browns of the woods are replaced by a sea of red/purple heather as the path emerges on the upper ridge. Silver and Great Coves lie to either side ahead, flanked by Tewit How immediately to the east. To the west, where the bare rock of Iron Crag protrudes above Ennerdale Fell's rich carpet, a sombre tone is added to an otherwise vividly painted canvas.

A view to the rear opens to reveal Ennerdale's fields with forested slopes beyond the lake. These rise to a long,

flowing line formed by the Great Borne/Starling Dodd ridge which leads on to the Buttermere Trio's loftier pinnacles. Grasmoor appears beyond these, while wide lowlands and the sea are revealed above Ennerdale Fell's lower northern slope.

The heather covering suddenly terminates in a distinct line that can be seen on all the surrounding fells. Rocks begin to protrude through turf and grasses as the route swings eastward on the ridge top, where Little Gowder lies immediately ahead. On the initial approach, there appears to be a curious, hook-shaped rock or

cairn atop the peak, but a short ascent reveals this to be an end-on view of the wall that passes directly over the summit.

One of the more surprising inclusions in the top 100, Little Gowder Crag stands at 733 metres (2404 ft) and is ranked as peak number 89. Haycock effectively blocks a sighting of Lakeland's major peaks, but from Illgill Head's screes in the south-east, the remaining southern outlook is wide open.

Middle Fell's western crags fall into Greendale's hollow, then the land rises to Seatallan. Immediately below, River

Bleng's long, wide valley rolls down to the lowlands and two large conifer plantations. A graceful outline formed by the Esk Estuary and the coast is somewhat tainted by Sellafield's intrusion before Ennerdale Fell introduces another section of coastline and Ennerdale Water.

In the north, Gavel Fell, Hen Comb and Mellbreak are prominent in that charming little cluster of fells between Ennerdale and Crummock Water. Whiteside, Grasmoor, Crag Hill, Sail and Causey Pike are all visible among the Derwent Fells above the Buttermere Trio. Great Cove and Tewit How's ridge form the foreground in this sector, before the eye passes round to nearby Steeple and Great Scoat Fell. A more distant Pillar is seen between these two, with Red Pike and Haycock completing the circle.

From Little Gowder, very little time or effort is required to conquer Haycock, where the top is covered by shattered rocks. A large stone shelter marks the summit at a height of 797 metres (2614 ft), qualifying this as peak number 47.

From now on, the Scafell range is on view, presenting a dramatic outline between the more distant Helvellyn range and Coniston group. Apart from this notable addition, one could be lulled into believing that nothing of further interest has entered the landscape. Owing to the summit shelter's location above the northern semi-circle, most visitors are unaware of a truly remarkable viewpoint at Haycock's southern cairn.

A short detour across the top enters a grassy area, then reaches the cairn atop a rocky knoll. Here Scoat Tarn can be seen nestled beneath Red Pike, and Illgill Head's screes are clear all the way down into Wast Water. Greendale Tarn lies in the saddle

On the ridge between Little Scoat Fell and Steeple.

between Middle Fell and Seatallan, before rolling moorlands, the estuary and a wide coastline complete the picture. Vigorous rock sculptures and contrasting textures of waters, grasslands and woods combine to generate a classic lakeland scene that should not be missed.

Comfortable turf lies underfoot as the route descends to a saddle between Haycock and Great Scoat Fell. The last major ascent of the day begins on a wide, grassy ridge leading to Great Scoat Fell, where the most spectacular scenery of the route begins to unfold.

The ridge narrows as Mirkiln Cove's crags encroach from below the left hand. Eventually, the way passes over a very narrow strip of turf between the precipitous crags and the wall that has been followed since Little Gowder. Suddenly, Steeple's crags and the Cove's buttresses present an awesome spectacle.

The drama continues as the route swings northwards onto a sharp ridge leading to Steeple's pointed pinnacle. With Mirkiln Cove below the left hand and Mirk Cove to the right, this short crossing is reminiscent of Striding Edge, with an equally acute sense of height.

Although the path over the jagged ridge is relatively easy to follow, this section must be treated with respect even in the most benign conditions. After the short climb to Steeple's summit, a measure of concentration is still required where the summit cairn stands directly above Mirk Cove at 819 metres (2687 ft).

Ranked as peak number 38, Steeple is simply a rock tower on Scoat Fell's northern spur, but possesses a spire-

On Steeple's summit looking back to Ennerdale Water.

like top that only Pillar Rock can equal. For most visitors, the abiding memory of this superb location is of peering nervously over broken crags that fall from beneath one's toes into Mirk Cove and thence into Ennerdale Forest. On the opposite side, Mirkiln Cove presents a similarly daunting scene, falling towards an almost full-length view of Ennerdale Water.

Among nearby landmarks, Black Crag forms the opposite flank of Mirk Cove, topped by Pillar. Great Gable is prominent above Little Scoat Fell, appearing in a cluster reaching from Glaramara to Scafell Pike.

Elsewhere, there are no significant changes to the landscape. Even if there were, it is highly unlikely that anybody's attention would be drawn from the magnificent spectacle of the immediate surroundings.

The route descends along Steeple's northern spur, heading directly toward Ennerdale. As the forest draws near, large areas of fresh saplings become increasingly obvious in the patchwork plantations. The path passes through salmon-pink coloured rocks, then re-enters the heather line before swinging westward over Low Beck. Steeple, Great Scoat Fell and Tewit How form Mirkiln Cove's arc above the left shoulder as the path moves parallel with the forest boundary, rising gently to Lingmell.

On passing over the hill crest, an impressive picture of the lake unfolds directly ahead. At this point, after such a lengthy and steep descent, it is surprising to see that the path is still at a considerable height above the valley. However, altitude is lost very rapidly from here. Re-entering the trees, the route returns to the confluence of Deep Gill and Silvercove Beck. Although there is still a lengthy walk to the car park, the going is comfortable as we retrace our earlier footsteps across the fields then alongside the relaxing shore.

Appendix

The Lakeland 100 in order of altitude

Ranking	Name	Altitude (metres)	Altitude (feet)	Walk	Ranking	Name	Altitude (metres)	Altitude (feet)	Walk
1	Scafell Pike	978	3208	2	33	Flesk	834	2736	5
2	Sca Fell	964	3162	2	34	Black Crag	828	2716	1
3	Symonds Knott	959	3146	2	35	High Street	828	2716	10
4	Helvellyn	950	3116	11	36	Red Pike (Mosedale)	826	2709	1
5	Ill Crag	935	3067	2	37	Hart Crag	822	2696	8
6	Broad Crag	934	3064	2	38	Steeple	819	2686	21
7	Skiddaw	931	3054	15	39	Shelter Crags	815	2673	5
8	Lower Man	925	3034	12	40	High Stile	807	2647	19
9	Great End	910	2985	2	41	The Old Man of Coniston	803	2634	3
10	Bow Fell	902	2959	5	42	High Raise (Eastern)	802	2631	10
11	Great Gable	899	2949	18	43	Kirk Fell	802	2631	1
12	Pillar	892	2926	1	44	Swirl How	802	2631	4
13	Nethermost Pike	891	2923	11	45	Green Gable	801	2627	18
14	Catstye Cam	890	2919	12	46	Lingmell	800	2624*	2
15	Esk Pike	885	2903	5	47	Haycock	797	2614	21
16	Raise	883	2896	12	48	Brim Fell	796	2611	3
17	Fairfield	873	2864	8	49	Green Side	795	2608	13
18	Blencathra	868	2847	14	50	Dove Crag	792	2598	8
19	Bowfell – North Top	866	2841	5	51	Rampsgill Head	792	2598	10
20	Little Man	865	2837	15	52	Grisedale Pike	791	2595	16
21	White Side	863	2831	1	53	Kirk Fell – East Top	787	2582	1
22	High Spying How	860	2821*	11	54	Allen Crags	785	2575	18
23	Crinkle Crags	859	2818	5	55	Great Carrs	785	2575	4
24	Dollywaggon Pike	858	2814	11	56	Thornthwaite Crag	784	2572	10
25	Great Dodd	857	2811	13	57	Glaramara	783	2568	18
26	Grasmoor	852	2795	20	58	Kidsty Pike	780	2559*	10
27	Gategill Fell Top	851	2791	14	59	Pillar Rock	780	2559	1
28	Atkinson Pike	845	2772	14	60	Dow Crag	778	2552	3
29	Stybarrow Dodd	843	2765	13	61	Harter Fell	778	2552	9
30	Little Scoat Fell	841	2759	1	62	Red Screes	776	2545	8
31	St Sunday Crag	841	2759	11	63	Looking Steads	775	2542	18
32	Crag Hill	839	2752	16	64	Shelter Crags – North Top	775	2542	5

Ranking	Name	Altitude (metres)	Altitude (feet)	Walk	Ranking	Name	Altitude (metres)	Altitude (feet)	Walk
65	Sail	773	2536	16	83	Hobcarton Crag	739	2424	16
66	Wandope	772	2532	16	84	Robinson	737	2417	17
67	Grey Friar	770	2526*	3	85	Harrison Stickle	736	2414	6
68	Hopegill Head	770	2526	20	86	Seat Sandal	736	2414	11
69	Great Rigg	766	2513	8	87	Combe Head	735	2411	18
70	Stony Cove Pike	763	2503	10	88	Long Side	734	2408	15
71	High Raise (Central)	762	2500	7	89	Little Gowder Crag	733	2404	21
72	Wetherlam	762	2500	4	90	Codale Head	730	2395*	7
73	Ill Bell	757	2483	9	91	Kentmere Pike	730	2395	9
74	Hart Side	756	2480	13	92	Hindscarth	727	2385	17
75	Sand Hill	756	2480	20	93	Clough Head	726	2381	13
76	Red Pike (Buttermere)	755	2477	19	94	Ullscarf	726	2381	7
77	Dale Head	753	2470	17	95	Thunacar Knott	723	2372	6
78	Carl Side	746	2447	15	96	Red Beck Top	721	2365	18
79	Black Sails	745	2444	4	97	Froswick	720	2362	9
80	High Crag	744	2440	19	98	Whiteside – East Top	719	2358	20
81	Round How	741	2431	2	99	Birkhouse Moor	718	2355	11
82	Little Stand	740	2427	5	100	Brandreth	715	2345	18

* No recorded spot heights. The given altitude is that of the highest contour on OS maps. The actual summit will be a little higher, but in no case can this exceed a further 9 metres.

Index